Microsoft® Official Academic Course:
Microsoft Office Excel 2003 Core Skills

Microsoft Corporation

PUBLISHED BY
Microsoft Press
A Division of Microsoft Corporation
One Microsoft Way
Redmond, Washington 98052-6399

This academic edition (2004) is printed under licence from Microsoft by

ITS-FEDA Ltd, Coombe lodge, Blagdon, Bristol BS40 7RG.

Printed in the UK by Basingstoke Press.

Library of Congress Cataloging-in-Publication Data pending.
    ISBN 1-904644-35-X
    (ITS - FEDA Ltd)
    ISBN 0-7356-2094-6
    (Microsoft Press)
    ISBN 0-07-225569-2
    (McGraw-Hill)

1 2 3 4 5 6 7 8 9   QWE   8 7 6 5 4 3

Distributed in Canada by H.B. Fenn and Company Ltd.

A CIP catalogue record for this book is available from the British Library.

Microsoft Press books are available through booksellers and distributors worldwide. For further information about international editions, contact your local Microsoft Corporation office or contact Microsoft Press International directly at fax (425)
936-7329. Visit our Web site at www.microsoft.com/learning/. Send comments to *mspinput@microsoft.com*.

AutoSum, Encarta, Microsoft, MSN, PowerPoint, Windows, and the Windows logo are either registered trademarks or
trademarks of Microsoft Corporation in the United States and/or other countries. Other product and company names men-
tioned herein may be the trademarks of their respective owners.

The example companies, organizations, products, domain names, e-mail addresses, logos, people, places, and events depicted
herein are fictitious. No association with any real company, organization, product, domain name, e-mail address, logo,
person, place, or event is intended or should be inferred.

This book expresses the author's views and opinions. The information contained in this book is provided without any
express, statutory, or implied warranties. Neither the authors, Microsoft Corporation, nor its resellers or distributors will be
held liable for any damages caused or alleged to be caused either directly or indirectly by this book.

Acquisitions Editor: Linda Engelman
Project Editor: Dick Brown

Body Part No. X10-34198

Excel

Contents

Course Overview

Welcome to the *Microsoft Official Academic Course* series for Microsoft Office System 2003 Edition. This series facilitates classroom learning, enabling you to develop competence and confidence in using Office applications. In completing courses taught with the *Microsoft Official Academic Course* series, you learn to use the software productively and discover how to make the software work for you. This series addresses core-level and expert-level skills in Microsoft Office Word 2003, Microsoft Office Excel 2003, Microsoft Office Access 2003, Microsoft Office PowerPoint 2003, Microsoft Office Outlook 2003, Microsoft FrontPage 2002/2003, and Microsoft Project 2002/2003.

The *Microsoft Official Academic Course* series provides:

- A time-tested, integrated approach to learning.
- Task-based, results-oriented learning strategies.
- Exercises based on realistic business scenarios.
- Complete preparation for Microsoft Office Specialist (MOS) certification.
- Attractive student guides with full-featured lessons.
- Lessons with accurate, logical, and sequential instructions.
- Comprehensive coverage of skills from the basic to the expert level.
- Review of core-level skills provided in expert-level guides.
- A CD-ROM with Microsoft's e-learning tool as well as practice files.

A Task-Based Approach Using Business Scenarios

The *Microsoft Official Academic Course* uses the time-tested approach of learning by doing. By studying with a task-based approach, you learn more than just the features of the software. You learn how to accomplish real-world tasks so that you can immediately increase your productivity using the software application.

The lessons are based on tasks that you might encounter in the everyday work world. This approach allows you to quickly see the relevance of the training beyond just the classroom. The business focus is woven throughout the series, from business examples within procedures, to scenarios chosen for practice files, to examples shown in the e-learning tool.

An Integrated Approach to Training

The *Microsoft Official Academic Course* series distinguishes itself from other series on the market with its consistent delivery and completely integrated approach to learning across print and online training media.

The textbook component of the *Microsoft Official Academic Course* series uses easily digested units of learning so that you can stop and restart lessons easily.

For those who prefer online training, this series includes an e-learning tool, the Microsoft e-Learning Library Version 2 (MELL 2). MELL 2 offers highly interactive online training in a simulated work environment, complete with graphics, sound, video, and animation. Icons in the margin of the textbook direct you to related topics within the e-learning tool so that you can choose to reinforce your learning more visually. MELL 2 also includes an assessment feature that students and teachers can use to gauge preliminary knowledge about the application.

Preparation for Microsoft Office Specialist (MOS) Certification

This series has been certified as approved courseware for the Microsoft Office Specialist certification program. Students who have completed this training are prepared to take the related MOS exam. By passing the exam for a particular Office application, students demonstrate proficiency in that application to their employers or prospective employers. Exams are offered at participating test centers. For more information, see *www.microsoft.com/traincert/mcp/officespecialist/requirements.asp*.

Designed for Optimal Learning

Lessons in the *Microsoft Official Academic Course* series are presented in a logical, easy-to-follow format, helping you find information quickly and learn as efficiently as possible. The colorful and highly visual series design makes it easy for you to see what to read and what to do when practicing new skills.

Lessons break training into easily assimilated sessions. Each lesson is self-contained, and lessons can be completed in sequences other than the one presented in the table of contents. Sample files for the lessons don't depend on completion of other lessons. Sample files within a lesson assume only that you are working sequentially through a complete lesson.

Each book within the *Microsoft Official Academic Course* series features:

- **Lesson objectives.** Objectives clearly state the instructional goals for the lesson so that you understand what skills you will master. Each lesson objective is covered in its own section, and each section or topic in the lesson is covered in a consistent way. Lesson objectives preview the lesson structure, helping you grasp key information and prepare for learning skills.

- **Key terms.** Terms with which you might not be familiar are listed at the beginning of the lesson. When these terms are used later in the lesson, they appear in boldface type and are defined. The Glossary contains all of the key terms and their definitions.

- **Informational text for each topic.** For each objective, the lesson provides easy-to-read, technique-focused information.

- **The Bottom Line.** Each main topic within the lesson has a summary of what makes the topic relevant to you.

- **Hands-on practice.** Numbered steps give detailed, step-by-step instructions to help you learn skills. The steps also show results and screen images to match what you should see on your computer screen. The accompanying CD contains the sample files needed for each lesson.

- **Full-color illustrations.** Illustrated screen images give visual feedback as you work through exercises. The images reinforce key concepts, provide visual clues about the steps, and give you something to check your progress against.

- **MOS icon.** Each section or sidebar that covers a MOS certification objective has a MOS icon in the margin at the beginning of the section. The complete list of MOS objectives and the location in the text where they are covered can be found in the MOS Objectives section of this book.

- **Reader aids.** Helpful hints and alternate ways to accomplish tasks are located throughout the lesson text. Reader aids provide additional related or background information that adds value to the lesson. These also include things to watch out for or things to avoid.

- **Check This Out.** These sidebars contain parenthetical topics or additional information that you might find interesting.

- **Button images in the margin.** When the text instructs you to click a particular button, an image of the button is shown in the margin.

- **Quick Reference.** Each main section contains a condensed version of the steps used in its procedures. This section is helpful if you want only a fast reminder of how to complete a certain task.

- **Quick Check.** These questions and answers provide a chance to review material covered in that section of the lesson.

- **Quick Quiz.** You can use the true/false, multiple choice, or short-answer Quick Quiz questions to test or reinforce your understanding of key topics within each lesson.

- **On Your Own exercises.** These exercises give you another opportunity to practice skills that you learned in the lesson. Completing these exercises helps you to verify whether you understand the lesson and to reinforce your learning.

- **One Step Further exercises.** These exercises give you an opportunity to build upon what you have learned by applying that knowledge in a different way. These might also require researching on the Internet.

- **Glossary.** Terms with which you might not be familiar are defined in the glossary. Terms in the glossary appear in boldface type within the lessons and are also defined within the lessons.

- **Index.** Student guides are completely indexed. All glossary terms and application features appear in the index.

- **MELL icons in the margin.** These icons direct you to related topics within the Microsoft e-Learning Library. For more information on MELL, please see the Microsoft e-Learning Library section later in this book.

Lesson Features

Lesson Objectives

Key Terms

Quick Reference

Quick Check

New for 2003

The Bottom Line

MELL Correlation

MOS Icon

Hands-on Practice

Buttons

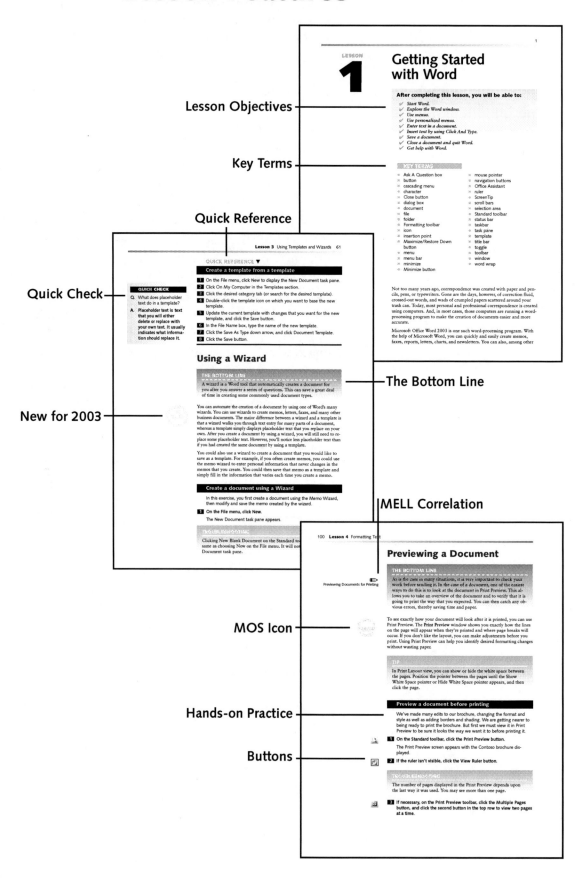

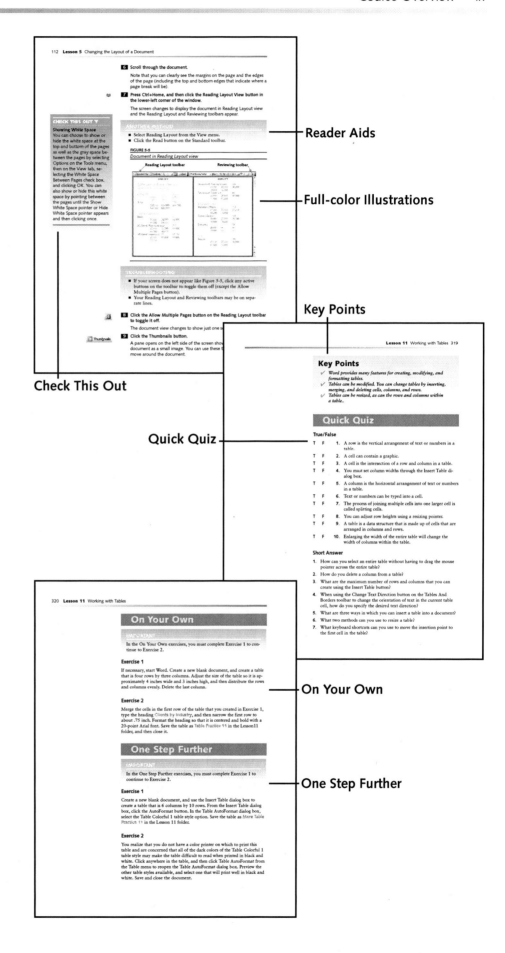

Reader Aids

Full-color Illustrations

Key Points

Check This Out

Quick Quiz

On Your Own

One Step Further

Conventions and Features Used in This Book

This book uses special fonts, symbols, and heading conventions to high-light important information or to call your attention to special steps. For more information about the features available in each lesson, refer to the "Course Overview" section.

Convention	Meaning
	This icon in the margin indicates a new or greatly improved feature in this version of the software.
	This icon indicates that the section where it appears covers a Microsoft Office Specialist (MOS) exam objective. For a complete list of the MOS objectives, see the "MOS Objectives" section.
THE BOTTOM LINE	These paragraphs provide a brief summary of the material to be covered in the section that follows.
◆ **Close the file.**	Words preceded by a yellow diamond in a black box give instructions for opening, saving, or closing files or programs. They also point out items you should check or actions you should carry out.
QUICK REFERENCE ▼	These provide an "at-a-glance" summary of the steps involved to complete a given task. These differ from procedures because they're generic, not scenario-driven, and they're brief.
QUICK CHECK	This is a quick question and answer that serves to reinforce critical points and pro-vides a chance to review the material covered.
TIP	Reader aids appear in green boxes. *Another Method* provides alternative pro-cedures related to particular tasks, *Tip* provides helpful hints related to particular tasks or topics, and *Troubleshooting* covers common mistakes or areas in which you may have trouble. *Important* highlights warnings or cautions that are critical to per-forming exercises.

Convention	Meaning
CHECK THIS OUT ▼	These notes in the margin area provide pointers to information elsewhere in the book (or another book) or describe interesting features of the program that are not directly discussed in the current topic or used in the exercise.
	When a toolbar button is referenced in the lesson, the button's picture is shown in the margin.
Alt+Tab	A plus sign (+) between two key names means that you must press those keys at the same time. For example, "Press Alt+Tab" means that you hold down the Alt key while you press Tab.
Boldface type	Indicates a key term entry that is defined in the Glossary at the end of the book.
Type Yes.	Anything you are supposed to type appears in red bold characters.
	This icon alongside a paragraph indicates reated coverage within the Microsoft e-Learning Library, (MELL)the e-learning tool. Find more information on MELL later in this book.

Using the CD-ROMs

There are two CD-ROMs included with this student guide. One contains the practice files that you'll use as you perform the exercises in the book. You can use the other CD-ROM, described below, to install a 180-day trial edition of Microsoft Office Professional Edition 2003. By using the practice files, you won't waste time creating the samples used in the lessons, and you can concentrate on learning how to use Microsoft Office Excel 2003. With the files and the step-by-step instructions in the lessons, you'll learn by doing, which is an easy and effective way to acquire and remember new skills.

System Requirements

Your computer system must meet the following minimum requirements for you to install the practice files from the CD-ROM and to run Microsoft Excel 2003.

IMPORTANT

This course assumes that Excel 2003 has already been installed on the PC you are using. Microsoft Office Professional Edition 2003— 180-Day Trial, which includes Excel, is on the second CD-ROM included with this book. Microsoft Product Support does not support these trial editions.

For information on how to install the trial edition, see "Installing or Uninstalling Microsoft Office Professional Edition 2003—180-Day Trial" later in this part of the book.

- A personal computer running Microsoft Excel 2003 on a Pentium 233-megahertz (MHz) or higher processor.
- Microsoft Windows® 2000 with Service Pack 3 (SP3), Windows XP, or later.
- 128 MB of RAM or greater.
- At least 2 MB of available disk space (after installing Excel 2003 or Microsoft Office).
- A CD-ROM or DVD drive.
- A monitor with Super VGA (800 X 600) or higher resolution with 256 colors.
- A Microsoft mouse, a Microsoft IntelliMouse, or other compatible pointing device.

If You Need to Install or Uninstall the Practice Files

Your instructor might already have installed the practice files before you arrive in class. However, your instructor might ask you to install the practice files on your own at the start of class. Also, if you want to work through any of the exercises in this book on your own at home or at your place of business after class, you will need to first install the practice files.

Install the practice files

1 Insert the CD-ROM in the CD-ROM drive of your computer.

A menu screen appears.

IMPORTANT

If the menu screen does not appear, start Windows Explorer. In the left pane, locate the icon for your CD-ROM, and click this icon. In the right pane, double-click the file StartCD.

2 Click Install Practice Files, and follow the instructions on the screen.

The recommended options are preselected for you.

3 After the files have been installed, click Exit.

A folder called Excel Core Practice has been created on your hard disk; the practice files have been placed in that folder.

4 Remove the CD-ROM from the CD-ROM drive.

Use the following steps when you want to delete the lesson practice files from your hard disk. Your instructor might ask you to perform these steps at the end of class. Also, you should perform these steps if you have worked through the exercises at home or at your place of business and want to work through the exercises again. Deleting the practice files and then reinstalling them ensures that all files and folders are in their original condition if you decide to work through the exercises again.

Unistall the practice files from the Windows XP or later operating system

1 On the Windows taskbar, click the Start button and then click Control Panel.

2 If you are in Classic View, double-click the Add Or Remove Programs icon. If you are in Category View, single-click the Add Or Remove Programs link.

3 In the Add Or Remove Programs dialog box, scroll down and select Excel Core Practice in the list. Click the Change/Remove button.

4 Click Yes when the confirmation dialog box appears.

> ### Uninstall the practice files from the Windows 2000 operating system
>
> **1** On the Windows taskbar, click the Start button, point to Settings, and then click Control Panel.
>
> **2** Double-click the Add/Remove icon.
>
> **3** Click Excel Core Practice in the list, and click the Remove or the Change/Remove button.
>
> **4** Click Yes when the confirmation dialog box appears.

Using the Practice Files

Each lesson in this book explains when and how to use any practice files for that lesson. The lessons are built around scenarios that simulate a real work environment, so you can easily apply the skills you learn to your own work. The scenarios in the lessons use the context of the fictitious Contoso, Ltd, a public relations firm, and its client, Adventure Works, a resort located in the mountains of California.

By default, Excel 2003 places the Standard and Formatting toolbars on the same row below the menu bar to save space. To match the lessons and exercises in this book, the Standard and Formatting toolbars should be separated onto two rows before the start of this course. To separate the Standard and Formatting toolbars:

- Position the mouse pointer over the move handle at the beginning of the Formatting toolbar until it turns into the move pointer (a four-headed arrow), and drag the toolbar down until it appears on its own row.

The following is a list of all files and folders used in the lessons.

File Name	Description
Lesson01 - folder	Folder used in Lesson 1
Employee Information	File used in Lesson 1
Lesson02 - folder	Folder used in Lesson 2
Percent Sales Increase	File used in Lesson 2
Five Years Sales02	File used in Lesson 2
Rentals	File used in Lesson 2
Monthly Sales	File used in Lesson 2
Lesson03 - folder	Folder used in Lesson 3
Lodging Analysis03	File used in Lesson 3
AW Guest Supplies	File used in Lesson 3
Lesson04 - folder	Folder used in Lesson 4
Sports Income	File used in Lesson 4

File Name	Description
Lesson05 - folder	Folder used in Lesson 5
Sports Income05	File used in Lesson 5
Food	File used in Lesson 5
Filter	File used in Lesson 5
Lesson06 - folder	Folder used in Lesson 6
Five Year Sales	File used in Lesson 6
Member Pledges	File used in Lesson 6
Lesson07 - folder	Folder used in Lesson 7
Lodging Usage	File used in Lesson 7
Activity Rentals	File used in Lesson 7
Food07	File used in Lesson 7
Lesson08 - folder	Folder used in Lesson 8
Financing	File used in Lesson 8
Lesson09 - folder	Folder used in Lesson 9
Intranet	File used in Lesson 9

Replying to Install Messages

When you work through some lessons, you might see a message indicating that the feature that you are trying to use is not installed. If you see this message, insert the Microsoft Office Excel 2003 CD or Microsoft Office CD 1 in your CD-ROM drive, and click Yes to install the feature.

Locating and Opening Files

After you (or your instructor) have installed the practice files, all the files you need for this course will be stored in a folder named Excel Core Practice located on your hard disk.

Navigate to the Excel Core Practice folder from within Excel and open a file

1 On the Standard toolbar, click the Open button.

2 In the Open dialog box, click the Look In down arrow, and click the icon for your hard disk.

3 Double-click the Excel Core Practice folder.

4 Double-click the file that you want to open.

All the files for the lessons appear within the Excel Core Practice folder.

If You Need Help with the Practice Files

If you have any problems regarding the use of this book's CD-ROM, you should first consult your instructor. If you are using the CD-ROM at home or at your place of business and need additional help with the practice files, contact McGraw-Hill for support:

E-mail: techsup@mcgraw-hill.com

Phone: (800) 331-5094

Post: McGraw-Hill Companies

       1333 Burr Ridge Parkway

       Burr Ridge, IL 60521

IMPORTANT

For help using Excel 2003, rather than this book, you can visit support.microsoft.com or call Microsoft Product Support at (425) 635-7070 on weekdays between 5 A.M. and 9 P.M. Pacific Standard Time or on Saturdays and Sundays between 6 A.M. and 3 P.M. Pacific Standard Time. Microsoft Product Support does not provide support for this course. Also please note that Microsoft Product Support does not support trial editions of Office.

Installing or Uninstalling Microsoft Office Professional Edition 2003—180-Day Trial

An installation CD-ROM for Microsoft Office Professional Edition 2003—180-Day Trial is included with this book. Before you install your trial version, please read this entire section for important information on setting up and uninstalling your trial software.

CAUTION

For the best performance, the default selection during Setup is to uninstall previous versions of Office. There is also an option not to remove previous versions of Office. With all trial software, Microsoft recommends that you have your original CDs available to reinstall if necessary. If you want to return to your previous version of Office, you need to uninstall the trial software. This should be done through the Add or Remove Programs icon in Microsoft Windows Control Panel.

Installation of Microsoft Office Professional Edition 2003—180-Day Trial software will remove your existing version of Microsoft Outlook. However, your contacts, calendar, and other personal information will not be deleted. At the end of the trial, if you choose to upgrade or to reinstall your previous version of Outlook, your personal settings and information will be retained.

Setup Instructions

1 Insert the trial software CD into the CD drive on your computer. The CD will be detected, and the Setup.exe file should automatically begin to run on your computer.

2 When prompted for the Office Product Key, enter the Product Key provided with the software, and then click Next.

3 Enter your name and organization user name, and then click Next.

4 Read the End-User License Agreement, select the I Accept The Terms In The License Agreement check box, and then click Next.

NOTE

Copies of the product License Agreements are also available for review at http://www.microsoft.com/office/eula.

5 Select the install option, verify the installation location or click Browse to change the installation location, and then click Next.

The default setting is Upgrade. You will have the opportunity to specify not to remove previous versions of Office from your computer later in the installation wizard.

6 Verify the program installation preferences, and then click Next.

CAUTION

For best performance, the default selection during setup is to uninstall (remove) previous versions of Office. There is also the option not to remove previous versions of Office. With all trial software, Microsoft recommends that you have your original CDs available to reinstall if necessary.

7 To finish Setup, select the check boxes you want so that you can receive the online updates and downloads or to delete the installation files, then click Finish.

Upgrading Microsoft Office Professional Edition 2003—180-Day Trial Software to the Full Product

You can convert the software into full use without removing or reinstalling software on your computer. When you complete your trial, you can purchase a product license from any Microsoft reseller and enter a valid Product Key when prompted during Setup.

Uninstalling the Trial Software and Returning to Your Previous Office Version

If you want to return to your previous version of Office, you need to uninstall the trial software. This should be done through the Add or Remove Programs icon in Control Panel.

1 Quit any programs that are running, such as Microsoft Excel or Outlook.

2 In control Panel, click Add or Remove Programs.

3 Click Microsoft Office Professional Edition 2003, and then click Remove.

NOTE

If you selected the option to remove a previous version of Office during installation of the trial software, you need to reinstall your previous version of Office. If you did not remove your previous version of Office, you can start each of your Office programs either through the Start menu or by opening files for each program, such as Word, Microsoft Excel, and Microsoft PowerPoint files. In some cases, you may have to recreate some of your shortcuts and default settings.

MOS Objectives
Core Skills

Objective	Activity	Page
XL03S-1	**Creating Data and Content**	
XL03S-1-1	Enter and edit cell contents	12-14, 17
XL03S-1-2	Navigate to specific cell content	8
XL03S-1-3	Locate, select, and insert supporting information	44
XL03S-1-4	Insert, position, and size graphics	152
XL03S-2	**Analyzing Data**	
XL03S-2-1	Filter lists using AutoFilter	127
XL03S-2-2	Sort lists-	124
XL03S-2-3	Insert and modify formulas	162, 171
XL03S-2-4	Use statistical, date and time, financial, and logical functions	177, 179, 188, 191, 195, 197
XL03S-2-5	Create, modify, and position diagrams and charts based on worksheet data	134-154
XL03S-3	**Formatting Data and Content**	
XL03S-3-1	Apply and modify cell formats	32, 41, 68, 72, 74-75, 79
XL03S-3-2	Apply and modify cell styles	83
XL03S-3-3	Modify row and column formats	37
XL03S-3-4	Format worksheets	68, 72, 74-75, 79, 81
XL03S-4	**Collaborating**	
XL03S-4-1	Insert, view, and edit comments	214
XL03S-5	**Managing Workbooks**	
XL03S-5-1	Create new workbooks from templates	4
XL03S-5-2	Insert, delete, and move cells	49, 53
XL03S-5-3	Create and modify hyperlinks	204, 206
XL03S-5-4	Organize worksheets	120, 123
XL03S-5-5	Preview data in other views	24, 102
XL03S-5-6	Customize window layout	118, 121
XL03S-5-7	Set up pages for printing	93-94, 97, 99, 104, 106
XL03S-5-8	Print data	24
XL03S-5-9	Organize workbooks using file folders	19
XL03S-5-10	Save data in appropriate formats for different uses	19

Taking a Microsoft Office Specialist Certification Test

The Microsoft Office Specialist (MOS) program is the only Microsoft-approved certification program designed to measure and validate your skills with the Microsoft Office suite of desktop productivity applications: Microsoft Word, Microsoft Excel, Microsoft PowerPoint, Microsoft Access, and Microsoft Outlook.

By becoming certified, you demonstrate to employers that you have achieved a predictable level of skill in the use of a particular Office application. Employers often require certification either as a condition of employment or as a condition of advancement within the company or other organization. The certification examinations are sponsored by Microsoft but administered through Nivo International.

The MOS program typically offers certification exams at the "core" and "expert" levels. For a core-level test, you demonstrate your ability to use an application knowledgeably and without assistance in a day-to-day work environment. For an expert-level test, you demonstrate that you have a thorough knowledge of the application and can effectively apply all or most of the features of the application to solve problems and complete tasks found in business.

Preparing to Take an Exam

Unless you're a very experienced user, you'll need to use a test preparation course to prepare to complete the test correctly and within the time allowed. The *Microsoft Official Academic Course* series is designed to prepare you for either core-level or expert-level knowledge of a particular Microsoft Office application. By the end of this course, you should have a strong knowledge of all exam topics, and with some additional review and practice on your own, you should feel confident in your ability to pass the appropriate exam.

After you decide which exam to take, review the list of objectives for the exam. This list can be found in the "MOS Objectives" section at the front of the appropriate *Microsoft Official Academic Course* student guide. You can also easily identify tasks that are included in the objective list by locating the MOS symbol in the margin of the lessons in this book.

For an expert-level test, you'll need to be able to demonstrate any of the skills from the core-level objective list, too. Expect some of these core-level tasks to appear on the expert-level test.

You can also familiarize yourself with a live MOS certification test by downloading and installing a practice MOS certification test from www.microsoft.com/traincert/mcp/officespecialist/requirements.asp.

To take the MOS test, first see www.microsoft.com/traincert/mcp/office-specialist/requirements.asp to locate your nearest testing center. Then call the testing center directly to schedule your test. The amount of advance notice you should provide will vary for different testing centers, and it typically depends on the number of computers available at the testing center, the number of other testers who have already been scheduled for the day on which you want to take the test, and the number of times per week that the testing center offers MOS testing. In general, you should call to schedule your test at least two weeks prior to the date on which you want to take the test.

When you arrive at the testing center, you might be asked for proof of identity. A driver's license or passport is an acceptable form of identification. If you do not have either of these items of documentation, call your testing center and ask what alternative forms of identification will be accepted. If you are retaking a test, bring your MOS identification number, which will have been given to you when you previously took the test. If you have not prepaid or if your organization has not already arranged to make payment for you, you will need to pay the test-taking fee when you arrive. The current test-taking fee is $75 (U.S.). Prices are subject to change and may vary depending on the testing center.

Test Format

All MOS certification tests are live, performance-based tests. There are no multiple-choice, true/false, or short-answer questions. Instructions are general: you are told the basic tasks to perform on the computer, but you aren't given any help in figuring out how to perform them. You are not permitted to use reference material other than the application's Help system.

As you complete the tasks stated in a particular test question, the testing software monitors your actions. An example question might be:

> Open the file named AW Guests and select the word Welcome in the first paragraph. Change the font to 12 point, and apply bold formatting. Select the words at your convenience in the second paragraph, move them to the end of the first paragraph using drag and drop, and then center the first paragraph.

The sample tests available from www.microsoft.com/traincert/mcp/office-specialist/requirements.asp give you a clear idea of the type of questions that you will be asked on the actual test.

When the test administrator seats you at a computer, you'll see an online form that you use to enter information about yourself (name, address, and other information required to process your exam results). While you complete the form, the software will generate the test from a master test bank and then prompt you to continue. The first test question will appear in a window. Read the question carefully, and then perform all the tasks stated in the test question. When you have finished completing all tasks for a question, click the Next Question button.

You have 45 to 60 minutes to complete all questions, depending on the test that you are taking. The testing software assesses your results as soon as you complete the test, and the test administrator can print the results of the test so that you will have a record of any tasks that you performed incorrectly. A passing grade is 75 percent or higher. If you pass, you will receive a certificate in the mail within two to four weeks. If you do not pass, you can study and practice the skills that you missed and then schedule to retake the test at a later date.

Tips for Successfully Completing the Test

The following tips and suggestions are the result of feedback received from many individuals who have taken one or more MOS tests:

- Make sure that you are thoroughly prepared. If you have extensively used the application for which you are being tested, you might feel confident that you are prepared for the test. However, the test might include questions that involve tasks that you rarely or never perform when you use the application at your place of business, at school, or at home. You must be knowledgeable in all the MOS objectives for the test that you will take.

- Read each exam question carefully. An exam question might include several tasks that you are to perform. A partially correct response to a test question is counted as an incorrect response. In the example question on the previous page, you might apply bold formatting and move the words at your convenience to the correct location, but forget to center the first paragraph. This would count as an incorrect response and would result in a lower test score.

- You are allowed to use the application's Help system, but relying on the Help system too much will slow you down and possibly prevent you from completing the test within the allotted time. Use the Help system only when necessary.

- Keep track of your time. The test does not display the amount of time that you have left, so you need to keep track of the time yourself by monitoring your start time and the required end time on your watch or a clock in the testing center (if there is one). The test program displays the number of items that you have completed along with the total number of test items (for example, "35 of 40 items have been completed"). Use this information to gauge your pace.

- If you skip a question, you cannot return to it later. You should skip a question only if you are certain that you cannot complete the tasks correctly.

- Don't worry if the testing software crashes while you are taking the exam. The test software is set up to handle this situation. Find your test administrator and tell him or her what happened. The administrator will work through the steps required to restart the test. When the test restarts, it will allow you to continue where you left off. You will have the same amount of time remaining to complete the test as you did when the software crashed.

■ As soon as you are finished reading a question and you click in the application window, a condensed version of the instruction is displayed in a corner of the screen. If you are unsure whether you have completed all tasks stated in the test question, click the Instructions button on the test information bar at the bottom of the screen and then reread the question. Close the instruction window when you are finished. Do this as often as necessary to ensure you have read the question correctly and that you have completed all the tasks stated in the question.

If You Do Not Pass the Test

If you do not pass, you can use the assessment printout as a guide to practice the items that you missed. There is no limit to the number of times that you can retake a test; however, you must pay the fee each time that you take the test. When you retake the test, expect to see some of the same test items on the subsequent test; the test software randomly generates the test items from a master test bank before you begin the test. Also expect to see several questions that did not appear on the previous test.

Microsoft e-Learning Library

Microsoft Learning is pleased to offer, in combination with our new *Microsoft Official Academic Course* for *Microsoft Office System 2003 Edition*, in-depth access to our powerful e-Learning tool, the Microsoft® e-Learning Library Version 2 (MELL 2) Desktop Edition for Office System 2003. The MELL Version 2 Desktop Edition for Office System 2003 will help instructors and students alike increase their skill and comfort level with Microsoft software and technologies—as well as help students develop the skills they need to succeed in today's competitive job market.

MELL Features

The MELL Version 2 Desktop Edition for Office System 2003 product included with this *Microsoft Official Academic Course* features:

- Fully customizable learning environments that help instructors pre-assess student's skill levels and direct them to the tasks that are appropriate to their needs.
- High-quality, browser-based training and reinforcement that offers students a familiar environment in which to acquire new skills.
- A powerful search tool that quickly scans a full library of learning materials and provides snappy answers to specific questions.
- Interactive exercises and focused lessons on specific subjects to help instructors direct their students quickly to exactly the content they need to know.
- Reliable, in-depth content, engaging simulations, automated support tools, and memorable on-screen demonstrations.
- An after hours and after class reference and reinforcement tool that students can take with them and use in their working lives.

Additionally, MELL Version 2 Desktop Edition for Office System 2003 fits easily into an existing lab and includes:

- Training solutions that are compatible with all existing software and hardware infrastructures.
- An enhanced learning environment that works without a separate learning management system (LMS) and runs in any SCORM-compliant LMS.
- The ability to send and receive shortcut links via e-mail to relevant help topics, which facilitates the learning experience in a classroom setting and encourages peer-to-peer learning.

Instructors who are preparing students for the MCSE/MCSA or MCAD credential can also use MELL 2 IT Professional Edition and MELL 2 Developer Edition to help students develop the skills they need to succeed in today's competitive job market. Both editions provide outstanding training and reference materials designed to help users achieve professional certification while learning real-world skills. Check out www.microsoft.com/mspress/business for more information on these additional MELL products.

Focused Students, Mastering Tasks

The MELL Version 2 Desktop Edition for Office System 2003 helps focus students on the tasks they need to know and helps them master those tasks through a combination of the following:

- Assessments that help determine the lessons that will require focus in the classroom or lab.
- Realistic simulations that mirror the actual software without requiring that it already be installed—making it ideal for students who may not have access to the latest Microsoft products outside of the classroom and labs.
- Within the simulation, the ability for a student to follow each step on his or her own, have the computer perform the step, or any combination of the two.

The MELL Version 2 Desktop Edition for Office System 2003 provides deep premium content that allows and encourages students to go beyond basic tasks and achieve proficiency and effectiveness—in class and eventually in the workplace. This depth is reflected in the fact that our desktop training titles are certified by the Microsoft Office Specialist Program.

The MELL Assessment Feature

MELL Version 2 Desktop Edition for Office System 2003 includes a skill assessment designed to help instructors identify topics and features that might warrant coverage during lecture or lab meetings. The skill assessment gives instructors an opportunity to see how much students already know about the topics covered in this course, which in turn allows instructors to devote meeting time to topics with which students are unfamiliar.

To use the assessment feature, follow these steps (note that the illustrations are specific to the Excel Core course, but the steps apply to all of the courses):

1 **Insert the Microsoft Official Academic Course companion CD that accompanies this textbook into your CD drive.**

2 From the menu, select "View e-Learning Course."

3 Click on the training course you are interested in via the left navigation pane.

4 Click on "Pre-Assessment" within any core training topic on the accompanying MELL Version 2 Desktop Edition for Office System 2003 CD-ROM.

5 Click on "Take the Pre-Assessment."

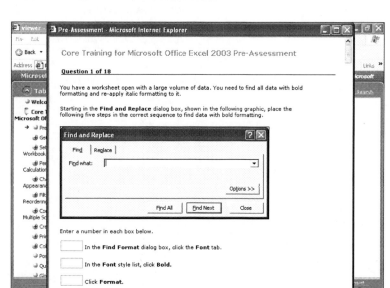

6 Input some correct answers and, if you choose, some incorrect answers as you move through the Pre-Assessment.

7 Click on "Show My Score" at the bottom of the Skills Assessment.

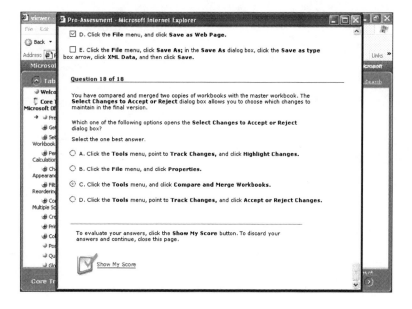

8 The "Show My Score" box details all the correct and incorrect answers and also provides correct answers for all the incorrect responses.

9 Additionally, the resultant table also provides a basic learning plan, directing you to areas you need to master while acknowledging the skills you already possess.

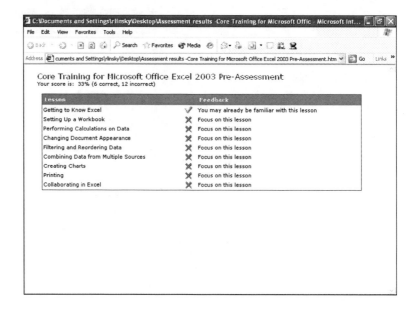

10 Click on either the "Print" or "Save" button to print or save to disk your Pre-Assessment results for future reference.

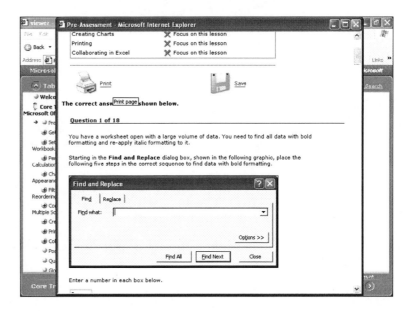

11 You are now ready to begin your interactive learning experience with MELL Version 2 Desktop Edition for Office System 2003!

1

Learning Worksheet Fundamentals

After completing this lesson, you will be able to:

✔ *Create a workbook.*
✔ *Understand Microsoft Excel window elements.*
✔ *Select cells.*
✔ *Enter text, numbers, and dates in a worksheet.*
✔ *Enter a range of data.*
✔ *Edit cell contents.*
✔ *Move between worksheets.*
✔ *Name and save a workbook.*
✔ *Open a workbook.*
✔ *Rename a worksheet.*
✔ *Preview and print a worksheet.*
✔ *Close a workbook and quit Excel.*

KEY TERMS

- active cell
- cell
- Print Preview
- range
- selecting

- task pane
- templates
- workbook
- worksheets

Introducing Excel

Microsoft Office Excel 2003 is a powerful spreadsheet program designed for organizing, formatting, and calculating numeric data. Excel displays data in a row-and-column format, with gridlines between the rows and columns, similar to accounting ledger books or graph paper. Consequently, Excel is well suited for working with numeric data for accounting, scientific research, statistical recording, and any other situation that can benefit from organizing data in a table-like format. Teachers often record student grade information in Excel, and managers often store lists of data—such as inventory records or personnel records—in Excel. As you work through this course, you'll learn how Excel makes it easy to perform calculations on numeric data and provides dozens of ways to format data for presentation purposes, including charts and reports.

IMPORTANT

Before you can use the practice files in this lesson, you must install them from the book's companion CD to their default location. For additional information on how to find and open files used in this book, see the "Using the CD-ROM" section at the beginning of this book.

Creating a Workbook

Creating a Workbook

When you start Excel, a new blank workbook opens automatically. The workbook contains three worksheets by default. Each workbook should contain information about a unique subject, such as inventory, employees, or sales. Each worksheet should hold a subset of information regarding that subject, such as inventory levels by location, salaried versus commissioned employees, or sales information for a given month.

You start Excel by using any of the methods that you use to start other Microsoft Windows programs. One common method is clicking the Start button, pointing to All Programs, pointing to Microsoft Office, and then choosing Microsoft Office Excel 2003 on the submenu. You can also click a shortcut icon, if one exists, on the desktop or on the Quick Launch bar.

TIP

Each open workbook is represented on the Excel button on the taskbar. It's easy to click a button to display a different workbook. When you have many open applications, each application has a button on which can be found a list of open files.

When you start Excel, a blank **workbook,** titled Book1, opens by default. A workbook is a file that can contain multiple **worksheets.** In turn, a worksheet is a grid of rows and columns in which you can enter data. For example, you might create four budget worksheets in a single workbook, with each worksheet containing a budget for one quarter of the upcoming fiscal year. If you're a teacher using Excel, you might create grading worksheets in the same workbook, with each worksheet storing grade records for a semester of the same class. As you can see, a workbook allows you to assemble worksheets that contain related data. After you create a workbook, you can save it as a single file on your hard disk.

◆ To complete the procedures in this lesson, you must use the practice file Employee Information in the Lesson01 folder in the Excel Core Practice folder that is located on your hard disk.

Start Excel, create a standard workbook, and close the workbook

In this exercise, you start Excel, create a standard workbook, and close the workbook.

1 On the Windows taskbar, click the Start button, point to All Programs, point to Microsoft Office, and click Microsoft Office Excel 2003.

Excel opens with Book1 ready for you to use.

FIGURE 1-1

Creating a new workbook

Other Task Panes button

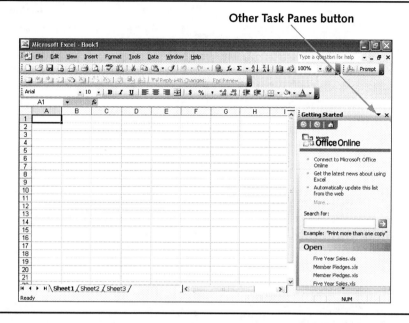

If the task pane is not displayed, open the View menu and click Task Pane.

2 Display the New Workbook task pane by clicking the Other Task Panes button and clicking New Workbook.

3 In the New section of the New Workbook task pane, click Blank Workbook.

Excel creates a workbook called Book2, and the task pane disappears.

Click Create A New Workbook at the bottom of the Getting Started task pane, and then choose Blank Workbook in the New Workbook task pane.

4 On the File menu, click Close.

Excel closes Book2, and Book1 reappears.

Click the workbook's Close Window button.

◆ Keep this file open for the next exercise.

QUICK CHECK

Q. By default, how many worksheets are in a new workbook?

A: **A new workbook contains three worksheets.**

CHECK THIS OUT ▼

Using Templates
Templates serve as a model for new workbooks and help automate common tasks such as formatting and calculating data. You can also find templates by clicking Templates On Office Online under the Templates section of the New Workbook task pane. Clicking this option takes you to Microsoft's Web site, which lists templates available for download. There are templates for a variety of tasks, from managing personal finances to tracking inventory to monitoring diet and exercise.

QUICK REFERENCE ▼

Start Excel, and create a new workbook

1 Click the Start button, point to All Programs, point to Microsoft Office, and click Microsoft Office Excel 2003.

2 On the New Workbook task pane, click Blank Workbook.

Creating a Workbook from a Template

Excel also provides **templates** that let you create workbooks already set up to track certain kinds of data, such as invoice and purchase order information. Templates are timesaving tools—they eliminate the need for you to spend time setting up the structure of a worksheet and applying complex formatting and formulas. All you need to do is enter the raw data. To create a workbook based on a template, click New on the File menu, which opens the New Workbook task pane. Under the Templates section, choose On My Computer.

FIGURE 1-2

Templates dialog box

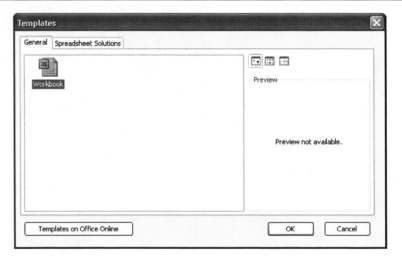

TROUBLESHOOTING

The templates you see in the Templates dialog box may be different than what is shown in Figure 1-2.

From the Templates dialog box, you can choose the General tab or the Spreadsheet Solutions tab and then select one of the templates shown.

Understanding Microsoft Excel Window Elements

THE BOTTOM LINE

The workbook window contains many of the same components that you use in other Windows applications. Being able to identify the main components of the Excel window will help you work more efficiently.

Many elements in the Excel window are similar to those in windows of other Windows programs. In Figure 1-3, the main components of the Excel window are identified.

FIGURE 1-3

Elements of the workbook window

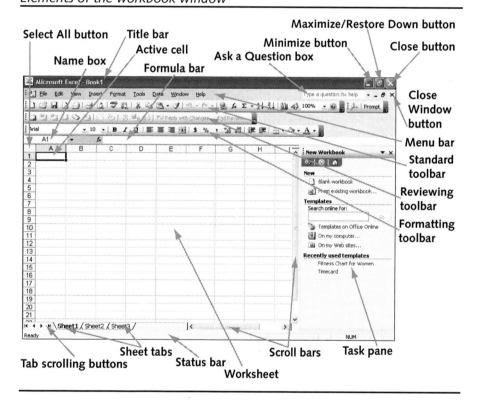

The following table describes the elements in the Excel window.

Element	Description
Title bar	Identifies the current program and the name of the current workbook
Menu bar	Lists the names of the menus in Excel
Toolbars	Give you quick access to functions that you use frequently, such as formatting, aligning, and totaling cell entries; the Standard and Formatting toolbars appear by default
Name Box	Displays the address of the active cell
Formula bar	Displays the contents of the active cell
Task pane	Lets you open files, paste data from the Clipboard, create blank workbooks, and create Excel workbooks based on existing files
Ask A Question box	Allows you to query the Help system; help topics that match your request are displayed in the task pane
Status bar	Displays information about a selected command; it also indicates the status (on or off) of the Caps Lock and Num Lock keys
Scroll bars	Include a vertical and a horizontal scroll bar and four scroll arrows, each used to display different areas of the worksheet
Select All button	Selects every cell in a worksheet
Sheet tabs	Identify the worksheets in the open workbook; click a tab to display a worksheet
Tab scrolling buttons	Let you display and navigate sheet tabs
Worksheet	A grid of vertical columns (identified by alphabetic characters) and horizontal rows (identified by numeric digits); columns and rows intersect to form cells; each cell can be identified by a full-cell reference, or address, consisting of the column and row coordinates of that cell—for example, B3
Active cell	The cell, designated by a thick border, that will be affected when you type or edit data
Minimize button	Minimizes the window to a button on the taskbar
Maximize/Restore Down	Toggles (switches back and forth) between maximizing a window and restoring a window to its previous size
Close Window button	Closes the current workbook window
ScreenTip	A small pop-up box that displays the name of an object or a toolbar button when you point to it with the mouse pointer

A great advantage of the **task pane** is that it groups many common actions, such as opening or creating new files, in one place and lets you perform them with a single mouse click. The only drawback of the task pane is that it takes up valuable screen space. Fortunately, you can show or hide the task pane easily. On the View menu, click Task Pane; Excel hides the task pane if it is currently displayed or shows it if it is currently hidden.

The benefit of placing the Ask A Question box in the main Excel window is that you can quickly and easily get help while your question is fresh in your mind, without adding any steps that might distract you from your question. With this feature, you no longer have to go to the Help menu or Office Assistant when you need help.

Become familiar with Excel window elements

In this exercise, you work with Excel window elements.

1 Point to the Chart Wizard button on the Standard toolbar for a few seconds.

A ScreenTip appears, displaying the words *Chart Wizard*.

2 Point to the Name Box, which contains the cell address A1.

A ScreenTip appears, displaying the title *Name Box*.

FIGURE 1-4

Displaying ScreenTips

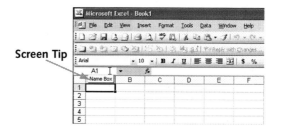

3 Click the Toolbar Options button at the end of the Formatting toolbar.

A menu with options appears.

FIGURE 1-5

Displaying Toolbar Options

4 Point to the Add Or Remove Buttons command.

A menu with additional commands appears.

5 **Point to Formatting on the submenu.**

A menu with the formatting button options appears.

FIGURE 1-6

Formatting button options

6 **Review the names of buttons on the menu.**

7 **When you are done, click somewhere outside of the open menus to close the menus.**

◆ **Keep this file open for the next exercise.**

Selecting Cells

THE BOTTOM LINE

Once you have opened a workbook, you can examine and modify its contents. To change specific data, you must first select the cell containing the data.

Before you can enter data in a worksheet, you must identify the **cell** (the intersection of a row and a column) in which you want to put the data. This is known as **selecting** the cell. You can select a single cell, a row, a column, and groups of adjacent and nonadjacent cells. You might select more than one cell in order to perform the same operation on all of them; for example, you might want to delete all of the data in a selected row.

To select a single cell, simply click that cell. When a cell is selected, a black border surrounds it, and that cell becomes the **active cell**, as shown in Figure 1-7.

FIGURE 1-7

Selecting a cell

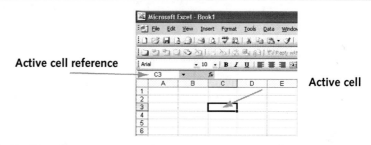

Active cell reference

Active cell

You can select all of the cells in a worksheet by clicking the Select All button at the top left corner of the worksheet.

FIGURE 1-8

Selecting all cells in a worksheet

Select All button

You can select a single row or column in a worksheet by clicking the corresponding row or column selector. For example, you might want to move an entire row of data to a new location in the worksheet, or you might want to apply a currency format to all of the data in a column.

FIGURE 1-9

Selecting a row or column

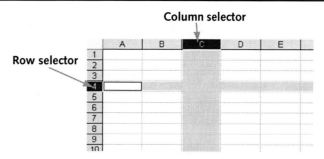

Column selector

Row selector

TIP

When you select a cell, the text on its row selector and its column selector appear shaded in orange instead of gray like the rest of the row and column selectors. That feature makes it easier to see the row and column "coordinates" of the selected cell. In addition, the cell address appears in the Name Box.

Select an entire row and an entire column in a worksheet

In this exercise, you select an entire row and an entire column in the current worksheet.

1 **Click the column selector for column D.**

Column D is selected.

2 **Click the row selector for row 1.**

Row 1 is selected.

3 **Click the column selector for column B, and drag the mouse pointer to the column selector for column E.**

The columns are selected.

4 **Click any cell in column G.**

Columns B, C, D, and E are deselected.

◆ **Keep this file open for the next exercise.**

ANOTHER METHOD

Another way to select a range of columns is to click the first column selector in the range, hold down the Shift key, and click the last column selector in the range. The same method works for selecting a range of rows.

QUICK REFERENCE ▼

Select a row or a column in a worksheet

Click the row or column selector.

QUICK CHECK

Q. What does a black border around a cell indicate?

A: A black border indicates that the cell is active.

Selecting a Range of Cells

THE BOTTOM LINE

Just as you can change the data in a single cell, you can also make changes to the data in a range, or contiguous group, of cells by selecting the range. Working with a range of cells saves you the time of performing the same operations, such as cutting, copying, or formatting, repeatedly on individual cells.

A **range** is normally identified by the references for its first and last cells, with a colon between them. For example, the vertical range extending from cell A1 to cell A9 is identified as A1:A9. Likewise, the horizontal range extending from cell C3 to cell G3 is identified as C3:G3. Ranges that extend across a block of columns and rows are identified by the addresses for the cells in the top left and bottom right corners of that block (B5:F9), as shown in Figure 1-10.

FIGURE 1-10

Selecting the range B5:F9

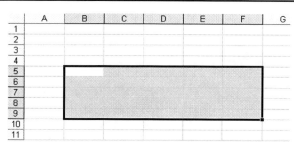

You select a range of cells by dragging the mouse pointer over the cells. When you select a range of cells, the first cell chosen becomes the active cell. The active cell is white, and the range of cells is blue. As you have learned, when you select more than one cell, you can perform the same operation on all of the cells at once.

Select a group of adjacent cells in the current worksheet

You've learned how to select a cell, a column, and a row. Now you will learn how to select a group of adjacent cells.

1 Click cell E3, hold down the mouse button, drag the mouse pointer down to cell E12, and release the mouse button.

The range E3:E12 is selected, and E3 remains the active cell.

2 Click cell A5, hold down the Shift key, and click cell H16.

The range is selected, and A5 remains the active cell.

FIGURE 1-11

Selecting the range A5:H16

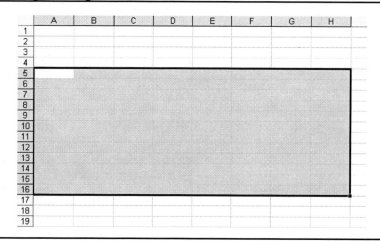

TIP

To select multiple nonadjacent cell ranges, select the first range, hold down the Ctrl key, and select any additional ranges.

3 Click cell F17, hold down the Shift key, and press the Down arrow key four times.

The range of cells from F17 to F21 (referred to as F17:F21) is selected.

QUICK REFERENCE ▼

Select a range of cells

1 Click the top left cell of the range of cells.

2 Drag the mouse to the bottom right cell in the range of cells.

Entering Text in a Worksheet

THE BOTTOM LINE

Worksheets contain three types of data: text, numbers, and formulas. Text values are sometimes referred to as "labels." These values can be the names of employees or a list of products. They are often used to help identify the numeric data contained in the worksheet, but they can also be used for other tasks, such as sorting and grouping data.

You can enter three basic categories of data in an Excel worksheet: text, numbers, and formulas. To enter text or numbers in a cell, you select the cell and type the information. As you type, each character appears in the Formula bar and in the active cell, along with the insertion point. The insertion point indicates where the next character will be inserted.

A text entry, which is sometimes called a label, is one that contains the characters *A* through *Z* or any other character that doesn't have a purely numeric value. Sometimes a text entry includes numbers, such as in a street address.

By default, a text entry appears left-justified in a cell. When the entry is longer than the defined width of the cell, it either "spills over" into the adjacent cell (if that cell is empty) or it appears in truncated form (if the adjacent cell is not empty). Internally, however, the text is stored in only one cell and includes each character originally entered.

Enter text in a worksheet

In this exercise, you enter text in a worksheet.

1 Click cell A1, type Sales, and press Enter.

The text is entered in cell A1, and A2 becomes the active cell.

ANOTHER METHOD

Press Tab or an arrow key to enter data and move to another cell.

2 Click cell A3, type Cabins, and press Enter.

Cell A3 contains the word *Cabins,* and the active cell moves to A4.

3 Type Condos, and press Enter.

The word *Condos* is entered in cell A4.

FIGURE 1-12

Entering text in a cell

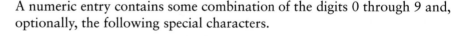

◆ Keep this file open for the next exercise.

Entering Numbers in a Worksheet

THE BOTTOM LINE

Once you enter numeric values in a worksheet, you can perform all kinds of calculations and analyses on them. Numbers can be formatted as currency, percentages, decimals, and fractions. Numeric values are also used to develop complex charts and graphs in Excel, which are useful tools for doing comparisons and making projections.

A numeric entry contains some combination of the digits 0 through 9 and, optionally, the following special characters.

Character	Used To
+	Indicate a positive value
- or ( )	Indicate a negative value
$	Indicate a currency value
%	Indicate a percentage
/	Indicate a fraction
.	Indicate a decimal value
,	Separate the digits of the entry
E or e	Display the entry in scientific (exponential) notation

When you start an entry with a plus sign to indicate a positive number, Excel ignores the sign. When you type parentheses to indicate a negative number, the number appears with a minus sign. When you include a dollar sign, a percent sign, a forward slash, a comma, or an exponential symbol, the program automatically assigns a numeric format to the entry.

QUICK CHECK

Q: Where are numeric entries aligned in a cell?

A: They are right-aligned, or right-justified.

By default, a numeric entry appears right-justified in a cell. When the entry is longer than the defined width of the cell, it appears in scientific notation, as pound signs (####), or rounded. Internally, however, Excel stores all numbers as originally entered.

ANOTHER METHOD

You can enter numbers by using the number keys above the letters on your keyboard or by pressing the Num Lock key and using the numeric keypad. Num Lock is a toggle key. An indicator light on your keyboard shines when Num Lock is on.

Enter sales figures in your worksheet

In this exercise, you enter numeric data in the worksheet.

1 Click cell B3, type 42848, and press Enter.

The number is entered in cell B3, and B4 becomes the active cell.

2 Type 92346, and press Enter.

The number is entered in cell B4, and B5 becomes the active cell.

◆ Keep this file open for the next exercise.

Entering Dates in a Worksheet

THE BOTTOM LINE

Dates are commonly used in worksheets to track data over a specified time period. Like other numeric values, they can be used in formulas and in developing charts and graphs.

Dates in Excel worksheets can be represented using only numbers or a combination of text and numbers. For example, *January 22, 2004*, and *1/22/04* are two ways of entering the same date. Like text, dates are often used as row and column labels. But unlike text, dates are considered *serial numbers*; they are sequential and can be added, subtracted, and used in calculations.

Be careful when representing a year with just the last two digits of the year. Excel interprets two-digit years from 00 to 29 to represent the years 2000 to 2029; two-digit years from 30 to 99 are interpreted as 1930 to 1999. The default year format uses two digits; however, it is a good idea to type four-digit years to avoid ambiguity.

By default, a date entry appears right-justified in a cell. After you type and enter a date in a cell, Excel might reformat the date and express it in a different way. The way in which a date is represented in a cell is initially based on your computer's default date setting. You will learn how to choose date formats, including the four-digit year options, in the next lesson.

Enter dates in a worksheet

You have learned how to enter text and numbers in a worksheet. Now you will enter dates in the worksheet.

1 Click cell B1, type January 2005, and press Tab.

Excel abbreviates the date to *Jan-05*, and C1 becomes the active cell.

2 Type Feb 2005, and press Tab.

Excel uses the same date formatting as above, and *Feb-05* is entered in cell C1. D1 is now the active cell.

◆ Keep this file open for the next exercise.

QUICK REFERENCE ▼

Enter data in a cell

1 Select a cell.
2 Type the data in the cell.
3 Press Enter.

Entering a Range of Data

THE BOTTOM LINE

When you select a range of cells first, the next cell in which you want to enter data automatically becomes active when you press the Enter key. This saves you the time of going to specific cells, such as the top of the next column in the range or the beginning of the next row in the range.

To enter data in an individual cell, you type the data and then press Enter. When you have several consecutive entries to make, you can select the range first to enter the data more quickly. For example, you might have several rows listing expenses and columns that label the expenses by day of the week. When you select the range first, you simply type the raw expense figures and press Enter. When you get to the bottom cell of a column in the range and press Enter, the insertion point automatically jumps to the first cell in the next column of the range.

Enter more sales figures in your worksheet

You have learned how to enter data by navigating to a selected cell and typing the data. In this exercise, you will learn how to enter a range of data.

1 Click cell C3, drag to cell D4, and release the mouse button.

Cells C3, C4, D3, and D4 are selected.

2 Type 39768, and press Enter.

The number is entered in cell C3, and C4 becomes the active cell.

3 Type 90426, and press Enter.

The number is entered in cell C4, and D3 becomes the active cell.

TIP

When entering text in a range of cells, you can press Tab to move from cell to cell horizontally and Enter to move from cell to cell vertically. When you reach the end of a column within a range, pressing Enter will take you to the cell at the top of the next column in the range.

4 Type 45122, and press Enter.

The number is entered in cell D3, and D4 becomes the active cell.

FIGURE 1-13

Entering a range of data

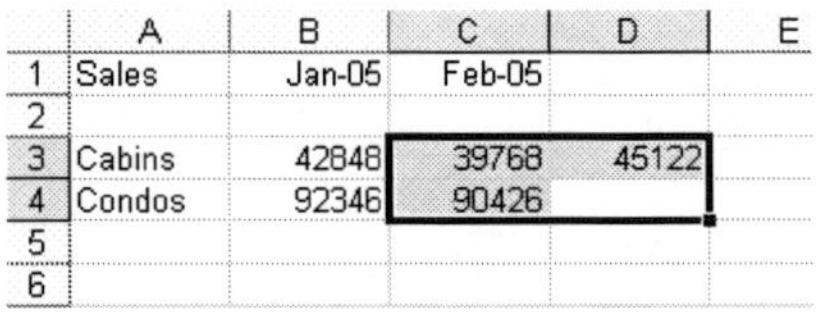

	A	B	C	D	E
1	Sales	Jan-05	Feb-05		
2					
3	Cabins	42848	39768	45122	
4	Condos	92346	90426		
5					
6					

5 Type 87409, and press Enter.

The number is entered, and cell C3 becomes the active cell.

◆ Keep this file open for the next exercise.

QUICK CHECK

Q. Which key do you press to move from cell to cell horizontally when entering data in a range of cells?

A: You press the Tab key.

QUICK REFERENCE ▼

Enter data in a range of cells

1. Select the range of cells.
2. Type the data in one of the cells, and press Enter.
3. Continue typing data and pressing Enter until the range of cells is filled.

Editing Cell Contents

THE BOTTOM LINE

Once you've entered values in a worksheet, you might want to delete them, add to them, or change them completely. Worksheets are not static, which makes it easy to correct a mistake or edit cell contents.

Checking and Correcting Data

After you have entered data in a cell, you can easily change the contents of the cell. However, you must first double-click the cell or click the cell and click in the Formula bar. Either of these actions puts Excel in Edit mode, which you can verify by checking that the word *Edit* appears in the status bar. After that, you type and press the Delete or Backspace key to edit the data in the cell. When Excel is in Edit mode, two buttons appear to the left of the Formula bar: Cancel and Enter.

FIGURE 1-14

Edit mode buttons on the Formula bar

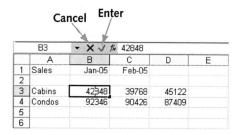

You can click the Cancel button or press the Esc key to cancel an entry before it is actually entered in the worksheet. Doing either of these deletes anything you have typed and brings Excel out of Edit mode. It also restores the previous contents of the active cell if that cell contained data. You can click the Enter button to complete an entry.

Revise entries in the current worksheet

In this exercise, you make changes to some of the entries in the current worksheet.

1 Click cell B3, position the mouse pointer between 2 and 8 in the Formula bar, and click.

Edit mode is activated, and the insertion point appears as an I-beam.

2 Press Backspace, type 6, and press Enter.

Cell B3 now contains the entry 46848.

ANOTHER METHOD

When you click a cell and then press F2, Edit mode is activated and the insertion point is placed at the end of the cell, allowing you to edit the current contents.

3 Click cell C4, type 92313, and press Enter.

Cell C4 now contains the entry 92313.

4 Click cell C3, type 65452, and click the Cancel button on the Formula bar.

The data entry is canceled, and the original value is restored.

◆ Keep this file open for the next exercise.

QUICK REFERENCE ▼

Edit the contents of a cell

1 Double-click the cell.

2 Edit the data by deleting, inserting, and replacing characters.

Moving between Worksheets

THE BOTTOM LINE

Often the workbooks you create will contain a number of worksheets. You can easily move between worksheets by clicking their sheet tabs at the bottom of the worksheet window.

As explained at the beginning of this lesson, each Excel workbook is made up of individual worksheets. This gives you the flexibility to group worksheets with similar subject matter together in one workbook. By default, a new workbook contains three blank worksheets. More worksheets can be added as needed, and unused worksheets can be deleted if desired. The names of the sheets appear in tabs along the bottom of the workbook window.

FIGURE 1-15

Sheet tabs

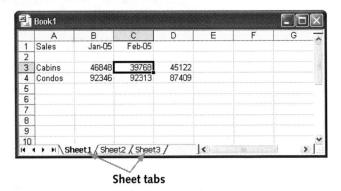

Sheet tabs

View two worksheets within the same workbook

You have learned how to move around in a worksheet. Now you will learn how to move between different worksheets within the same workbook.

1 Click the Sheet2 tab at the bottom of the workbook window.

Sheet2 and its contents appear. The worksheet is blank.

2 Click the Sheet1 tab at the bottom of the workbook window.

Sheet1 and its contents reappear.

◆ Keep this file open for the next exercise.

Right-click a sheet tab to display a shortcut menu that allows you to, among other options, insert or delete worksheets.

QUICK REFERENCE ▼

Move to another worksheet in the same workbook

Click the sheet tab for the worksheet.

Naming and Saving a Workbook

THE BOTTOM LINE

Like any data you enter in a computer file, you'll want to save your workbook files so that you can work with them later. Excel allows you to save workbooks in a variety of formats so that they can be opened and used in different spreadsheet programs and even in non-spreadsheet programs, such as in Microsoft Word and Access and on the Web.

Saving Changes to an Existing Workbook

When you finish entering and editing data in a workbook, you need to name and save the workbook on your hard disk so that the information will be available the next time you start your computer. Saving workbook files is similar to saving other types of files in Windows programs. The first time you save a workbook, you need to name it and specify in which folder you want to save it. You can save it in a folder on your computer's hard disk or, if your computer is connected to a network, on a hard disk in a different computer. You can even create a folder in which to save the workbook by using tools within Excel. After you've saved a workbook, you just click the Save button on the Standard toolbar to save any changes you made after the last time you saved. The workbook will be saved with the same name and in the same place.

When you want to save the workbook with a different name or in a different folder, you make those changes by performing the same steps that you performed when you saved the workbook for the first time. As with any other Windows file, a workbook's name can be up to 255 characters long, but it can't contain any of the following characters:

/ \ > < * ? " | : ;

You can also use the controls in the Save As dialog box to specify a different format for the new file. For example, you might need to save an Excel file in a different format so that you can share the file with another person who uses a different spreadsheet program, such as Lotus, or even for use in a non-spreadsheet program.

The Places bar in the Open and Save As dialog boxes gives you convenient access to files stored in your My Documents folder, in your Favorites folder, and on your desktop. The History folder on the Places bar also provides easy access to recently opened workbooks.

Save a workbook to a folder, and save a workbook as a Lotus file

In this exercise, you save your workbook into a folder you create within Excel. You also save the workbook as a Lotus file.

1 **On the File menu, click Save As.**

Excel displays the Save As dialog box. The files and folders that appear in this dialog box will depend on the folder that was last used to save a workbook on your computer.

FIGURE 1-16

Save As dialog box

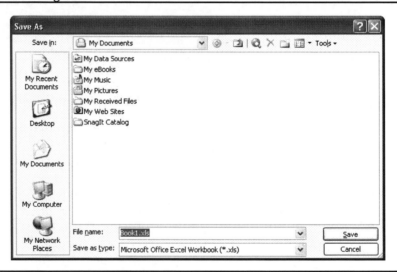

2 **Click the Save In down arrow, and click the icon for your local hard disk (probably drive C).**

3 **Double-click the Excel Core Practice folder.**

4 **Click the Create New Folder button in the dialog box.**

The New Folder dialog box appears.

5 **Type 2005 Sales, and click OK.**

The New Folder dialog box closes, and the Save As dialog box displays the 2005 Sales folder. The name Book1 appears in the File Name text box because Book1 is the open file.

ANOTHER METHOD

You can also create folders using Windows Explorer. You don't need to create them within Excel.

6 **Select the text in the File Name text box, type** Lodging Sales, **and then click Save.**

The file is named and saved.

7 **On the File menu, click Save As.**

8 **In the Save As dialog box, click the down arrow in the Save As Type text box.**

9 **Scroll and select the WK4(1-2-3)(*.wk4) option.**

10 **Click Save.**

A message box appears explaining that there may be some features in your file that are not supported in the format you have chosen.

11 **Click Yes in the message box.**

Your file is now saved with the same name but as a Lotus spreadsheet, so it has a different file name extension.

◆ **Close Lodging Sales.wk4. Leave Excel open for the next exercise.**

QUICK REFERENCE ▼

Create a folder

1 On the File menu, click Save As.

2 Navigate to the location where you want to create the folder.

3 Click the Create New Folder button in the Save As dialog box.

4 In the New Folder dialog box, type a name for the folder in the Name Box and click OK.

QUICK **CHECK**

Q. How many characters can be in the file name for a workbook?

A: **A file name can have up to 255 characters.**

Opening a Workbook

THE BOTTOM LINE

After you save an Excel workbook, you can reopen it at any time to review its contents and make changes.

Once you've saved a workbook to disk, you can open it in a number of ways. You can click the Open button or select Open on the File menu and then select the file from the Open dialog box. Or you can open it from the Getting Started task pane. If the workbook is one of the last four you've worked on, it will be listed at the bottom of the File menu, and all you need to do is click it to open it.

Open an existing workbook

You have learned how to create a new blank workbook. Now you will learn how to open an existing workbook.

1 **On the Standard toolbar, click the Open button.**

The Open dialog box appears.

- ■ Click Open on the File menu.
- ■ Press Ctrl+O.

2 **Click the Look In down arrow, click the icon for your hard disk, and double-click the Excel Core Practice folder.**

The contents of the Excel Core Practice folder appear in the Open dialog box.

FIGURE 1-17

Opening an existing workbook

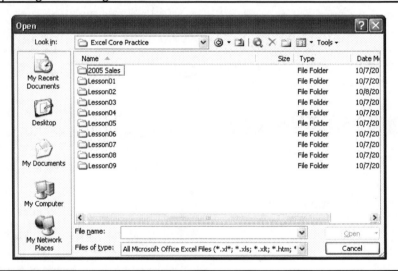

3 **Double-click the Lesson01 folder.**

The names of the files stored in the Lesson01 folder appear.

If you open an existing workbook, Excel closes the blank Book1 workbook that appeared when you started the program.

4 **Click the Employee Information file, and click Open.**

The Open dialog box closes, and the Employee Information file appears.

ANOTHER METHOD

Double-click the Excel icon next to the file name in the Open dialog box.

5 **On the File menu, click Close.**

Excel closes the Employee Information workbook.

ANOTHER METHOD

Click the workbook's Close Window button.

6 **Click File on the menu bar.**

Excel displays a list of recently opened workbooks at the bottom of the File menu.

7 **On the File menu, click Employee Information.**

The file opens.

◆ **Keep this file open for the next exercise.**

QUICK REFERENCE ▼

Open a previously created workbook

1 On the File menu, click Open.

Or

Click More on the Getting Started task pane.

2 Browse to the location of the file.

3 Click the file name.

4 Click Open.

Renaming a Worksheet

THE BOTTOM LINE

In workbooks that contain more than one worksheet with data, you'll probably want to assign names to the sheets that help identify the data that's on them.

Making Workbooks Easier to Work With

By default, the worksheets in each Excel workbook are named Sheet1, Sheet2, and Sheet3. Just as giving a unique name to your workbook helps you remember what is in it, renaming a worksheet can remind you of its contents. For example, a chain of restaurants might have a budget workbook that contains a worksheet for each restaurant location. The sheets are named according to location.

Rename a worksheet

In this exercise, you give a worksheet a different name.

1 Double-click the Sheet1 sheet tab.

Sheet1 is selected within the tab.

2 Type Directory, and press Enter.

Directory appears on the sheet tab.

◆ **Keep this file open for the next exercise.**

ANOTHER METHOD

Right-click a sheet tab, and then click Rename.

QUICK REFERENCE ▼

Rename a worksheet within a workbook

1 Double-click the sheet tab at the bottom of the worksheet.

2 Type a new name, and press Enter.

Previewing and Printing a Worksheet

THE BOTTOM LINE

You can see how a worksheet looks before printing it by displaying it in the Print Preview window. Previewing the worksheet can help you spot formatting inconsistencies and irregular page breaks, which you can then correct before printing. Having a printout of a worksheet can also help you identify errors or formatting problems, but it's also useful when you want to distribute copies to people who don't have access to the electronic file.

After a worksheet is complete, you can preview and print its contents. To print a worksheet, you begin by displaying the Print dialog box. In this dialog box, you can change most print settings, preview the data, and print the worksheet.

You should check the spelling in a worksheet before printing it. Click the Spelling button on the Standard toolbar to begin checking the worksheet.

Also, before printing a worksheet, you can preview it. The **Print Preview** window, shown in Figure 1-18, displays a full-page view of the file just as it will be printed so that you can check the format and overall layout before actually printing.

FIGURE 1-18

Print Preview window

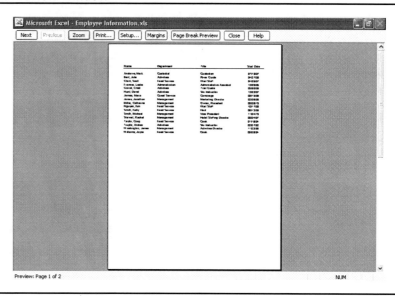

Commands available in the Print Preview window appear as buttons across the top of the window. The current page number and total number of pages in the worksheet appear in the bottom left corner of the window.

Printing Worksheets

When you're ready to print, you can decide to print the entire workbook, a single sheet in a workbook, or just a selected range of data. You can select the range of cells you want to print before displaying the Print dialog box, or you can specify the range you want to print in the Print dialog box.

Preview and print the current worksheet

Now that you've entered data in a worksheet and saved it, you'll preview and print it.

1 **Click the Print Preview button on the Standard toolbar.**

The file appears in the Print Preview window.

ANOTHER METHOD

Click Print Preview on the File menu.

2 **Click anywhere in the worksheet.**

The zoom factor is increased, and the preview is enlarged.

3 **Click anywhere in the worksheet again.**

The zoom factor is decreased, and the preview is reduced.

TIP

To print a file from the Print Preview window, click Print on the Print Preview toolbar to display the Print dialog box.

4 Click the Close button on the Print Preview toolbar.

The Print Preview window closes.

5 On the File menu, click Print.

The Print dialog box appears.

ANOTHER METHOD

Press Ctrl+P.

6 Click OK.

The current worksheet is printed.

7 Click the Save button on the Standard toolbar.

The worksheet is saved using the current name.

ANOTHER METHOD

Click Save on the File menu.

◆ Keep this file open for the next exercise.

IMPORTANT

The Close button above the Close Window button is used to quit Excel. Be careful not to click Close instead of Close Window. When you're not sure which button to click, position the mouse pointer over the button for a moment. A ScreenTip will appear, telling you the name of the button on which the mouse pointer is positioned.

QUICK REFERENCE ▼

Preview and print a worksheet

1 Click the Print Preview button on the Standard toolbar.

2 On the File menu, click Print.

Or

Press Ctrl+P to open the Print dialog box.

3 Make selections as desired, and click OK.

QUICK **CHECK**

Q. When you are in the Print Preview window, which button do you click to return to Normal view?

A: **You click the Close button.**

Closing a Workbook and Quitting Excel

THE BOTTOM LINE

When you are done working in a file, you should close it to keep your taskbar and desktop uncluttered. This also helps eliminate the possibility of someone else making unwanted changes to the file.

You can remove a workbook from the window by closing the workbook or by quitting Excel. Closing the current workbook leaves Excel running, while closing quits the Excel program.

After a workbook is saved on your hard disk, you can clear it from the screen by closing the workbook window. If the workbook has not been saved, Excel will prompt you to save it before closing the window. When you have finished using Excel, you need to close it using Excel commands. Do not turn off your computer while a program is running.

TIP

To close all open workbooks at once, hold down the Shift key and then click Close All on the File menu.

Close a workbook, and quit Excel

In this exercise, you close a workbook and quit Excel.

1 Click the Close Window button in the top right corner of the work-book window.

The workbook closes.

2 Click the Close button in the top right corner of the Excel window.

Excel closes.

ANOTHER METHOD

Click Exit on the File menu.

◀◆▶ If you are continuing to other lessons, restart Excel.

Key Points

✓ *Excel is a powerful spreadsheet program you use to organize and calculate data.*

✓ *Before you can enter data or make modifications to it, you must first select the cell or range containing the data.*

✓ *You enter data in a worksheet by simply typing in the selected cell. Often you will want to make changes to the data you enter. All you need to do is select the cell and type your changes directly in the cell or in the Formula bar.*

✓ *You will likely enter data on a number of worksheets within a workbook. You can switch to a different sheet by clicking its sheet tab.*

✓ *As with just about any computer file, you will want to save a workbook to disk so that you can open it and work with it again.*

✓ *In workbooks that have more than one worksheet containing data, you should name the worksheets so that you can easily identify the data that they contain. You also might want to print individual worksheets so that you can review a hard-copy printout of data or distribute them to others to review.*

Quick Quiz

True/False

T F 1. You can move between worksheets by clicking the scroll arrows.

T F 2. You can create a workbook from templates that are stored on your computer or from templates you find online.

T F 3. By default, a new workbook contains three worksheets.

T F 4. The title bar contains the names of Excel's menus.

T F 5. The columns in a worksheet are identified by numbers.

T F 6. You cannot print a worksheet while in the Print Preview window.

Multiple Choice

1. Which key can you press to put Excel in Edit mode?
   a. Esc
   b. F1
   c. F2
   d. F3

2. How is the active cell in a worksheet identified?
   a. It has a black border surrounding it.
   b. It is white, while the rest of the cells are gray.
   c. It is shaded in orange.
   d. It is shaded in black.

3. Which element in the Excel window displays information about a selected command?
   a. Formula bar
   b. horizontal scroll bar
   c. Name Box
   d. status bar

4. Which element in the Excel window displays the contents of the active cell?
   a. Formula bar
   b. horizontal scroll bar
   c. Name Box
   d. status bar

Short Answer

1. How can you select all cells in a worksheet simultaneously?

2. How can you open an existing workbook?

3. What is the easiest way to enter data in a range of cells?

4. How can you rename a worksheet?

5. How can you close all open workbooks at once?

6. What are two ways to select a range of cells?

7. How can you select nonadjacent ranges of cells?

8. What's the difference between clicking New on the File menu and clicking the New button?

9. What are three characters that can't be used in the name of a workbook?

10. What information does the Name Box display?

IMPORTANT

In the On Your Own section below, you must complete Exercise 1 before continuing to Exercise 2.

On Your Own

Exercise 1

Create a workbook named **MyFirst**. In cells B1, C1, and D1, type the names and years of the next three months, such as July 2004, August 2005, and September 2005. Select the range B2:D3, and enter numbers in the cells.

Exercise 2

Click cell C3, and use the Formula bar to change the number in the cell. Rename Sheet1 MyFirstSheet. Select column B, and then select row 5. Simultaneously select the ranges B1:D2 and B5:D7. Preview your worksheet, print it, and save it.

One Step Further

Exercise 1

This lesson discussed the fact that Excel provides a number of predesigned templates for your use. Open the Loan Amortization template (in the Spreadsheet Solutions templates), and give a brief description of its purpose. If you don't have the Loan Amortization template, open another one. Enter data in the worksheet to explore how the spreadsheet works. How would a template like this be useful to you?

Exercise 2

You may have noticed in the Templates section of the New Worksheet task pane that there are two other sources of templates besides those that were installed on your computer with the Excel application. One is Web sites that you may learn of, and the other is Microsoft's Web site. If you have Internet access, click the Templates on Office Online option and explore the templates available there. (*Hint:* You may wish to explore the templates that deal with your personal interests and hobbies.)

Exercise 3

In this lesson, you learned how to select a range of cells. Use the Ask A Question box to find out how to deselect some portion in a range without deselecting the entire range and reselecting the desired cells.

LESSON

2

Editing and Formatting Worksheets

After completing this lesson, you will be able to:

✔ *Format numeric data.*
✔ *Adjust the size of rows and columns.*
✔ *Align cell contents.*
✔ *Find and replace cell contents.*
✔ *Insert and delete cells, rows, and columns.*
✔ *Cut, copy, paste, and clear cells.*
✔ *Use additional paste techniques.*

KEY TERMS

- clear
- collect and paste
- column width
- copy
- cut
- Office Clipboard

- paste
- Paste Special
- points
- row height
- string

Microsoft Excel provides tools that give you great flexibility in changing the appearance of your data and the structure of your worksheets. With a little effort, you can adjust spacing, alignment, and the look of type to make a worksheet easier to view, follow, and update; they're easier for others to use, too.

You can change the way numbers are displayed so that their appearance corresponds with the type of numbers you are using. For instance, if you enter sales amounts in a worksheet, you can format them so that they look like monetary values. That is, if you enter *1455* in a worksheet, you can format this number so that it appears as *$1,455*.

You can also change the width of columns so that the data in the column fits appropriately, and you can increase the height of a particular row to call attention to the data in the row. As you work with worksheets, you'll often find that you must move or copy data to other locations—a feature that is easy to perform in Excel. In fact, Excel provides numerous techniques you can use to copy or move data to a different location in a worksheet or even to a different worksheet.

You can also use Excel to look for specific data in a worksheet and then display the cell where the data appears. When you want to replace data with different data, Excel provides a way to automate this process as well.

Formatting Numbers

Making Numbers
Easier to Read

THE BOTTOM LINE

Numeric values can be used for various types of data—currency, percentages, decimals, and more. Applying accurate formatting to numeric data makes it more useful and easier to interpret and analyze.

Most of the data that you use in Excel is numeric. This data includes financial figures, dates, fractions, percentages, and other information that usually appears with a mix of numerals and symbols. To be more meaningful, most numeric data needs some special touches—a dollar sign, a certain number of decimal places, or a percent sign, for example.

At a resort hotel, for example, the bookkeeper tracks room sales collected per week. She wants the sales amounts to look like monetary amounts; for example, *$53.00*, not just *53*. In entering the sales amounts, she could type a dollar sign, followed by the number of dollars, followed by a decimal point, followed by the number of cents. But she knows that it's much easier to enter the raw sales amounts and let Excel add these currency formats.

To quickly change how your numeric data appears, you can select one of Excel's options for formatting numbers, either before or after you enter the number in the cell. These options automatically insert and delete symbols and digits to reflect the format you choose. By default, all data you enter is formatted with the General option, which shows the data exactly as you enter it. If you include a date or a special character ($ % / , E e) when entering a number, Excel automatically formats it with the appropriate option. When you want entries to appear differently, you can choose from the following formats, organized by category.

Category	Appearance	If You Type	It Looks Like
General	Displays data exactly as you enter it	1234	1234
Number	Displays two decimal places by default	1234	1234.00
Currency	Displays currency and other symbols appropriate for various regions of the world (including the euro)	1234	$1,234.00
Accounting	Displays currency symbols and aligns decimal points of entries in a column	1234 12	$1,234.00 $12.00
Date	Displays days, months, and years in various formats, such as *May 18, 2005, 18-May,* and *3/14/2001*	1234	May 18, 1903 18-May 5/18/1903
Time	Displays hours, minutes, and seconds in various formats, such as *8:47 PM, 20:47,* and *8:47:56*	12:34	12:34 AM 12:34 12:34:00
Percentage	Multiplies cell values by 100 and displays the result with a percent sign	1234	123400.00%
Fraction	Displays entries as fractions in various denominations and to various degrees of accuracy	12.34	12 1/3
Scientific	Displays entries in scientific or exponential notation	1234	1.23E+03
Text	Displays entries exactly as they were entered, even if the entry is a number	1234	1234
Special	Displays and formats list and database values, such as Zip Codes, phone numbers, and U.S. Social Security numbers	12345 123-555-1234 000-00-0000	12345 123-555-1234 000-00-0000
Custom	Allows you to create formats that aren't available in any of the other categories		Appearance varies based on format you create

After you choose an option, you might need to further specify how you want the numbers to appear; for example, you can choose how many decimal places to use, select international currency symbols, and set the format for negative numbers.

◆ To complete the procedures in this lesson, you must use the practice files **Percent Sales Increase, Five Years Sales02, Rentals,** and **Monthly Sales** in the Lesson02 folder in the Excel Core Practice folder that is located on your hard disk.

◆ Open **Percent Sales Increase** from the Excel Core Practice/Lesson02 folder.

Format several numeric entries in a worksheet

In this exercise, you apply formats to raw numeric data that's already been entered.

1 **Make sure that cell A1 is currently selected, and on the Format menu, click Cells.**

The Format Cells dialog box appears.

ANOTHER METHOD

- Press Ctrl+1.
- Right-click a cell, and choose Format Cells on the shortcut menu.

2 **Click the Number tab, if necessary, and in the Category list, click Date.**

The Number tab is displayed, and the Type list is filled with options for formatting dates.

FIGURE 2-1

Number tab in the Format Cells dialog box

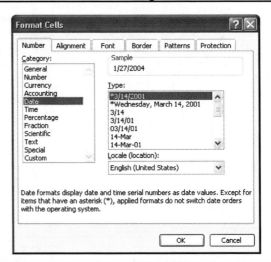

3 **In the Type list, click 3/14/01, and click OK.**

The date in cell A1 changes to match the date format that you selected.

4 **Select the range B3:F8.**

5 **On the Format menu, click Cells, and then click Currency in the Category list.**

The Format Cells dialog box appears with formatting options for Currency (monetary values) shown. Notice that the default format for currency includes the dollar sign ($), a thousands comma separator, and two decimal places.

FIGURE 2-2

Currency formats

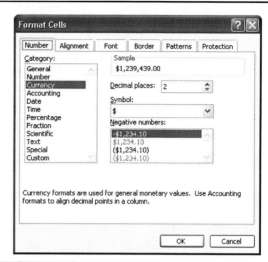

IMPORTANT

Make sure that you type a zero at step 6, *not* the letter O.

6 **Double-click in the Decimal places box, type 0, and press Enter.**

The selected cells are now in currency format, with no decimal places.

7 **Select the range C10:F10.**

8 **On the Format menu, click Cells, and then click Percentage in the Category list.**

The Format Cells dialog box appears with Percentage selected, and the dialog box shows the sample format for the first cell in the selected range. The only option you can change for the percentage format is the number of decimal places.

FIGURE 2-3

Applying the Percentage format

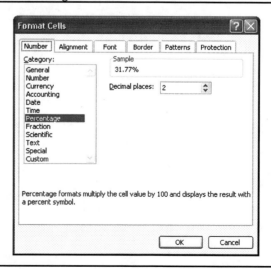

9 **Click OK.**

The selected cells appear in percentage format, with two decimal places.

10 **Click any blank cell in the worksheet.**

The selected range is deselected. The worksheet looks similar to that shown in Figure 2-4.

FIGURE 2-4

Applying number formats to data

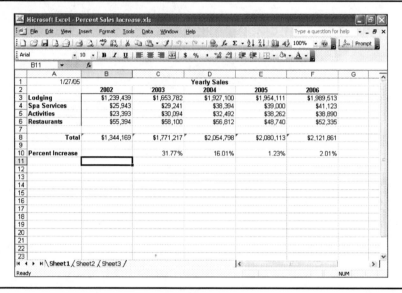

You can also use the Formatting toolbar to specify some of the more widely used number formats. Lesson 3, "Formatting Cells," explains how to use the Formatting toolbar to format numbers.

11 **On the File menu, click Save.**

- Click the Save button on the Standard toolbar.
- Press Ctrl+S.

◆ **Close Percent Sales Increase, and leave Excel open for the next exercise.**

QUICK REFERENCE ▼

Format numeric entries in a worksheet

1 Select the cell or cells to be formatted.

2 On the Format menu, click Cells; or right-click the selection and click Format Cells on the shortcut menu.

QUICK CHECK

Q: Which tab in the Format Cells dialog box contains options for applying formats, such as Currency and Accounting, to numeric values?

A: The Number tab contains options for applying formats to numeric values.

3 Click the Number tab, if necessary.

4 Select the formatting options you want.

5 Click OK.

Adjusting the Size of Rows and Columns

Making Data Easier to Read

THE BOTTOM LINE

Modifying column width and row height can make a worksheet's contents easier to read and work with.

Although a cell entry can include up to 32,000 characters, the default **column width** is only 8.43 characters. For some number formats, when you enter a value that won't fit within the default column width, the number "spills over" into the next column. For other number formats, a number that won't fit within a column is displayed as a series of pound signs (######), indicating that the number is too long for the current column width. For example, as shown in Figure 2-5, when the bookkeeper for Adventure Works enters a sales amount for *Lodging* in currency format, the number appears in the cell as a series of pound signs because the total, $1,239,439, is 10 characters wide—too large to fit within the default column width of 8.43 characters.

FIGURE 2-5

Entries that are too long for the column width

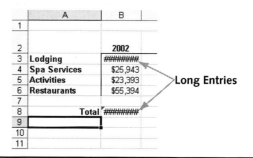

When a number appears as a series of pound symbols, it doesn't affect the value that is stored internally; you can view any of these entries by selecting the cell and looking at the value displayed in the Formula bar or by simply widening the column so that entries appear in full and as entered.

On the other hand, at times, the default column width will be wider than you need it to be. For instance, the bookkeeper at Adventure Works creates a column that stores only Yes or No entries for each sales amount, indicating whether the actual sales amount met or exceeded the projected amount. In this case, the column width doesn't need to be 8.43 characters—three or four characters would probably be wide enough. By reducing the width of the column, you can view more columns on your screen at a time.

Excel provides three methods for adjusting column width:

- You can use the Column Width dialog box (available on the Format menu) to enter the character width that you want.
- You can drag the right edge of the column selector to the right or to the left to increase or decrease the column width. When you position the mouse pointer on the right edge of a column selector, a resize pointer appears, indicating that you can resize the column. For instance, when you click the right edge of the column selector for column G and drag the selector to the right, the column is widened as you drag, as shown in Figure 2-6. As you drag, the width of the column in characters and pixels appears in a yellow ScreenTip above the column selector. Similarly, when you drag the column selector to the left, the column is narrowed as you drag.

FIGURE 2-6

Resizing a column

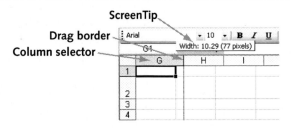

- You can automatically adjust a column to fit the longest entry in the column by double-clicking the right edge of a column selector.

ANOTHER METHOD

You can also click AutoFit Selection (on the Column submenu on the Format menu) to adjust the column width to accommodate the entry in the active cell or the longest entry in a selected range.

You can also adjust the **row height** for a particular row by using the same basic methods. That is, you can use the Row Height dialog box (also available from the Format menu) to specify the height of a row in **points.** One point is equal to 1/72 inch. So a row height of 12 points is equal to 1/6 inch. You can also change the height of a row by clicking the bottom of the row selector and dragging it up or down.

FIGURE 2-7

Resizing a row

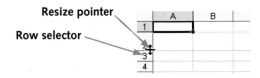

You might want to adjust row height to accommodate larger characters, such as a worksheet title or row headings that appear in larger type. However, it is more common to adjust column width to account for lengthy or short labels or numbers.

◆ **Open Five Year Sales02 from the Excel Core Practice/Lesson02 folder.**

Resize columns and rows

In this exercise, you resize columns and rows. For this exercise, the width of columns in the practice file has been preset to 15 characters.

1 **Select the range B4:F4. On the Format menu, point to Column, and then click Width.**

The Column Width dialog box appears, showing the current column width.

FIGURE 2-8

Column Width dialog box

ANOTHER METHOD

Drag the right border of one of the column selectors in the selected range to the desired width.

TIP

To specify a standard width for all columns in a workbook, on the Format menu, point to Column, and click Standard Width. Type the desired width, and click OK.

2 **Type 13 in the Column Width text box, and click OK.**

The width of columns B through F decreases from 15 characters to 13 characters.

3 **Click any cell.**

The range B4:F4 is no longer selected.

4 **Point to the bottom of the row selector for row 2.**

The mouse pointer changes to a double-headed arrow—the resize pointer—as shown below.

5 **Drag the row selector down until the row has a height of about 20.25 points (27 pixels, or screen picture elements). Use the ScreenTip to achieve the exact height.**

The height of row 2 increases.

FIGURE 2-9

Increasing the height of a row

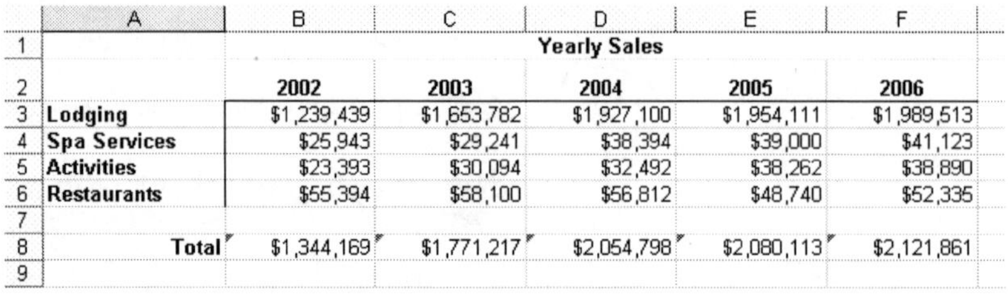

	A	B	C	D	E	F
1				Yearly Sales		
2		2002	2003	2004	2005	2006
3	Lodging	$1,239,439	$1,653,782	$1,927,100	$1,954,111	$1,989,513
4	Spa Services	$25,943	$29,241	$38,394	$39,000	$41,123
5	Activities	$23,393	$30,094	$32,492	$38,262	$38,890
6	Restaurants	$55,394	$58,100	$56,812	$48,740	$52,335
7						
8	Total	$1,344,169	$1,771,217	$2,054,798	$2,080,113	$2,121,861
9						

ANOTHER METHOD

Select the row, open the Format menu, click Row, click Height, and enter the desired height in the Row Height dialog box.

6 Point to the right edge of the column selector for column D.

The mouse pointer changes to a double-headed arrow.

7 Double-click the right edge of the column selector for column D.

The width of column D decreases to better fit the column contents.

FIGURE 2-10

Decreasing the width of a column

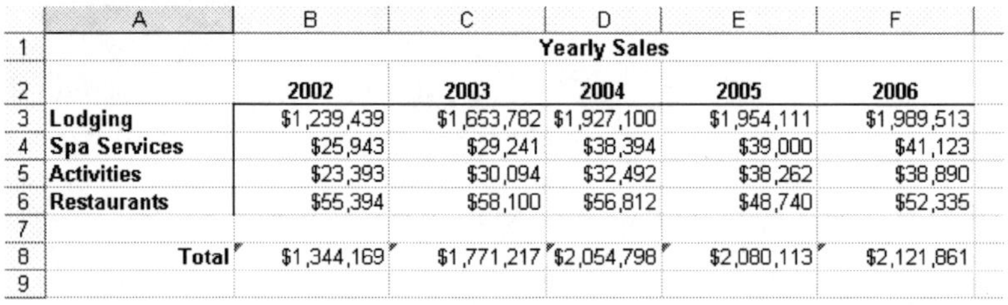

	A	B	C	D	E	F
1				Yearly Sales		
2		2002	2003	2004	2005	2006
3	Lodging	$1,239,439	$1,653,782	$1,927,100	$1,954,111	$1,989,513
4	Spa Services	$25,943	$29,241	$38,394	$39,000	$41,123
5	Activities	$23,393	$30,094	$32,492	$38,262	$38,890
6	Restaurants	$55,394	$58,100	$56,812	$48,740	$52,335
7						
8	Total	$1,344,169	$1,771,217	$2,054,798	$2,080,113	$2,121,861
9						

◆ Keep this file open for the next exercise.

QUICK REFERENCE ▼

Adjust the size of a column or row

1 Position the mouse pointer on the right border of the column selector or on the bottom border of the row selector.

2 Drag the border to the desired width.

Or

Double-click the right border of the column selector or the bottom border of the row selector to adjust the size to match the longest or largest entry.

Adjust the size of multiple columns or multiple rows

1 Select at least one cell from each column or at least one cell from each row.

2 On the Format menu, point to Column, and click Width, or point to Row, and click Height.

3 Type the new width in the Column Width box or the new height in the Row Height box.

4 Click OK.

Aligning Cell Contents

THE BOTTOM LINE

Text entries are normally aligned to the left, and numeric entries are normally aligned to the right. Proper alignment of data enhances readability and ensures that the data conforms to customary standards of displaying data (i.e., aligning decimal points in entries that are used for accounting purposes).

In addition to formatting numbers, you can also change the way they align relative to the edges of cells. You can change the horizontal alignment of selected cells to the left, right, or center. Text entries are normally left-aligned horizontally in a cell, meaning the first character in the cell appears next to the left edge of the cell. Numeric entries are normally right-aligned, meaning the last character in the cell appears next to the right edge of the cell. In a center-aligned cell, the characters in the cell are centered evenly between the left and right edges of the cell. Normally right alignment works best for numbers because all of the numbers in a column are aligned under the same digit positions, as shown in Figure 2-11.

FIGURE 2-11

Numbers aligned right

	A	B	C
1	1,400,342		
2	842		
3	1,952		
4			
5			

However, you might want to left-align or center-align numbers to achieve a different effect. For instance, you might want to left-align dates because the digit position of dates is generally not important. Or you might want to center-align numbers to achieve a stylized look. For example, the sales manager at Adventure Works tracks sales for different categories (room charges, gift shop sales, horse stable rentals, kennel charges, and so on) and creates a column that provides a ranking (based on which category has the most sales) for each category. A center-aligned effect can enhance the appearance of the column, as shown in Figure 2-12.

FIGURE 2-12

Centering numeric data

	A	B	C
1		**Ranking**	
2	Kennel	12	
3	Lodging	4	
4	Weight Room	32	
5	Jukebox	101	
6			
7			

You also can change the vertical alignment of cell contents; that is, the way in which a cell entry is positioned between the top and bottom edges of the cell. The default alignment for text and numbers is bottom, which means characters are placed just above the bottom edge of the cell. You can also change the vertical alignment of cells to the top or center. Center alignment often looks good when you want to increase the height of a row to call attention to labels or values stored in the row, but keep the entries centered between the top and bottom of the row.

Align cell contents horizontally and vertically

In this exercise, you set the vertical and horizontal alignment of cell contents. You also use the Undo and Redo buttons to see how changes can be undone and reapplied as desired.

1 Select the range B3:B6.

2 On the Format menu, click Cells.

The Format Cells dialog box appears.

3 Click the Alignment tab.

The Alignment tab appears.

FIGURE 2-13

Alignment tab in the Format Cells dialog box

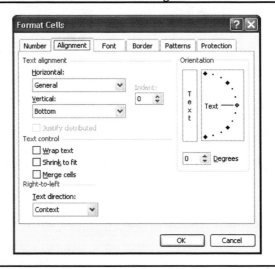

4 Click the Horizontal down arrow, and click Left (Indent) in the list.

5 Click the Vertical down arrow, and view the list choices.

Choices on the Vertical list let you align the data up and down inside the cell. Vertical alignment becomes more apparent when your rows are significantly taller than the data they contain.

6 Click the Vertical down arrow again to close the list without changing the vertical alignment.

7 Click OK.

The contents of the selected cells are aligned to the left.

8 On the Standard toolbar, click the Undo button.

Excel returns the cells to their previous formatting.

ANOTHER METHOD

- Select Undo on the Edit menu.
- Press Ctrl+Z.

9 On the Standard toolbar, click the Redo button.

Excel reapplies the cell formatting.

ANOTHER METHOD

- Select Redo on the Edit menu.
- Press Ctrl+Y.

10 On the Standard toolbar, click the Undo button.

Excel undoes the cell formatting again.

11 Click the Save button on the Standard toolbar.

ANOTHER METHOD

- Click Save on the File menu.
- Press Ctrl+S.

◆ Close Five Year Sales02. Leave Excel open for the next exercise.

IMPORTANT

Once you save a workbook, you can no longer undo or redo changes. If you think you might want to undo or redo a particular action, don't save changes to the workbook until you are satisfied with the results.

QUICK CHECK

Q: In what three ways can data be horizontally aligned within a cell?

A: Data can be left-, right-, or center-aligned.

QUICK REFERENCE ▼

Align one or more cell entries

1 Select the cell or cells to be aligned.

2 On the Format menu, click Cells.

3 Click the Alignment tab.

4 Click the Horizontal or Vertical down arrow, and choose options from the lists.

5 Click OK.

Finding and Replacing Cell Contents

THE BOTTOM LINE

The Find and Replace options let you locate specified data quickly and, if necessary, replace it with different data. These features are most effective in large worksheets in which all of the data is not visible on the screen, thus saving you the time of scanning through vast amounts of data to find what you're looking for.

A single worksheet can contain more than 65,000 rows and 256 columns. You probably won't work with too many worksheets that have data in all of the rows and columns, but you likely will use worksheets in which the content of some rows or columns do not fit on one screen. You can use Excel's Find and Replace features to find data and, if desired, replace it with different data.

Finding Data

If you want to locate a particular item of data that isn't immediately visible—for example, you might want to search a list of several hundred employees to find those who are in the Accounting Department—you can scan the worksheet visually to look for the item. A much easier and quicker way, though, is to use the Find tab of the Find And Replace dialog box. When you enter the text or number that you want to find, Excel locates the first occurrence of this search **string**. A string is any sequence of letters or numbers that you type. When the first entry found isn't the one you want, you can continue to the next entry.

◆ **Open Rentals from the Excel Core Practice/Lesson02 folder.**

Find text

In this exercise, you find a word in a worksheet.

1 On the Edit menu, click Find.

The Find And Replace dialog box appears.

Press Ctrl+F.

2 **Click the Options button, if necessary, to expand the dialog box.**

FIGURE 2-14

Find And Replace dialog box

3 **In the Find What text box, type** Ski.

It does not matter which cell is currently the active cell. If you don't select a range of cells, Excel will search the entire worksheet.

2 **Click the Search down arrow, and, if necessary, click By Rows.**

Excel will search across successive rows rather than down successive columns.

5 **Click the Look In down arrow, and click Values.**

Excel will search cells for values rather than formulas.

If you are searching for a value—either text or numeric—rather than a formula, make sure you click Values in the Look In box. If Formulas is currently selected in the Look In box and you want to find a value, the search will not locate any matches. You will learn about formulas in Lesson 7.

6 **Click Find Next.**

Excel selects the cell that contains the first occurrence of *Ski*.

Press Enter.

If you can't see the search results in the worksheet, drag the title bar of the Find And Replace dialog box to move the dialog box out of the way.

7 **Click Find Next.**

Excel selects the cell that contains the next occurrence of *Ski*.

◆ Leave the Find And Replace dialog box open for the next exercise.

QUICK REFERENCE ▼

Find occurrences of a specific value in your worksheet

1 Click any cell.

2 On the Edit menu, click Find.

3 In the Find What box, type the value to find.

4 Click the Search down arrow, and choose to search by rows or columns.

5 Click the Look In down arrow, and click Values.

6 Click the Find Next button. You can click the Find Next button until there are no more matches.

Finding and Replacing Formats

You can use a distinctive text format to identify data that you may need to change later or that you want to highlight. For example, in the Rentals workbook, you could apply an italic format to all equipment items that were rented more than 20 times a month. If you wanted to find all of these items, you could use the Find Format dialog box, accessible through the Find And Replace dialog box, to seek out that specific format. In the Find And Replace dialog box, you'd click the Format button, click the Font tab, and select the Italic font

You can narrow the focus of a find operation by selecting the Match Case and Match Entire Cell Contents check boxes in the Find And Replace dialog box. The Match Case check box, when selected, requires that the text in cells match the uppercase and lowercase characters that you enter for the search string. Select the Match Entire Cell Contents check box when you want to specify that the search string be the *only* contents in a cell for it to be considered a match.

Replacing Data

When you edit worksheets, you might need to find a certain character string within the worksheet and replace it with a different character string. For example, the sales manager at Adventure Works wants to change the Rental workbook so that all prices that end with *.95* as the decimal amount are changed to *.99*. (For example, an item that currently rents for $4.95 per hour would now cost $4.99 per hour.) The change doesn't appreciably increase rental costs for visitors, but over time, it can significantly increase the total revenue from rentals.

You can quickly find and replace all or some occurrences of a character string in a worksheet using the Replace tab of the Find And Replace dialog box. Being able to replace data with the click of a button can save you the time of finding occurrences of the data and repeatedly typing replacement data.

Replace data in a worksheet

In this exercise, you find and replace the first occurrence of a search string and then replace every occurrence of a string in the worksheet with a different string.

1 In the Find And Replace dialog box, click the Replace tab.

FIGURE 2-15

Replace tab in the Find And Replace dialog box

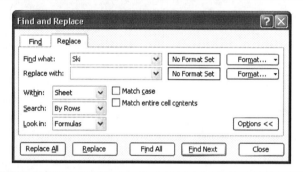

2 In the Find What text box, replace Ski with .95, and press Tab.

The search string that you want to locate is entered, and the insertion point is positioned in the Replace With text box.

3 In the Replace With text box, type .99.

The contents of the Replace With text box will be used to replace occurrences of the specified search string.

4 Click the Search down arrow, and click By Columns.

Excel will search down successive columns rather than across successive rows.

5 Click Find Next.

Excel locates the first occurrence of the search string .95.

ANOTHER METHOD

Press Enter.

6 Click Replace.

Excel replaces the first occurrence of .95 with .99 and locates the next occurrence of the search string.

7 **Click Replace All.**

Excel replaces all occurrences of *.95* with *.99*—the values in the Price per Rental column.

8 **Click OK to close the message box that tells you how many replacements were made.**

9 **Click Close.**

The Find And Replace dialog box is closed.

10 **On the File menu, click Save As, type** Rentals 2, **and click Save.**

The workbook is saved with the new name.

◆ **Keep this file open for the next exercise.**

TIP

You might wonder why you can't just enter *95* as the search string and *99* as the replacement string—without including the decimal point. If you were to do this, Excel would replace any value in the worksheet that contained *95*, rather than only those values that include the decimal point in front of *95*. For example, if the quantity *95* appeared in any of the Rentals per Month columns, Excel would replace it with *99*, which is not what you want. When you want to replace only the partial contents of a cell, as you do in this exercise, be as specific as possible in entering the search string; otherwise, Excel might make incorrect replacements.

QUICK REFERENCE ▼

Find and replace all occurrences of a specific value in your worksheet

QUICK CHECK

Q: The Find and Replace commands are on which menu?

A: **The commands are on the Edit menu.**

1 Click any cell.

2 On the Edit menu, click Replace.

3 In the Find What box, type the value to find.

4 In the Replace With box, type the new value.

5 Click the Search down arrow, and choose to search by rows or columns.

6 Click Replace All.

7 Click Close.

Inserting and Deleting Cells, Rows, and Columns

THE BOTTOM LINE

You can insert rows or columns in which you want to enter new data, or you can insert rows and columns and leave them blank to enhance the appearance of the worksheet or to serve as dividers between sections of data. You can also easily delete cells and entire rows and columns.

After setting up a worksheet, you might find that you need to insert a blank cell, column, or row to create space for entering additional information. For instance, if the sales manager wants to add new rental items in the Rentals worksheet, he'll need to insert a new row for each new rental item. Alternatively, he might want to delete an existing cell, column, or row to eliminate unnecessary information. In the Rentals worksheet, column C is used to indicate the total number of rentals for each item in the year. The sales manager finds that this column is unnecessary and wants to delete it.

You can insert cells, columns, or rows using the Insert menu, and you can delete them using the Edit menu. When you insert a cell or a range of cells in a worksheet, you either shift the existing cells in that row to the right or shift the existing cells in the column down. To insert one or more rows, begin by selecting the number of rows that you want to insert. You do this by clicking and dragging across at least one cell for each row that you want to add. The number of rows that you select is then inserted *above* the first row that you selected, as shown in Figure 2-16.

FIGURE 2-16

Inserting rows

In this example, cells in rows 5, 6, and 7 were selected, as shown in the illustration on the left. When you click Rows on the Insert menu, three new rows are inserted above the first selected row, as shown in the illustration on the right.

Inserting columns is similar. When you want to insert one or more columns, you begin by selecting the number of columns that you want to insert. You do this by clicking and dragging at least one cell for each column that you want to add. In the following illustration on the left, cells in columns C and D are selected. When you click Columns on the Insert menu, Excel inserts two new columns—to the *left* of column C, as shown in the illustration on the right.

FIGURE 2-17

Columns are inserted to the left

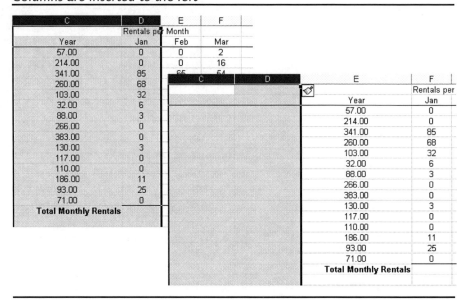

When you insert a row, column, or cell in a worksheet with existing formatting, such as the Currency format, the Insert Options button appears. Clicking the Insert Options button displays a list of choices about how the inserted row or column should be formatted. These options are summarized in the following table.

Option	Action
Format Same As Above	Apply the format of the row above the inserted row to the new row
Format Same As Below	Apply the format of the row below the inserted row to the new row
Format Same As Left	Apply the format of the column to the left of the inserted column to the new column
Format Same As Right	Apply the format of the column to the right of the inserted column to the new column
Clear Formatting	Apply the default format to the new row or column

Insert and delete rows, columns, and cells

In this exercise, you delete a column, insert cells (shifting the adjacent cells in the same row to the right), and insert rows.

1 Click cell C3.

C3 is now the active cell.

2 On the Edit menu, point to Clear, and click Contents.

The contents of the active cell are deleted, but the column is not removed.

Right-click the selection, and click Clear Contents on the shortcut menu.

3 **On the Edit menu, click Delete.**

The Delete dialog box appears.

Right-click the cell, and select Delete on the shortcut menu.

FIGURE 2-18

Delete dialog box

4 **Click the Entire Column option, and click OK.**

The Year column, along with all of its contents, is deleted.

5 **Select C1:F1.**

Four cells are selected.

6 **On the Insert menu, click Cells.**

The Insert dialog box appears.

Right-click the selection, and select Insert on the shortcut menu.

FIGURE 2-19

Insert dialog box

7 **Click the Shift Cells Right option, and click OK.**

Excel inserts four new cells and shifts the contents of existing cells (in the same row) to the right.

8 **Select cells A10:A12.**

Three rows are selected.

TIP

It does not matter which column you use to select cells when you want to insert rows.

9 **On the Insert menu, click Rows.**

Excel inserts three rows above what was row 10 (now row 13). You now have room to add three new rental items.

FIGURE 2-20

Inserting three rows

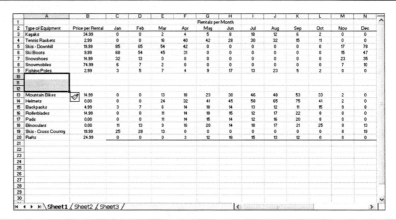

10 **Click the Undo button twice.**

Excel removes the inserted rows and cells.

11 **On the Standard toolbar, click the Save button.**

The workbook is saved with the current name.

◆ **Close Rentals 2. Keep Excel open for the next exercise.**

QUICK REFERENCE ▼

Insert a cell in a worksheet

1 Select the cell or cells above or to the left of where you want to insert the cell.

2 On the Insert menu, click Cells.

3 Choose whether to shift the cells down or to the right.

4 Click OK.

Or

1 Select the cell or cells above or to the left of where you want to insert the cell.

2 Right-click the selection.

3 Click Insert on the shortcut menu.

4 Make a selection, and click OK.

Insert a column or row

1 Select a cell to the left of the column or above the row where you want to insert the column or row.

2 On the Insert menu, click Columns or Rows, as appropriate.

Or

3 Right-click the column or row heading.

4 Click Insert on the shortcut menu.

5 In the Insert dialog box, click Entire Row or Entire Column, and click OK.

Cutting, Copying, Pasting, and Clearing Cells

THE BOTTOM LINE

Once you've entered raw data in a worksheet, you'll probably want to rearrange or reorganize some of it to make the worksheet, as a whole, easier to read and interpret. You might want to move sections of data to another location in the worksheet or copy existing data to another location so you don't need to retype it. You also might want to "clear" cells of values, formats, or both.

When you're entering data in a worksheet, you might find yourself changing your mind about where you've placed the contents of a cell, row, or column. Or you might simply make a mistake by entering data in a particular row or column when you meant to place it in a different row or column.

When you want to change where you've placed data in your worksheet, you do not need to delete the existing data and then retype the data at the new locations. Excel lets you move the existing contents of one or more cells to a different location. This approach is called **cut** and **paste** because you cut (remove) data from its original location and then paste (insert) the data at a different location. When you cut data, Excel stores it in the Windows Clipboard, a temporary storage location in your computer's memory. The data is removed from the worksheet but is still available for you to paste at a different location. You can even paste data from the Clipboard into a file created by a different application, such as Microsoft Word or Microsoft PowerPoint.

At times, you'll want to reuse data that you've already entered. For instance, the sales manager at Adventure Works has created a worksheet containing sales amounts for the first quarter. He wants to **copy** many of the cells from one worksheet and paste them in another worksheet, which he'll use to create sales amounts for the second quarter. In Figure 2-21, the illustration on the left shows that the range A3:A7 on sheet Q1 has been selected and copied. The illustration on the right shows the same range pasted to sheet Q2.

FIGURE 2-21

Copying data from one location to another

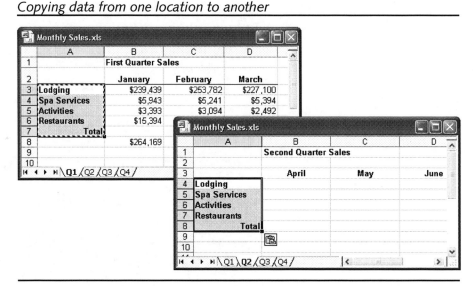

This approach is especially useful when you've applied number formatting to cells or text formatting to titles and labels. The sales manager can copy many of the labels and sales amounts (formatted as currency) to a different worksheet for the second quarter. He can then change the text labels without losing the current text formatting, and he can **clear** the sales amounts without losing the currency formatting stored in the cells. When you clear cells, you can specify whether you want to clear the values stored in the cells but keep the formatting, clear any formulas stored in the cells, clear the formatting in the cells but keep the values, or clear everything in the cells.

TIP

When you are pasting a range of cells—for example, a selection that contains three cells across in two adjacent rows—select an area with the same number of cells across and down as the data you cut or copied. You can also select a single cell to paste into; the pasted data will fill cells below and to the right of the selected cell.

◆ **Open Monthly Sales from the Excel Core Practice/Lesson02 folder.**

Copy, move, and clear data

In this exercise, you move and copy data to a new location, clear the formatting in a selected range, and clear the contents in a selected range.

1 **Click cell A7, and on the Standard toolbar, click the Cut button.**

The contents of cell A7 are copied to the Windows Clipboard, and a flashing marquee appears around cell A7, as shown in the following illustration. The marquee indicates the contents that will be cut.

ANOTHER METHOD

- Click Cut on the Edit menu.
- Right-click the selection, and click Cut on the shortcut menu.
- Press Ctrl+X.

FIGURE 2-22

Cutting data

	A	B	C	D
1		First Quarter Sales		
2		January	February	March
3	Lodging	$239,439	$253,782	$227,100
4	Spa Services	$5,943	$5,241	$5,394
5	Activities	$3,393	$3,094	$2,492
6	Restaurants	$15,394	$12,100	$12,812
7	Total			
8		$264,169	$274,217	$247,798
9				

2 **Click cell A8, and on the Standard toolbar, click the Paste button.**

The contents of the Windows Clipboard (from cell A7) are pasted in cell A8, and the marquee no longer appears around cell A7.

ANOTHER METHOD

- Click Paste on the Edit menu.
- Right-click the cell, and click Paste on the shortcut menu.
- Press Ctrl+V.

3 **Select B3:D6, and on the Standard toolbar, click the Copy button.**

The contents of the selected cells are copied to the Windows Clipboard, and a flashing marquee appears around the selected cells, indicating what has been copied to the Windows Clipboard.

ANOTHER METHOD

- Click Copy on the Edit menu.
- Right-click the selection, and click Copy on the shortcut menu.
- Press Ctrl+C.

TIP

If you decide you don't want to cut or copy data after you've already executed the Cut or Copy command, simply press the Esc key to abort the procedure.

4 **Click the Q2 sheet tab near the bottom of the Excel window.**

Excel displays the Q2 worksheet.

ANOTHER METHOD

Another way to cut and paste data is to select the cells and drag the selection by its border to the cells where you want to paste the data. To copy using the same method, hold down the Ctrl key while you drag.

5 **Click cell B4, and on the Standard toolbar, click the Paste button.**

The contents of the Windows Clipboard are copied to the Q2 worksheet, starting at the location of the active cell (B4).

6 **On the Edit menu, point to Clear, and click Formats.**

The currency formatting is removed from the selected cells.

7 **On the Standard toolbar, click the Undo button.**

The currency formatting is reapplied to the selected cells.

8 **On the Edit menu, point to Clear, and click Contents.**

The contents are removed from the selected cells, but the formats are still present and will be applied to any data entered in those cells.

9 **Type** 3444**, and press Enter.**

Excel converts your entry to currency format.

10 **On the File menu, click Save As, type** Monthly Sales 2**, and click Save.**

The workbook is saved with the new name.

◆ **Keep this file open for the next exercise.**

QUICK REFERENCE ▼

Cut or copy and then paste data in a worksheet

1 Select the desired cell or cells.

2 On the Standard toolbar, click the Cut button to remove the data or the Copy button to make a duplicate of the data.

3 Select the cell or cells into which you want to paste the data.

4 On the Standard toolbar, click the Paste button.

Or

1 Select the desired cell or cells.

2 On the Edit menu, click Cut or click Copy.

3 Select the cell or cells into which you want to paste the data.

4 On the Edit menu, click Paste.

Clear a cell or range of cells

1 Select the desired cell or range of cells.

2 On the Edit menu, point to Clear and click Formats to clear the formatting only, or click Contents to clear the contents only, or click All to clear both the contents and formatting.

Using Additional Paste Features

THE BOTTOM LINE

Excel provides a number of other features for organizing and customizing the data you paste to a new location. The Paste Special command lets you choose among values, formats, formulas, and other options to paste. The Paste Options button lets you specify how the data you paste is formatted. And the Office Clipboard allows you store up to 24 cut or copied items, any of which you can retrieve to paste in a new location. These features give you greater control over the appearance of data and help eliminate the need to repeatedly apply the same formatting to data that's copied.

As illustrated in the previous section, you can use the Standard toolbar buttons for cutting, copying, and pasting text. Excel provides other useful techniques that extend your editing capabilities. When you cut or copy text, you can use the **Paste Special** command (on the Edit menu) to display the Paste Special dialog box.

FIGURE 2-23

Paste Special dialog box

This dialog box gives you a number of options for specifying what you want to paste. For instance, if you copy a range of cells from one worksheet, you can use the Paste Special command to paste only the formatting from the copied cells to a different location. In the previous exercise, you pasted a range of cells to a different worksheet; then you used the Clear command to clear the contents from the pasted cells without losing the cell formatting. The Paste Special dialog box provides a more efficient way to achieve the same result.

An even more efficient and convenient way to perform some of these actions is through the Paste Options button. This button appears next to data you copy from a cell and paste in another cell.

FIGURE 2-24

Paste Options button

July	August	June
$239,439	$253,782	$227,100
$5,943	$5,241	$5,394
$3,393	$3,094	$2,492
$15,394	$12,100	$12,812

Clicking the Paste Options button displays a list of actions Excel can take regarding the pasted cells. The formatting options are valuable tools in helping to achieve a consistent look among the worksheets in a workbook.

FIGURE 2-25

Paste Options menu

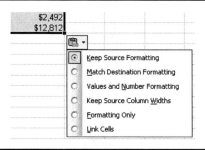

The options you see in your Paste Options list will vary depending on the content of the cell you are pasting.

These options are summarized in the following table.

Option	Action
Keep Source Formatting	Paste the contents of the Clipboard (which holds the last information selected via the Cut or Copy commands) in the target cells, and format the data as it was formatted in the original cells
Match Destination Formatting	Paste the contents of the Clipboard in the target cells, keeping any numeric formats
Values And Number Formatting	Paste the contents of the Clipboard in the target cells, and resize the columns of the target cells to match the widths of the columns of the source cells
Keep Source Column Widths	Paste the contents of the Clipboard in the target cells, and resize the columns of the target cells to match the widths of the columns of the source cells
Formatting Only	Apply the format of the source cells to the target cells, but do not copy the contents of the source cells
Link Cells	Display the contents of the source cells in the target cells, updating the target cells whenever the content of the source cells changes
Values Only	Paste the values from a column in the target column, and use the existing format to the target column
Values And Source Formatting	Paste a column of cells in the target column, and apply the format of the copied column to the new column

TROUBLESHOOTING

If the Paste Options button does not appear, you can turn the feature on by clicking Options on the Tools menu. In the dialog box that appears, click the Edit tab; then select the Show Paste Options buttons check box.

Use Paste Options

In this exercise, you use the Paste Options button to paste only the formatting of the data that's been copied.

1 **Click the Q1 sheet tab.**

Excel displays the Q1 worksheet. The range B3:D6 should still be selected. If this range is not selected, select it now.

 2 **On the Standard toolbar, click the Copy button.**

The contents of the selected range are copied to the Windows Clipboard.

3 **Click the Q3 sheet tab, and click cell B4.**

Excel displays the Q3 worksheet, and B4 is the active cell.

4 **On the Standard toolbar, click the Paste button.**

The selected cells are pasted in the Q3 worksheet.

5 **Click the Paste Options button.**

6 **Click the Formatting Only option.**

Excel pastes the formatting from the copied cells, starting at the location of the active cell, but does not paste the contents.

7 **Type 3444, and press Enter.**

Excel converts your entry to currency format.

8 **Click the Q1 sheet tab.**

Excel displays the Q1 worksheet.

◆ **Keep this file open for the next exercise.**

QUICK REFERENCE ▼

Copy the formatting in a cell or range of cells

1 Select the cell or range of cells whose formatting you want to copy.

2 On the Standard toolbar, click the Copy button.

3 Select the cell or range of cells into which you want to paste the formatting.

4 On the Standard toolbar, click the Paste button.

5 Click the Paste Options button.

6 Click the Formatting Only option.

QUICK CHECK

Q: What happens if you apply the Match Destination Formatting paste option?

A: **The contents of the Clipboard are pasted in the target cells, keeping any numeric formats.**

Working with the Office Clipboard

The **Office Clipboard** provides additional features for pasting data. Although the Office Clipboard has a name similar to the Windows Clipboard, it works in a different way. The Windows Clipboard stores the contents from only one copy or cut operation at a time. When you copy or cut another selection, the contents of the Windows Clipboard are replaced with the new contents. By contrast, the Office Clipboard can store the contents of up to 24 copy or cut operations at one time from any Office application.

Why is this valuable? Consider that the sales manager at Adventure Works wants to create a worksheet for third-quarter sales. However, he wants to see how the worksheet will look if each row label is separated by a blank row. He could copy the row labels from the Q1 worksheet, paste them in the Q3 worksheet, and insert a blank row between each row label. But the Office Clipboard, which has its own task pane, provides an easier way. The sales manager displays the Clipboard task pane and then quickly copies the row labels in Q1, one row at a time. The Office Clipboard stores each row as a separate entry. The sales manager then switches to the Q2 worksheet and uses the Office Clipboard to paste each entry, one at a time, where he wants the entry to appear. The ability to copy multiple selections, store them collectively in the Office Clipboard, and paste each selection separately is called **collect and paste.**

As shown in Figure 2-26, the Clipboard task pane includes two buttons—Paste All and Clear All. Each selection on the Clipboard appears as a page icon (with some portion of the copied information) on the task pane and indicates from which application the selection was cut or copied. When the task pane is open, any time you use the Copy button the selected cells are copied to the Office Clipboard. Use the Paste All button to paste all of the selections from the Office Clipboard at one time. Use the Clear All button to empty the contents of the Office Clipboard. Click one of the page icons to paste the selection in the current cell or range of cells. When you want to delete specific items from the Clipboard, point to the item and click on the arrow that appears next to it. From the menu that opens, you can select Delete to remove a specific item from the Clipboard.

FIGURE 2-26

Clipboard task pane

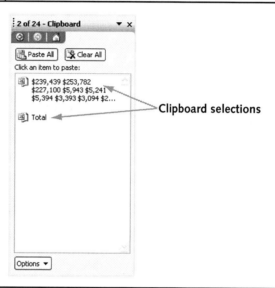

Clipboard selections

Paste selections to and from the Clipboard

In this exercise, you use the Office Clipboard to organize and manage items to paste.

1 To display the Office Clipboard task pane, on the Edit menu, click Office Clipboard.

The Clipboard task pane appears.

2 If you see any page icons on the Clipboard task pane, click the Clear All button.

 3 In the worksheet, click cell A3, and on the Standard toolbar, click the Copy button.

The contents of the cell are copied as a selection to the Office Clipboard, and the Clipboard task pane shows a page icon for the copied selection.

4 In the worksheet, click cell A4, and then click the Copy button.

The contents of the cell are copied as a selection to the Office Clipboard, and the Clipboard task pane shows two page icons.

FIGURE 2-27

Pasting selections to the Clipboard

5 In the worksheet, click cell A5, and then click the Copy button.

The contents of the cell are copied as a selection to the Office Clipboard, and the Clipboard task pane shows three page icons.

6 In the worksheet, click cell A6, and then click the Copy button.

The contents of the cell are copied as a selection to the Office Clipboard, and the Clipboard task pane shows four page icons.

7 Click the Q4 sheet tab, and click cell A5.

Excel displays the Q4 worksheet, and A5 is the active cell.

8 On the Clipboard task pane, click the Spa Services icon.

The selection is pasted in cell A5.

9 Click cell A7, and on the Clipboard task pane, click the Lodging icon. The selection is pasted in cell A7.

10 Repeat step 9 to paste Activities to cell A9 and Restaurants to cell A11.

Your worksheet should look similar to the following illustration.

FIGURE 2-28

Selections pasted to the worksheet

11 On the Clipboard task pane, click the Clear All button.

The Office Clipboard is now empty.

 12 Click the Save button to save your changes.

◆ Close Monthly Sales 2. If you are continuing to other lessons, leave Excel open. If you are not continuing to other lessons, click the Close button in the title bar of the Excel window.

QUICK REFERENCE ▼

Copy and paste multiple objects using the Office Clipboard

1 If necessary, click Office Clipboard on the Edit menu to display.

2 Select the cell or range of cells whose contents you want to copy.

3 On the Standard toolbar, click the Copy button.

4 Repeat steps 1 and 2 for up to 23 more cells (or ranges of cells) whose contents you want to copy.

5 Select the cells into which you want to paste the data.

6 On the Clipboard task pane, click the object you want to paste.

7 Repeat steps 4–5 for the remaining items on the Clipboard task pane.

QUICK CHECK

Q: How many cut and/or copy operations can the Office Clipboard hold?

A: It can hold 24.

Key Points

✔ *Applying accurate formatting to numeric data makes the data more useful and easier to interpret and analyze.*

✔ *Modifying column width and row height can make a worksheet's contents easier to read and work with.*

✔ *Proper alignment of data enhances readability and ensures that the data conforms to customary standards of displaying data (i.e., aligning decimal points in entries that are used for accounting purposes).*

✔ *The Find and Replace options let you locate specified data quickly and, if necessary, replace it with different data. These features are most effective in large worksheets where it can take a significant amount of time to scan numerous rows and/or columns to find the data you're looking for.*

✔ *You can insert rows or columns in which you want to enter new data, or you can insert rows and columns and leave them blank to enhance the appearance of the worksheet. You can also easily delete cells and entire rows and columns.*

✔ *Once you've entered raw data in a worksheet, you'll probably want to rearrange or reorganize some of it to make the worksheet, as a whole, easier to read and interpret. You might want to move sections of data to another location in the worksheet or copy existing data to another location so you don't need to retype it. You can copy and paste cell formats.*

These features give you greater control over the appearance of data and help eliminate the need to repeatedly apply the same formatting to data that's copied.

✔ *The Office Clipboard allows you store up to 24 cut or copied items, any of which you can retrieve at any time to paste in a new location.*

Quick Quiz

True/False

T　F　　**1.** The Number format displays data exactly as you enter it.

T　F　　**2.** You can apply only those formats that are available in the Category list box of the Format Cells dialog box.

T　F　　**3.** A series of pound signs (#####) in a cell indicates that the entry is too long for the current column width.

T　F　　**4.** You can manually adjust the width of a column, but not the height of a row.

T　F　　**5.** The Office Clipboard holds up to 24 items that you've cut or copied, whereas the Windows Clipboard holds only the most recent item.

Multiple Choice

1. Which number format would you apply to display values as currency?
   a. Number
   b. Currency
   c. Monetary
   d. Financial

2. Which of the following is *not* a method for opening the Format Cells dialog box?
   a. Select Cells on the Format menu.
   b. Press Ctrl+1.
   c. Click the Format Cells button on the Formatting toolbar.
   d. Right-click the selection, and select Cells on the shortcut menu.

3. To find data using the Find and Replace dialog box, you must enter a sequence of characters called a(an)
   a. string.
   b. range.
   c. address.
   d. condition.

4. When you insert a cell in a worksheet with existing formatting, which button appears, giving you options about how the inserted cell should be formatted?
   a. Paste Options
   b. Paste Special
   c. Insert Options
   d. Format Options

5. Which Clipboard can store up to 24 items?
   a. Windows
   b. Excel
   c. Collect and Paste
   d. Office

Short Answer

1. If you wanted to insert two rows above row 7 in your current worksheet, what steps would you use?

2. What is the difference between the Accounting and Currency number formats?

3. How can you drag to change the height of a row or the width of a column?

4. How do you display the Office Clipboard task pane?

5. How can you find the third occurrence of a value in your worksheet?

On Your Own

◆ **Open Five Year Sales02 from the Excel Core Practice/Lesson02 folder.**

Exercise 1

Insert a row between rows 1 and 2. Resize row 1 to a height of 25 pixels. Move the *Yearly Sales* title text to cell A1. Delete the row you added.

Exercise 2

Still using the Five Year Sales02 workbook, format cells B3:F6 as Accounting. Replace every occurrence of *12* in the worksheet with 13. Find all entries that are bold, and change the formatting to bold italics.

Exercise 3

Still using the Five Year Sales02 workbook, in Sheet1, copy the range A3:F7 to the Office Clipboard. Switch to Sheet2, and paste the selected cells beginning at cell A3. In Sheet2, change the width of columns A through F to 15 characters. Then select the range B3:F6, delete its contents, but retain the formatting.

◆ **Save and close Five Years Sales02.**

One Step Further

Exercise 1

Create a worksheet to track your physical activity on a weekly basis. The rows should be the days of the week; the physical activities you do on a regular basis (walking, running, specific sports, aerobics, and so on) should go in the columns. Insert a row above row 1, and center the heading *Minutes per Day* above the days of the week. Improve the appearance of the worksheet by adjusting column widths, changing font colors, and so on. Change the name of the sheet to reflect the ending date for this week. Save the workbook as My Physical Activity. Use this worksheet to log how many minutes you spend on physical activity each day.

Exercise 2

Continuing with the workbook you created in Exercise 1, select all of the content from your first worksheet and copy it to Sheet 2. Clear any of the minute values that were entered. Rename this sheet with the date of the ending day for next week. Copy the contents of the second sheet to Sheet 3, and rename that sheet to reflect the ending date for two weeks from now. Save your worksheets. Use these sheets to log your physical activity for the next several weeks. If desired, add additional sheets to continue monitoring your activity level.

Formatting Cells

After completing this lesson, you will be able to:

✔ *Format text.*
✔ *Format numbers as currency.*
✔ *Use Format Painter.*
✔ *Add borders to cells.*
✔ *Add shading to cells.*
✔ *Use AutoFormat.*
✔ *Create and apply styles.*
✔ *Merge cells.*

KEY TERMS

▪ attribute
▪ AutoFormat
▪ font

▪ Format Painter
▪ merge cells
▪ style

Excel provides dozens of ways to format labels and values in a worksheet. If your worksheet or workbook will be printed or viewed by others, especially if it is part of a report or presentation, you'll want it to look as attractive and comprehensible as possible. For example, to improve the design, you can enlarge the text for headings and format the headings and labels in bold, italics, or both. You can also format text in different fonts (type styles) and in different colors.

In this lesson, you will learn how to format text and numbers, including headings, labels, and values. You will learn how to use Excel's Format Painter feature, which allows you to quickly pick up all of the formatting for selected text and then apply the same formats to different text. You will also learn how to add borders and shading around selected cells. Then you will learn how to apply one of Excel's built-in worksheet designs to add colors and design effects to a worksheet using only a few mouse clicks. Next you will learn how to create a style, which is a collection of formatting characteristics that can be applied at any time simply by clicking the name of the style in a list. Finally, you will learn how to combine multiple cells into a single cell.

IMPORTANT

Before you can use the practice files in this lesson, you must install them from the book's companion CD to their default location. For additional information on how to find and open files used in this book, see the "Using the CD-ROM" section at the beginning of this book.

Formatting Text

Making Data Easier to Read
Changing the Appearance of
Data

THE BOTTOM LINE

Excel's formatting tools enable you to give your worksheets a professional, customized look. You can use certain formats to call out important or unique data, such as the title of the worksheet. You can also use formatting that matches what's used in other documents, such as letterhead, to give all of your documents a consistent look.

In Lesson 2, you learned that applying certain formats to numeric data can make it more meaningful and easier to interpret. You also learned how alignment and spacing can improve the readability of data. Now you will see how applying different fonts in different sizes and styles can add a professional, polished look to your worksheets.

A **font** is the design of type, including letters, numbers, and other character symbols. The different characters of a particular font have a similar design to provide a consistent look. Excel's default font is 10-point Arial. In typography, one point is 1/72 inch. So characters in a 10-point font are about 1/6 inch high.

You can change to different fonts and different font sizes to add visual interest to a worksheet and to call attention to specific data. For example, in a budget worksheet, you might use a font in a large point size, in bold, and in a different color to make the title stand out. You might use a different font, such as the default 10-point Arial, for the budget data and the same font but in a different style, such as bold italics, for the column and row labels.

The Font tab of the Format Cells dialog box contains options to change the font, the font style (such as bold and italics), and the point size of a cell entry. You can apply some of these same formatting options by selecting buttons on the Formatting toolbar. You'll use this toolbar throughout this lesson.

FIGURE 3-1

Selected buttons on the Formatting toolbar

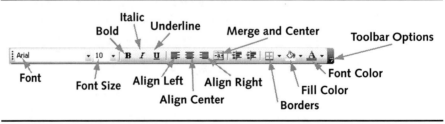

◆ To complete the procedures in this lesson, you must use the practice files Lodging Analysis03 and AW Guest Supplies in the Lesson03 folder in the Excel Core Practice folder that is located on your hard disk.

◆ Open Lodging Analysis03 from the Excel Core Practice/Lesson03 folder.

Format text

In this exercise, you format text in a worksheet.

B

1 Click cell B1, and on the Formatting toolbar, click the Bold button.

The title appears in bold, making it easier to determine the kind of data on the worksheet.

ANOTHER METHOD

Select Cells on the Format menu; or right-click the selection, and click Format Cells on the shortcut menu; or press Ctrl+1. In the Format Cells dialog box, click the Font tab, and click Bold in the Font Style list box.

Press Ctrl+B.

2 Select the range B3:E3, and on the Formatting toolbar, click the Center button.

The year labels are centered.

ANOTHER METHOD

Select Cells on the Format menu; or right-click the selection, and click Format Cells on the shortcut menu; or press Ctrl+1. In the Format Cells dialog box, click the Alignment tab, and click Center in the Horizontal list box.

TIP

You can customize the Formatting toolbar by placing buttons on it that you use frequently and removing those you don't. To customize your toolbar, click the Toolbar Options button, and then click Add or Remove Buttons. Click menu options to select or deselect the buttons on the list.

B

3 Click the Bold button on the Formatting toolbar.

The year labels appear in bold.

4 Right-click the area you've selected, click Format Cells on the shortcut menu, and click the Font tab.

The Font tab of the Format Cells dialog box appears.

FIGURE 3-2

Font tab in the Format Cells dialog box

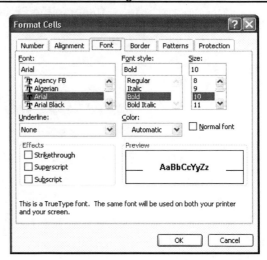

- Select Cells on the Format menu.
- Press Ctrl+1.

5 **On the Font list, scroll down and click Times New Roman.**

Click the Font button down arrow, and select Times New Roman.

6 **On the Size list, scroll down and click 12.**

Click the Font Size down arrow, and select 12.

7 **Click the Color down arrow, click the Red square (third row, first square), click OK, and click a blank area of the worksheet.**

The range is deselected and appears in 12-point, red, Times New Roman text. The new formats applied to the year labels make them stand out.

Click the Font Color button down arrow, and select Red.

B

8 **Select the range A4:A8, and click the Bold button.**

The row labels appear in bold.

9 **On the Format menu, click Cells, and click the Alignment tab.**

The Format Cells dialog box appears with the Alignment tab on top.

10 **Double-click in the Indent box, type 1, and click OK.**

The sales categories in the selected cells are indented one character to the right.

FIGURE 3-3

Indenting entries

	A	B	C	D	E
1		Yearly Income - Lodging			
2					
3		2002	2003	2004	2005
4	Teepees	23393	30094	32492	38262
5	Cabins	75943	79241	88394	89000
6	Condos	239439	653782	927100	954111
7					
8	Total	338775	763117	1047986	1081373
9					

ANOTHER METHOD

Click the Increase Indent button.

11 **On the File menu, click Save As, type Lodging Analysis, and click Save.**

The workbook is saved with the new name.

◆ **Keep this file open for the next exercise.**

ANOTHER METHOD

You can also change the file name by selecting only the numbers *03* at the end of the current file name, deleting them, and clicking the Save button.

QUICK CHECK

Q: What is a commonly used font style?

A: **Bold, italic, and underline are commonly used font styles.**

QUICK REFERENCE ▼

Format text

1. Select the cell or cells to be formatted.
2. On the Format menu, click Cells.
3. Click the Font tab.
4. Select the desired font, style, and size options.
5. Click OK.

Or

Select the cell or cells to be formatted, and click the appropriate button on the Formatting toolbar.

Formatting Numbers as Currency

THE BOTTOM LINE

You might use a worksheet to track your investments, to set your income and expenses, or to list the value of household items. Worksheets such as these contain monetary, or currency, values. Applying the appropriate currency format to these values makes them more meaningful and easier to interpret.

When you type numbers in worksheet cells, Excel formats the cells in the General format by default—which means that all text and numeric entries appear exactly as you've entered them. In the previous lesson, you learned about the various formats, such as Currency, Date, and Percentage, that you can apply to numbers using the Number tab in the Format Cells dialog box. For example, you can display large numbers with comma separators between thousands digit positions, you can display numbers as currency with dollar signs and decimal positions for fractions of a dollar, and you can display numbers as fractions or even percentages.

Some common number formats can be applied to selected cells more easily by using the Formatting toolbar. The following table shows some of the buttons on the Formatting toolbar that you can click to format numbers.

Button	Button Name	Description
$	*Currency Style*	Formats numbers with dollar signs, comma separators for thousands, and two decimal places
%	*Percent Style*	Multiplies numbers by 100 and displays them with percent signs
,	*Comma Style*	Inserts commas between groups of thousands
←.0 .00	*Increase Decimal*	Adds one decimal position each time you click the button
.00 →.0	*Decrease Decimal*	Removes one decimal position each time you click the button

Format numbers using the Formatting toolbar

In this exercise, you use the Formatting toolbar to format numbers as currency and to remove decimal positions.

1 **Select the range B4:E8, and on the Formatting toolbar, click the Currency Style button.**

The numbers in the selected cells appear with dollar signs, comma separators, and two decimal positions. Notice that none of the numbers includes fractions of a dollar, so the decimal positions are not necessary.

Select Cells on the Format menu; or right-click the selection, and click Format Cells on the shortcut menu; or press Ctrl+1. In the Format Cells dialog box, click the Number tab, and click Currency in the Category list box.

2 **Click the Decrease Decimal button twice, and click an empty cell in the worksheet.**

The decimal positions are removed from the selected range of numbers, and the range is deselected. Your worksheet should look similar to the following illustration:

FIGURE 3-4

Numbers with decimals removed

	A	B		C		D		E
1		Yearly Income - Lodging						
2								
3		2002		2003		2004		2005
4	Teepees	$	23,393	$	30,094	$	32,492	$	38,262
5	Cabins	$	75,943	$	79,241	$	88,394	$	89,000
6	Condos	$	239,439	$	653,782	$	927,100	$	954,111
7								
8	Total	$	338,775	$	763,117	$	1,047,986	$	1,081,373

Select Cells on the Format menu; or right-click the selection, and click Format Cells on the shortcut menu; or press Ctrl+1. In the Format Cells dialog box, click the Number tab, and change the value in the Decimal Places text box to the desired number.

Q: By default, how many decimal places appear in a value when you format it using the Currency Style button on the Formatting toolbar?

A: The value has two decimal places by default.

◆ **Keep this file open for the next exercise.**

QUICK REFERENCE ▼

Use the Formatting toolbar to apply number formatting to a range of cells

1 Select the range of cells to which you want to apply number formatting.

2 On the Formatting toolbar, click the desired number format button (Currency Style, Percent Style, or Comma Style).

Using Format Painter

THE BOTTOM LINE

The Format Painter allows you to quickly copy the attributes, or characteristics, of data that you have already formatted and apply these attributes to other data, thus eliminating the need for you to apply the same formats repeatedly.

The **Format Painter** feature is available in most Microsoft Office programs. It allows you to copy formatting from a cell or range of cells and apply it to another cell or range of cells.

You can copy formats, including font, font size, font style, font color, alignment, indentation, number formats, and borders and shading, which you'll learn about in the next section. To apply all of these formats, you must make a number of selections, either from the Formatting toolbar or from the Format Cells dialog box. For example, in a sales worksheet, you record sales data at the end of each month in the next open column and label the column with the name of the month. You can use the Format Painter to copy the formatting on the previous month's column to the current month's column. This feature saves you time and helps ensure formatting consistency.

TROUBLESHOOTING

If the Format Painter button doesn't appear on the Standard toolbar, click the Toolbar Options button to display the rest of the buttons; then click the Format Painter button.

Use the Format Painter to apply formats

In this exercise, you use the Format Painter button to copy a format from one cell to a range of cells.

1 **Click cell B3.**

The first column label cell is selected.

 2 **Click the Format Painter button on the Standard toolbar.**

A flashing marquee appears around the selected cell, and the mouse icon changes to a plus sign with a paintbrush next to it.

FIGURE 3-5

Copying a format with the Format Painter

Flashing marquee

	A	B	C	
1		Yearly Income - Lodging		
2				← Format Painter mouse icon
3		2002	2003	
4	Teepees	$ 23,393	$ 30,094	
5	Cabins	$ 75,943	$ 79,241	
6	Condos	$ 239,439	$ 653,782	
7				
8	Total	$ 338,775	$ 763,117	

3 Select the range A4:A8 (the row labels).

Excel copies the formatting in cell B3 to the range you selected. The row labels now appear in red, bold, and 12-point Times New Roman font.

4 On the Standard toolbar, click the Save button.

The workbook is saved with the current name.

- Select Save on the File menu.
- Press Ctrl+S.

◆ Keep this file open for the next exercise.

TIP

You can use the Format Painter to copy formatting to more than one nonadjacent cell or range of cells. Just *double-click* the Format Painter button, and then click the individual cells or ranges you want to format. When you are done, click the Format Painter button again to deactivate it.

QUICK CHECK

Q: What does the mouse pointer icon look like when you've clicked the Format Painter button?

A: It changes to a plus sign with a paintbrush next to it.

QUICK REFERENCE ▼

Use Format Painter to copy formats from one cell to other cells

1 Select a cell that contains formatting that you want to copy.

2 On the Standard toolbar, click the Format Painter button.

3 Select the cell or range to which you want to apply the format.

Adding Borders to Cells

THE BOTTOM LINE

You can emphasize a cell or range of cells by adding borders. Borders are especially useful for demarcating sections in a worksheet, such as a row of labels or totals.

Adding borders to a cell or range of cells can enhance the visual appeal of your worksheet, make it easier to read, and highlight specific data. Borders can also clearly separate sections of a worksheet. For example, in a sales worksheet, you might add a border under the cells containing the names of each month in the year, you might add a border between each column of monthly sales data, and you might add a border around the row containing the sales totals for each month.

Excel provides more than a dozen border styles—including single lines of varying widths, dotted lines, and dashed lines. You can also change the color of a border. When you create a border for a cell or range of cells, you don't need to apply the border to all four sides. You can specify that the border be applied to any side or combination of sides. For instance, you can apply a double line border to only the bottom border of the first row of a worksheet to separate the title from the rest of the worksheet.

Excel provides three methods for applying borders:

- You can select the cell or cells to which you want to add the border and use the options available under the Formatting toolbar's Borders button.
- You can draw borders directly on the worksheet using the Borders toolbar, as shown in Figure 3-6. To draw a border around a group of cells, click the mouse pointer at one corner of the group and drag it to the diagonal corner. You will see your border expand as you move the mouse pointer. When you want to add a border in a vertical or horizontal line, drag the mouse pointer along the target grid line. You can also change the characteristics of the border you draw through the options on the Borders toolbar.

FIGURE 3-6

Borders toolbar

TIP

You display the Borders toolbar by opening the View menu, pointing to Toolbars, and clicking Borders.

- You can apply borders using the Borders tab in the Format Cells dialog box. With this method, you choose where you want the border, the line style, and the line color all from one tab.

Add borders

In this exercise, you use all three methods to add borders to your worksheet.

1 Select the range B8:E8.

2 On the Formatting toolbar, click the down arrow to the right of the Borders button.

A menu of border line styles and locations appears.

FIGURE 3-7

Borders menu

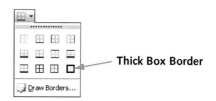

Thick Box Border

3 Click the Thick Box Border button (fourth button, third row, as identified in Figure 3-7).

A thick border is added around all sides of the selected cells.

4 Select the range A3:E3.

5 On the Format menu, click Cells, and click the Border tab.

The Format Cells dialog box appears with the Border tab on top.

FIGURE 3-8

Border tab in the Format Cells dialog box

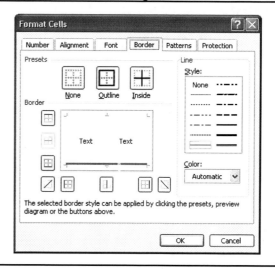

ANOTHER METHOD

Right-click the selection, and click Format Cells on the shortcut menu; or press Ctrl+1. In the Format Cells dialog box, click the Border tab.

6 In the Style list, click the second line style in the second column.

7 Click the Color down arrow, and click the Blue square (second row, sixth square).

8 In the Border section of the dialog box, click the bottom border.

In the dialog box, Excel shows a preview of what the chosen border will look like.

FIGURE 3-9

Preview of borders

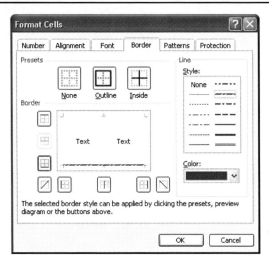

9 Click OK, and click a blank cell in the worksheet.

The Format Cells dialog box closes, and the blue border is added to your worksheet.

10 Point to Toolbars on the View menu, and click Borders to open the Borders toolbar.

ANOTHER METHOD

Click the Borders button down arrow, and select Draw Borders.

11 Click the down arrow on the Line Style button, and select the double line.

The mouse pointer changes to a pencil with a line next to it, and the Line Style button reflects the selection you have made.

12 Click and drag under the text in cell B1. Then click the Draw Border button on the Borders toolbar to toggle the mouse icon back to the regular selection arrow.

A double line is drawn under the text, and your worksheet should look similar to the following illustration.

FIGURE 3-10

Adding more borders

	A	B	C	D	E
1		Yearly Income - Lodging			
2					
3		2002	2003	2004	2005
4	Teepees	$ 23,393	$ 30,094	$ 32,492	$ 38,262
5	Cabins	$ 75,943	$ 79,241	$ 88,394	$ 89,000
6	Condos	$ 239,439	$ 653,782	$ 927,100	$ 954,111
7					
8	Total	$ 338,775	$ 763,117	$ 1,047,986	$ 1,081,373

◆ Keep this file open for the next exercise.

QUICK CHECK

Q: What are two ways to display the Borders toolbar?

A: You can display the Borders toolbar by se-lecting Toolbars on the View menu and then clicking Borders or by clicking the Borders button down arrow and selecting Draw Borders.

Adding Shading to Cells

Shading can draw attention to selected data as well as add color to your worksheet. Applying a light shade to every other column or row in a large worksheet is a good technique for improving the readability of data.

As with borders, you can add shading and patterns to one cell or a range of cells to set off the selection. For example, you might have a worksheet with numerous rows of data that span across 15 columns. You could apply a light shade of color to every other row so that it's easier to follow the data for a certain entry across the long series of columns, as shown in Figure 3-11.

FIGURE 3-11

Using shading to make data easier to read

	Type of Equipment	Price per Rental	Year	Jan	Feb	Mar	Apr	May	Jun	Jul	Aug	Sep
2												
3	Kajaks	34.95	57.00	0	0	2	4	5	8	18	12	6
4	Tennis Rackets	2.95	214.00	0	0	16	40	42	28	30	32	15
5	Skis - Downhill	19.95	341.00	85	65	54	42	0	0	0	0	0
6	Ski Boots	9.95	260.00	68	54	45	31	0	0	0	0	0
7	Snowshoes	14.95	103.00	32	13	0	0	0	0	0	0	0
8	Snowmobiles	74.95	32.00	6	7	2	0	0	0	0	0	0
9	Fishing Poles	2.95	86.00	3	5	7	4	9	17	13	23	5
10	Mountain Bikes	14.95	266.00	0	0	10	18	23	30	46	48	53
11	Helmets	0.00	383.00	0	0	24	32	41	45	58	65	75
12	Backpacks	4.95	130.00	3	7	6	14	18	14	13	12	11
13	Rollerblades	14.95	117.00	0	0	11	14	18	15	12	17	22
14	Pads	0.00	110.00	0	0	11	14	15	14	12	16	20
15	Binoculars	0.00	186.00	11	13	9	16	20	14	18	17	21
16	Skis - Cross Country	19.95	93.00	25	28	13	0	0	0	0	0	0
17	Rafts	24.95	71.00	0	0	0	3	12	16	15	13	12

Shading can be a shade of gray or a color. Although colors can add significantly to the appearance of a worksheet, colors appear in a printed worksheet only when you are using a color printer. A pattern is a set of lines or dots that fill selected cells. Applying patterns is especially useful when you want to call attention to one or more cells in a printed worksheet but you do not have a color printer. If you have a color printer or plan to view your worksheet only on the screen, you can combine color shading with a pattern in selected cells. However, make sure the text in the cells is still easy to read.

Apply shading and patterns to cells

In this exercise, you add shading to cells in the worksheet and preview the patterns that you can apply to cells.

1 Select the range B8:E8.

You will add shading to the cells that show total projected income for each year.

2 On the Format menu, click Cells, and click the Patterns tab.

The Format Cells dialog box appears with the Patterns tab on top.

FIGURE 3-12

Patterns tab in the Format Cells dialog box

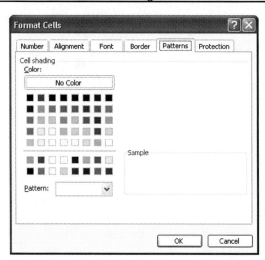

ANOTHER METHOD

Right-click the selection, and click Format Cells on the shortcut menu; or press Ctrl+1. In the Format Cells dialog box, click the Patterns tab.

3 In the Color area, click the Yellow square in the bottom row of colors.

ANOTHER METHOD

Click the Fill Color button's down arrow, and click Yellow.

4 Click the Pattern down arrow.

The fill patterns that you can add to cells appear.

FIGURE 3-13

Available fill patterns

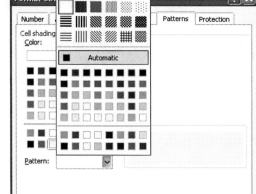

Patterns work best with row and column labels—especially for labels that are in a large font size or that are bold. When a pattern is applied to cells that contain numbers, the numbers can often be difficult to read.

5 Click the Pattern down arrow again.

The Pattern list closes without a pattern selected.

6 Click OK, and click a blank area of the worksheet.

The cells are deselected and appear with yellow shading.

7 On the Standard toolbar, click the Save button.

The workbook is saved with the current name.

◆ Keep this file open for the next exercise.

Using AutoFormat

THE BOTTOM LINE

The AutoFormat feature is another of Excel's handy time-saving devices. Simply select a range of cells and choose from among a number of predesigned formats to apply to it. This saves you the time of adding worksheet formats such as borders, shading, and font styles and sizes.

Applying Styles and
Formats to Data

With the **AutoFormat** feature, you can format the data in your worksheets using a professionally designed template. The AutoFormat feature is ideal for a range of data that consists of these basic components:

- A top row with labels
- A first column with labels
- The raw data that's being stored
- A row or column (or both) with totals

When you apply an AutoFormat to a range with these components, they are automatically identified and formatted with the borders, shading, and font effects that are appropriate for that type of data. An AutoFormat is not permanent—you can modify it or change it completely using any formatting techniques you choose.

Apply an AutoFormat to a worksheet

In this exercise, you explore the AutoFormat dialog box and format a worksheet area with AutoFormat.

1 Select the range A3:E8.

All of the row labels, column labels, and data cells are selected.

2 **On the Format menu, click AutoFormat.**

The AutoFormat dialog box appears.

FIGURE 3-14

AutoFormat dialog box

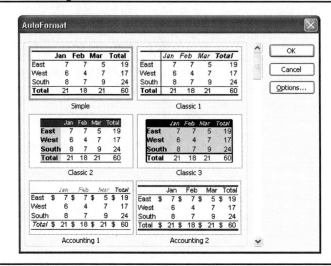

3 **Scroll down on the formats list to view all of the available formats.**

4 **Scroll back to the top of the formats list, click the Classic 2 format preview, click OK, and click a blank area of the worksheet.**

The range is deselected and appears in the Classic 2 format.

FIGURE 3-15

Applying the Classic 2 format

	A	B	C	D	E
1		Yearly Income - Lodging			
2					
3		2002	2003	2004	2005
4	Teepees	$ 23,393	$ 30,094	$ 32,492	$ 38,262
5	Cabins	$ 75,943	$ 79,241	$ 88,394	$ 89,000
6	Condos	$239,439	$653,782	$ 927,100	$ 954,111
7					
8	Total	$338,775	$763,117	$1,047,986	$1,081,373

TIP

When an AutoFormat is applied, Excel removes any existing formatting in the selected cells so that the AutoFormat can be applied correctly.

5 **On the Standard toolbar, click the Save button.**

The file is saved with the current name.

◆ **Keep this file open for the next exercise.**

Applying Styles and Formats to Data

Creating and Applying Styles

THE BOTTOM LINE

Styles, which are a defined set of formats, can save you time and provide consistency in the look of your worksheets.

A **style** is a set of formatting attributes that you can apply to a cell or range of cells more easily than setting each attribute individually.

Excel comes with several ready-made styles that you can use to format data quickly. You've already learned that the raw data you enter is formatted by default in the Arial 10- point font. This is Excel's "Normal" style. You can create a style that incorporates any of the following formatting attributes:

- Number
- Alignment
- Font
- Border
- Patterns
- Protection

An **attribute** is a formatting characteristic of a cell (such as a dotted line border) or the data in a cell (such as a font or font size). You can modify the attributes of the Normal style or Excel's other ready-made styles, or you can create your own styles. For example, the financial manager for a chain of fast-food restaurants records receipts by month on a separate worksheet for each location. The worksheet titles, subtitles, and row and column labels are basically the same in each worksheet. He creates a style for the title, a style for the subtitle, a style for the row labels, and a style for the column labels. All he does is select the data and apply the appropriate style. He doesn't need to spend time applying the individual formats that make up the style, and all the worksheets are consistent in their appearance.

When you create a new style, you must base it on an existing style; however, you don't need to keep any of the formatting that composes the original style.

Create and apply styles

In this exercise, you create a style that applies a font, a font size, alignment, and a font style to the contents of selected cells. You then apply the new style to other cells.

1 Click cell B1, and on the Format menu, click Style.

The Style dialog box appears, with Normal as the default style, as shown in Figure 3-16.

FIGURE 3-16

Style dialog box

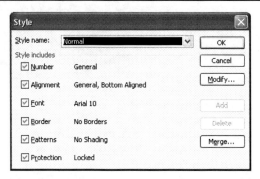

2 Click in the Style Name box at the end of the word Normal, type 2, and click the Add button.

A style named Normal2 is created.

3 Click the Modify button.

The Format Cells dialog box appears. In this dialog box, you define the attributes of the style.

4 Click the Font tab, click Times New Roman on the Font list, click Bold on the Font Style list, and click 14 on the Size list.

The contents of any cell to which you apply the Normal2 style will appear in 14-point, Times New Roman, bold text.

5 Click OK.

The Style dialog box reappears, showing the changes you made to the Normal2 style.

6 Click OK again.

The contents of cell B1 appear with the formatting you specified for the Normal2 style.

7 Click cell A8, and on the Format menu, click Style.

The Style dialog box appears.

TIP

You can apply styles more easily when you add the Style list to the Formatting toolbar. To do so, on the Tools menu, click Customize to display the Customize dialog box. Click the Commands tab, click Format on the Categories list, and drag the Style list box from the Commands list to the Formatting toolbar.

8 **Click the Style Name down arrow, click Normal2, and click OK.**

The contents of cell A8 appear with the formatting you specified for the Normal2 style.

FIGURE 3-17

Applying a new style to a cell

	A	B	C	D	E
1		Yearly Income - Lodging			
2					
3		2002	2003	2004	2005
4	Teepees	$ 23,393	$ 30,094	$ 32,492	$ 38,262
5	Cabins	$ 75,943	$ 79,241	$ 88,394	$ 89,000
6	Condos	$239,439	$653,782	$ 927,100	$ 954,111
7					
8	Total	$338,775	$763,117	$1,047,986	$1,081,373

9 **On the Edit menu, click Undo Style.**

The contents of cell A8 appear with the previous formatting.

ANOTHER METHOD

- Click the Undo button on the Standard toolbar.
- Press Ctrl+Z.

10 **On the Standard toolbar, click the Save button.**

The file is saved.

ANOTHER METHOD

- Select Save on the File menu.
- Press Ctrl+S.

◆ **Close Lodging Analysis.**

QUICK REFERENCE ▼

Create and apply a style

1 On the Format menu, click Style.

2 Click the Style Name down arrow, and click the style on which you want to base the new style.

3 Type a name for the new style on the Style Name list.

4 Click OK.

5 Select the cell or range of cells to which you want to apply the style.

6 On the Format menu, click Style.

7 Click the style you want to apply on the Style Name list.

8 Click OK.

Merging Cells

THE BOTTOM LINE

Merging multiple cells into a single cell gives you control over the alignment and spacing of a data entry that might be unusually long—such as a worksheet title—in comparison to other entries in the same row or column.

You already know that you can adjust the width of a column so that the longest number or text entry in the column fits within the column width. You can also **merge cells** to support additional formatting capabilities. Merging cells combines two or more cells into a single cell so that the text or value within the cell can be formatted more easily. For example, you might want to merge several cells in the title row of a worksheet so that the title is contained within a single cell. Then you could align the title so that it's centered within the cell and over the worksheet data.

You can also merge cells in adjoining rows so that you have more control over the alignment and placement of text in the cells. For example, suppose several of the column labels for your worksheet are lengthy. If you widen the columns to fit the lengthy column labels, the columns might be much longer than the longest value in the column. For example, suppose you have a column label called *Quantity Ordered*. This label occupies 16 character positions. Now consider that the largest order amount is 9,999— five character positions. If you widen the *Quantity Ordered* column to fit the column label, the column is wider than necessary. You'll see how this technique works in the following exercise.

A better approach is to merge the *Quantity Ordered* cell with the cell below it. After you've merged the cells, you can use the Format Cells dialog box to format *Quantity Ordered* so that the text wraps from the top line into the line below it and is centered horizontally and vertically in the merged cell. You can then narrow the column so that the values fit better within the column.

◆ **Open AW Guest Supplies from the Excel Core Practice/Lesson03 folder.**

Merge cells

In this exercise, you merge cells horizontally (multiple cells in the same row) and vertically (multiple cells in the same column) and reformat the merged cells.

1 **Click cell A1 to select it, if necessary.**

2 **Hold down the Shift key, and click cell F1.**

The range A1:F1 is selected.

Although you can click and drag to select any range of cells, the technique used in steps 2 and 3 provides an easier way to select a lengthy range of cells.

3 **Click the Merge And Center button.**

The selected cells are merged into one cell, and the text is centered in the cell.

To open the Format Cells dialog box, select Cells on the Format menu; right-click the selection, and select Format Cells on the shortcut menu; or press Ctrl+F1. Click the Alignment tab; click the Horizontal down arrow, and select Center Across Selection; and click Merge Cells in the Text Control section.

4 **Click cell A3, hold down the Shift key, and click cell F3.**

The range A3:F3 is selected.

5 **Click the Merge And Center button.**

The selected cells are merged into one cell, and the text is centered in the cell.

FIGURE 3-18

Merging cells and centering their content

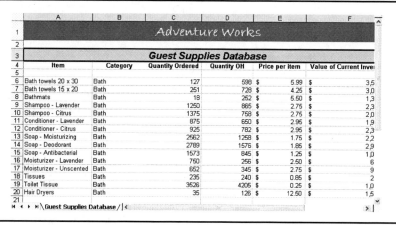

6 **Select the range C4:C5; right-click the selected cells; and on the shortcut menu, click Format Cells.**

The Format Cells dialog box appears.

7 **Click the Alignment tab.**

The Alignment tab of the Format Cells dialog box appears on top.

FIGURE 3-19

Alignment tab in the Format Cells dialog box

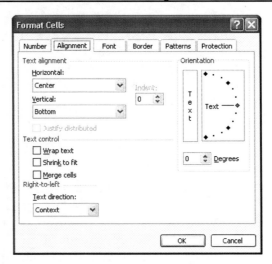

8 **Click the Vertical down arrow, and click Center.**

The selected cells will be centered vertically in the merged cell.

9 **In the Text control section of the dialog box, select the Wrap text check box.**

The text in the selected cells will wrap to two or more lines if the text does not fit on one line.

TIP

You can unmerge a merged cell at any time by selecting the cell, displaying the Alignment tab of the Format Cells dialog box, and clearing the Merge Cells check box.

10 **In the Text control section of the dialog box, select the Merge Cells check box, and click OK.**

The cells are now merged into a single cell, and the text is centered vertically and horizontally in the merged cell.

11 **Click the right edge of the column selector for column C, and drag to the left until the column is about 9 characters in width.**

The text in the merged cell wraps to a second line.

FIGURE 3-20

Wrapping text

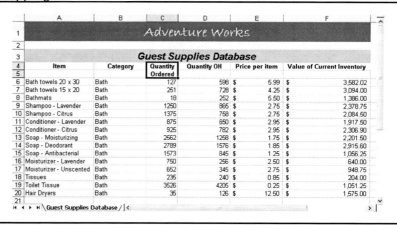

TIP

The column width, measured in the number of characters, appears and changes as you drag the column selector.

 12 On the Standard toolbar, double-click the Format Painter button. Select the range D4:D5, then E4:E5, and finally F4:F5.

Excel copies the merge formatting to the selected cells.

 13 Click the Format Painter button.

Excel copies the merge formatting to the selected cells, the Format Painter is no longer activated, and the cell selection marquee around cell C4 disappears.

14 On your own, use the column selectors to reduce the width of columns D, E, and F so that the text in the merged cells wraps to two lines for each column.

FIGURE 3-21

Decreasing column width to wrap column labels

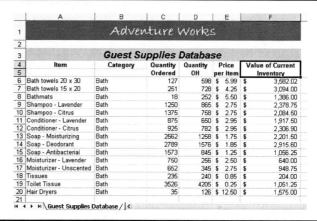

15 On the File menu, click Save As, type AW Guest Supplies 03, **and click the Save button.**

The file is saved with the new name.

◆ **Close AW Guest Supplies 03. If you are continuing to other lessons, leave Excel open. If you are not continuing to other lessons, save and close all open workbooks. Click the Close button in the top right corner of the Excel window.**

QUICK REFERENCE ▼

Merge cells

1 Select the range of cells that you want to merge into a single cell.

2 On the Formatting toolbar, click the Merge and Center button.

Or

Display the Alignment tab of the Format Cells dialog box, and select the desired merge options.

Key Points

✔ *Excel's formatting tools enable you to give your worksheets a professional, customized look. You can format text and numbers using the Format Cells dialog box or buttons on the Formatting toolbar.*

✔ *The Format Painter allows you to quickly copy the attributes, or characteristics, of data that you have already formatted and apply these attributes to other data, thus eliminating the need for you to apply the same formats repeatedly.*

✔ *You can emphasize a cell or range of cells by adding borders or shading. Borders are especially useful for demarcating sections in a worksheet, such as a row of labels or totals. You can use shading to draw attention to selected data as well as add color to your worksheet.*

✔ *You can automatically apply professionally designed formats to a range by using the AutoFormat feature. This saves you the time of adding worksheet formats such as borders, shading, and font styles and sizes.*

✔ *Styles, which are a defined set of formatting options, can save you time and provide consistency in the look of your worksheets.*

✔ *Merging multiple cells into a single cell gives you control over the alignment and spacing of a data entry that might be unusually long in comparison to other entries in the same row or column.*

Quick Quiz

True/False

T   F   **1.** You cannot change the alignment of numeric values.

T   F   **2.** Bold and italics are examples of font styles.

T   F   **3.** By default, the General format is applied to numbers you enter in a cell.

T   F   **4.** The best way to add a line under a row of column labels is to apply the Underline font style.

T   F   **5.** To modify a style, open the AutoFormat dialog box and make your changes there.

T   F   **6.** You can merge cells horizontally, but not vertically.

Multiple Choice

1. Which of the following is *not* an alignment option?
   a. Underline
   b. Align Left
   c. Alight Right
   d. Center

2. Which of the following is the measurement unit for font sizes?
   a. leader
   b. tick
   c. millimeter
   d. point

3. If you wanted to change the entry *131.2543* to *131.25*, which button on the Formatting toolbar would you click?
   a. Increase Decimal
   b. Decrease Decimal
   c. Align Right
   d. Increase Indent

4. Which feature lets you apply a predesigned format to a range?
   a. AutoFormat
   b. Format Painter
   c. Format Wizard
   d. Style Painter

Short Answer

1. What is the easiest way to convert selected cells to currency format?

2. What are two ways to apply shading to selected cells?

3. How can you display a button that isn't showing on a toolbar?

4. What purpose do styles serve?

5. How can you apply a border to a cell or range of cells you've selected?

On Your Own

◆ **Open Lodging Analysis03 from the Excel Core Practice/Lesson03 folder.**

Exercise 1

Move the title text to cell A1, and then merge and center it over the worksheet data. Right-align the column headings. Change the column headings to a size, font, and style that you like. Then use the Format Painter to copy the format of the column labels to the row labels.

Exercise 2

Using the Lodging Analysis03 workbook, select the labels and data in the worksheet. Apply different AutoFormats to see how they look. Then create a style, and apply it to the Total row.

◆ **Save and close Lodging Analysis03.**

One Step Further

Exercise 1

Create a worksheet in which to log your daily physical activities. (If you created this worksheet in the previous lesson, you can continue to use that worksheet.) This worksheet should contain a list of your regular physical activities in column A and should include a column for each day of the week. In a row above the days of the week, insert a heading that reads Minutes per Day. Merge and center this heading. Change the heading format to 14-point, Arial, bold. Select the entire range that includes all of the days of the week and all of the activities (do not include the heading), and apply the Colorful 1 AutoFormat.

Exercise 2

In reviewing the worksheet that you created in Exercise 1, you decide that you like the basic Colorful 1 format; however, you're not fond of the colors and think you would like the borders to be somewhat different. What methods can you use to alter these features? Which method do you like the best? Write a brief answer to these questions.

Exercise 3

While learning to format cells in a worksheet, you have selected individual cells as well as ranges of cells. Use Excel's Help files to determine if there is a quick way to select an entire worksheet and apply formatting changes to all of the cells at once. Write a brief explanation of your findings.

Changing Print Options

After completing this lesson, you will be able to:

✔ *Add a header and footer to a worksheet.*
✔ *Change margins and center a worksheet.*
✔ *Change the orientation and the scale of a worksheet.*
✔ *Add and delete page breaks.*
✔ *Set and clear a print area.*
✔ *Set other print options.*

KEY TERMS

▪ footer
▪ header
▪ orientation

▪ resolution
▪ scaling

One of the easiest ways to share information in a worksheet or workbook is to print copies for others to review. For instance, every year at the annual briefing for the Adventure Works resort, the activities coordinator passes out copies of an Excel worksheet that summarizes the yearly revenue for sports equipment rentals. She takes advantage of several Excel features that make worksheets more readable and more attractive.

By adding headers and footers, the activities coordinator can print information about the worksheet (such as the title, the date the worksheet was printed, and the author) on every page. She can adjust the size of the margins and change the orientation of the worksheet. She can even enlarge or reduce the size of the worksheet so all of the information fits on one page. She can center the content on a page for readability. To keep some worksheet information confidential, she can specify which parts of the worksheet to print and which parts not to print. Finally, she can insert page breaks to improve readability.

IMPORTANT

Before you can use the practice files in this lesson, you must install them from the book's companion CD to their default location. For additional information on how to find and open files used in this book, see the "Using the CD-ROM" section at the beginning of this book.

Adding a Header and Footer

THE BOTTOM LINE

Headers and footers are useful for documenting important information about a worksheet, such as the date it was created or last modified, who prepared it, the page number, and so on.

A **header** is a line of text that appears at the top of each page of a printed worksheet. A **footer** is a line of text that appears at the bottom. Headers and footers commonly contain information such as a page number, the title of a worksheet, and the date a worksheet was printed. This information provides another tool for helping users identify the contents, author, and status of a worksheet.

You can create headers and footers by picking from a list of header and footer options that Excel provides. These options include page numbers, workbook names, worksheet names, author names, company names, and combinations of these. The same options are available for both headers and footers.

You also can create headers and footers by typing the text that you want to appear or by clicking buttons to insert codes that form your own combinations of the options Excel provides. Then whenever you print the worksheet, Excel replaces the codes with the name of the workbook, the current page number, the current date, and so on. Doing this is an easy way to ensure that header and footer information is up to date.

The Header dialog box, where you create custom headers, looks similar to Figure 4-1

CHECK THIS OUT ▼

Enhancing Headers and Footers
You can insert a graphic in the header or footer. Adding a graphic, such as a logo, to a worksheet can help further identify it, and it can add color and dimension to the appearance of the worksheet. To insert a graphic, click the Custom Header or Custom Footer buttons in the Page Setup dialog box. Click the Insert Picture button, and then locate the graphic you want to insert. After you insert a graphic into a header or footer, the Format Picture button becomes available. Clicking that button will open a dialog box with tools to edit your graphic.

FIGURE 4-1

Header dialog box

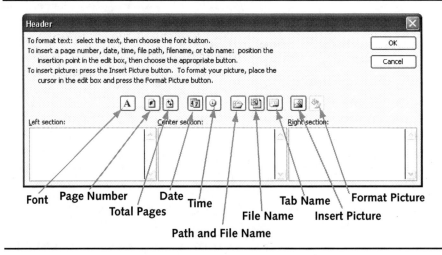

Information in the Left Section box is aligned with the left margin of the worksheet, information in the Center Section box is centered, and text in the Right Section box is aligned with the right margin. When you want to change the font, font size, or font style of a header or footer, click the Font button to open the Font dialog box.

◆ To complete the procedures in this lesson, you must use the practice file Sports Income in the Lesson04 folder in the Excel Core Practice folder that is located on your hard disk.

◆ Open Sports Income from the Excel Core Practice/Lesson04 folder.

Add a header and footer

In this exercise, you add a header and footer to a worksheet.

1 On the View menu, click Header And Footer.

The Page Setup dialog box appears with the Header/Footer tab displayed.

FIGURE 4-2

Page Setup dialog box

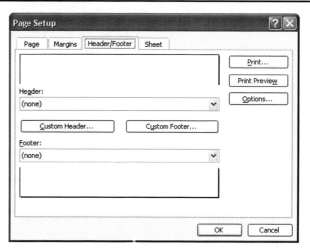

2 Click the Custom Header button.

The Header dialog box appears.

3 Click in the Right Section box, and click the Date button. Refer to Figure 4-1, where the buttons are identified.

A code for the date is inserted.

TIP

If you want to use an ampersand (&) within the text of a header or a footer, type two ampersands (&&). Otherwise, Excel interprets the single ampersand as part of the code.

4 In the Header dialog box, click OK.

The Header dialog box closes. The current date appears in the Header preview box in the Page Setup dialog box.

5 Click the Footer down arrow. On the list that appears, scroll down and click Sports Income.xls, Page 1.

The footer you chose appears in the Footer preview box.

6 Click OK.

The Page Setup dialog box closes. The header and footer would appear on a printed copy of the worksheet, although you can't see them on the screen.

7 On the Standard toolbar, click the Print Preview button.

The worksheet appears in the Preview window with the header and footer you specified, as shown in Figure 4-3.

FIGURE 4-3

Previewing a worksheet with the header and footer

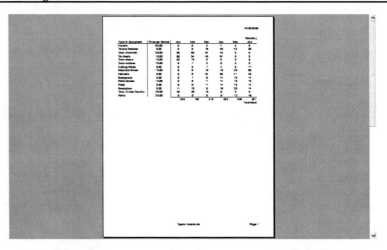

8 On the Print Preview toolbar, click the Next button.

Note that the header and footer also appear on the second page of the worksheet.

9 On the Print Preview toolbar, click the Close button.

The workbook window appears.

10 Save the workbook with the current name.

◆ Keep this file open for the next exercise.

QUICK REFERENCE ▼

Select a header or a footer

1 On the View menu, click Header And Footer.

2 Click the Header or Footer down arrow, and click the desired header or footer.

3 Click OK.

Customize a header or footer

1 On the View menu, click Header And Footer.

2 Click the Custom Header button or the Custom Footer button.

3 In the Header or Footer dialog box, type the desired text, and click buttons to enter codes in the Left, Center, or Right sections.

4 Format the text, if desired, and click OK twice.

Changing Margins

Making Printed Worksheets
Easier to Read

THE BOTTOM LINE

Margins are an effective way to control and optimize the white space on a printed worksheet. Achieving balance between data and white space adds considerably to the readability and appearance of a worksheet.

By default, worksheet margins are 1 inch on the top and the bottom and 0.75 inch on the left and right. When you add a header or footer to the worksheet, it is separated from the body of the worksheet by 0.5 inch.

You can change the margins to suit the needs of each workbook. For example, the activities coordinator at Adventure Works wants to print the Sports Income worksheet on company letterhead for the annual briefing, so she sets the top margin of the worksheet to 1.5 inches, leaving room for the company logo, address, and phone number.

Another technique for adding balance to a worksheet is centering its contents on the page. You can center the contents vertically between the top and bottom edges of the page or horizontally between the left and right edges of the page.

Change margins and alignment

In this exercise, you change the margins of a worksheet and center the worksheet on the page.

1 On the File menu, click Page Setup.

The Page Setup dialog box appears.

2 Click the Margins tab, if necessary.

The current margins are listed in the Top, Bottom, Right, Left, Header, and Footer boxes.

FIGURE 4-4

Margins tab in the Page Setup dialog box

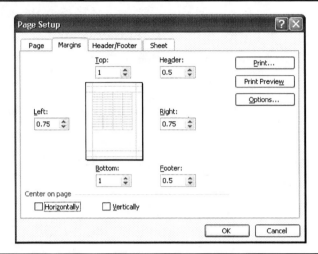

3 Click the up arrow in the Top box twice.

The top margin changes to 1.5 inches.

4 Click the up arrow in the Bottom box twice.

The bottom margin changes to 1.5 inches.

ANOTHER METHOD

You also can alter the margins in the Print Preview window by clicking the Margins button on the Print Preview toolbar and dragging the dotted margin indicators.

5 In the Center On Page section at the bottom of the dialog box, select the Horizontally and Vertically check boxes.

6 Click the Print Preview button in the dialog box.

The preview shows this change, as shown in Figure 4-5.

FIGURE 4-5

Previewing page setup

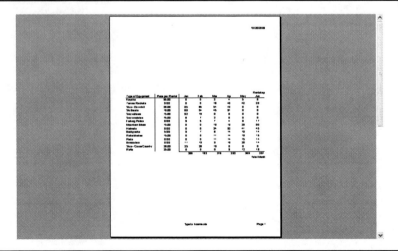

7 On the Print Preview toolbar, click the Close button.

The Print Preview window closes.

◆ Keep this file open for the next exercise.

QUICK REFERENCE ▼

Change margin settings, and center a worksheet on a page

1 On the File menu, click Page Setup, and click the Margins tab.

2 In the Top, Bottom, Left, Right, Header, or Footer boxes, click the arrow buttons, or type a new margin.

3 Select the Horizontally and Vertically check boxes, and click OK.

Changing the Orientation and Scale

THE BOTTOM LINE

Printed worksheets are easiest to read and analyze when all of the data appears on one piece of paper. Excel's orientation and scaling features give you more control over the number of pages that worksheet data prints on.

Positioning Data on a Printed Page

You can change the **orientation** of a worksheet so that it prints either vertically or horizontally on a page. A worksheet printed vertically uses the Portrait setting and looks like the document shown in Figure 4-5. Portrait orientation is the default setting. A worksheet printed horizontally uses the Landscape setting, shown in Figure 4-6.

FIGURE 4-6

Landscape orientation

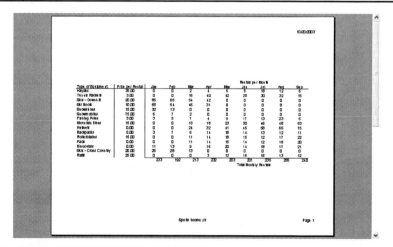

You may decide to use the Landscape setting if the width of the area you want to print is greater than the height. For example, the Sports Income workbook is currently set to print in Portrait orientation, and it needs two pages to accommodate all of the columns of data. The data would be much easier to read if it were all on one page. This can be accomplished by changing the orientation to landscape.

If you still can't fit all of the data on one printed page by changing the orientation, you can shrink or reduce it by using Excel's **scaling** options. The most common reason for scaling a worksheet is to shrink it so that you can print it on one page, but you also can enlarge the sheet so that data appears bigger and fills up more of the printed page. To scale a worksheet, you specify how much to enlarge or shrink it or you specify the number of pages on which you want it to fit.

Change the orientation and scaling of a worksheet

In this exercise, you change the orientation of a worksheet and set it up to print on one page.

1 On the File menu, click Page Setup.

The Page Setup dialog box appears.

2 Click the Page tab.

FIGURE 4-7

Page tab in the Page Setup dialog box

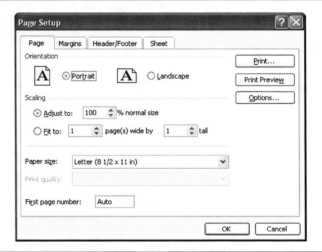

3 Click the Landscape option.

The orientation of the worksheet changes from portrait to landscape.

4 On the Page tab, click the Print Preview button.

The preview displays the first page of the worksheet.

5 On the Print Preview toolbar, click the Close button.

The Print Preview window closes.

6 On the File menu, click Page Setup.

The Page tab of the Page Setup dialog box appears.

7 **In the Scaling section in the middle of the tab, click the Fit To option. Keep the default settings of 1 page wide by 1 page tall.**

The worksheet is scaled to fit on one page.

8 **On the Page tab, click the Print Preview button.**

The scale of the worksheet decreases so that the worksheet fits on one page. It should look similar to the following illustration.

FIGURE 4-8

Setting up the data to fit on one page

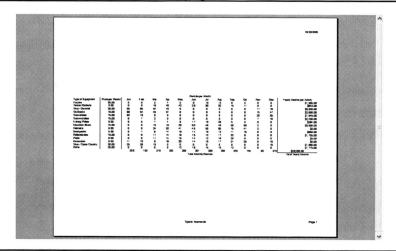

9 **On the Print Preview toolbar, click the Close button.**

The Print Preview window closes.

10 **Save the workbook with the current name.**

◆ **Keep this file open for the next exercise.**

QUICK CHECK

Q. What is the difference between orientation and scaling?

A: Orientation refers to the direction in which the worksheet prints—either portrait, in which the sheet is longer than it is wide, or landscape, in which the sheet is wider than it is long. Scaling refers to enlarging or reducing the data.

QUICK REFERENCE ▼

Change the page orientation of a worksheet

1 On the File menu, click Page Setup, and click the Page tab.

2 In the Orientation section, click the Portrait or Landscape option, and click OK.

Scale a worksheet

1 On the File menu, click Page Setup, and click the Page tab.

2 Click the Adjust To option. In the Adjust To box, enter the percentage of the normal size at which you want the worksheet to appear.

Or

Click the Fit To option. In the two Fit To boxes, enter the number of pages wide by the number of pages tall that you want the worksheet to appear.

3 Click OK.

Adding and Deleting Page Breaks

THE BOTTOM LINE

When worksheet data prints on more than one page, you can control where the page breaks occur. This allows you to break data where it's most logical, resulting in a well-organized, easy-to-read document.

Excel determines the number of pages on which a worksheet will print based on the size of the worksheet, the margin settings, the orientation, and the scaling. The places where Excel breaks the content from one page to the next are called automatic page breaks, and Excel adjusts these automatically when you add and delete worksheet content.

You also can add and delete your own page breaks, but Excel won't adjust them as you change worksheet content. When you want to change your own page break positions, you must do it manually in the Page Break Preview window. Manual page breaks help you organize the content by letting you break pages based on content rather than dimensions. For instance, the activities coordinator at the Adventure Works wants to see how a worksheet would look if she added a page break between the rentals per month for each type of equipment and the total monthly rentals for all equipment.

Add and delete page breaks

In this exercise, you insert and delete page breaks.

1 the File menu, click **Page Setup**.

The Page Setup dialog box appears with the Page tab displayed.

2 In the Adjust To box, type 100, and then click **OK**.

The worksheet scale returns to 100%.

3 Click cell A18. On the Insert menu, click **Page Break**.

Excel inserts a page break in the worksheet below row 17. The page break appears as a dashed line on the worksheet, similar to that shown in Figure 4-9.

FIGURE 4-9

Inserting a page break

	A	B	C	D	E	F	G	H	I	J
1								Rentals per Month		
2	Type of Equipment	Price per Rental	Jan	Feb	Mar	Apr	May	Jun	Jul	Aug
3	Kayaks	35.00	0	0	2	4	5	8	18	12
4	Tennis Rackets	3.00	0	0	16	40	42	28	30	32
5	Skis - Downhill	20.00	85	65	54	42	0	0	0	0
6	Ski Boots	10.00	68	54	45	31	0	0	0	0
7	Snowshoes	15.00	32	13	0	0	0	0	0	0
8	Snowmobiles	75.00	6	7	2	0	0	0	0	0
9	Fishing Poles	3.00	3	5	7	4	9	17	13	23
10	Mountain Bikes	15.00	0	0	13	18	23	30	46	48
11	Helmets	0.00	0	0	24	32	41	45	59	65
12	Backpacks	5.00	3	7	6	14	18	14	13	12
13	Rollerblades	15.00	0	0	11	14	18	15	12	17
14	Pads	0.00	0	0	11	14	15	14	12	16
15	Binoculars	0.00	11	13	9	16	20	14	18	17
16	Skis - Cross Country	20.00	25	28	13	0	0	0	0	0
17	Rafts	25.00	0	0	0	3	12	16	15	13
18			233	192	213	232	203	201	235	255
19								Total Monthly Rentals		
20										

IMPORTANT

A manual page break occurs immediately above and to the left of the selected cell.

 4 **On the Standard toolbar, click the Print Preview button.**

A preview of the worksheet appears with the page break you just inserted.

5 **On the Print Preview toolbar, click the Close button.**

The Print Preview window closes.

TIP

You must select a cell directly below the manual page break in order for the Remove Page Break option to appear on the Insert menu.

6 **On the Insert menu, click Remove Page Break.**

The manual page break is removed, and the page breaks return to their default positions.

ANOTHER METHOD

You can move page breaks by dragging them in the Page Break Preview window. You display this window by clicking the Page Break Preview button on the Print Preview toolbar or by clicking Page Break Preview on the View menu.

7 **Save the workbook with the current name.**

◆ **Keep this file open for the next exercise.**

QUICK CHECK

Q. If you want to insert a page break between columns G and H and rows 20 and 21, which cell should you select before executing the Page Break command on the Insert menu?

A: You should click cell H21.

QUICK REFERENCE ▼

Add a page break

1 Select the cell directly below and to the right of where you want the page break.

2 On the Insert menu, click Page Break.

Delete a page break

1 Select the cell directly below and to the right of the page break you want to delete.

2 On the Insert menu, click Remove Page Break.

Setting and Clearing a Print Area

Printing Part of a Worksheet

THE BOTTOM LINE

Defining an area or a section in a worksheet to print gives you more control over exactly what shows up on the printed page.

If you don't want to print an entire worksheet, you can print only an area you specify by setting a print area. For example, you might have a worksheet in which you're recording data for each month in the year. You want to print only data recorded for the first three months. You can set the print area to include this data only. Any other printing options you've set, such as margins or orientation, apply to the print area. The print area you set is the only part of the worksheet that prints until you clear it or change it.

TIP

Setting a print area works differently from choosing to print a selection using the Print dialog box. If you set a print area, only cells in that area will print, regardless of what cells are selected when you execute the Print command. Also, when you set a print area, you do not need to select a range before you print.

The activities coordinator at Adventure Works decides to scale the worksheet to fit on one page. She also sets a print area to print only the revenue generated by sports equipment rentals and not the maintenance cost of the equipment.

Set and clear a print area

In this exercise, you set and clear a print area in a worksheet.

1 On the File menu, click Page Setup.

The Page Setup dialog box appears with the Page tab displayed.

2 In the Scaling section in the middle of the tab, click the Fit To option. Keep the default settings of 1 page wide by 1 page tall.

The worksheet is scaled to fit on one page.

You also can specify a print area in the Page Setup dialog box. On the Sheet tab, enter the cell range in the Print Area box.

3 Click OK.

4 Select the range A2:E18.

5 On the File menu, point to Print Area, and click Set Print Area.

 6 Click in any cell, and on the Standard toolbar, click the Print Preview button.

The Print Preview window appears, showing what would print if you printed the worksheet with the current settings.

FIGURE 4-10

Previewing the sheet

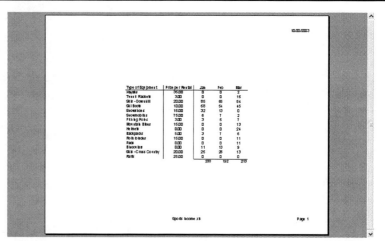

7 On the Print Preview toolbar, click the Print button. In the Print dialog box that appears, click OK.

The selection prints.

8 On the File menu, point to Print Area, and click Clear Print Area.

The print area is cleared.

9 Save the workbook with the current name.

◆ Keep this file open for the next exercise.

To print an area of a worksheet without setting a print area, select the area. On the File menu, click Print. In the Print dialog box in the Print What section, click Selection, and click OK.

QUICK REFERENCE ▼

Set and clear a print area

1 Select the portion of the worksheet you want to print.

2 On the File menu, point to Print Area, and click Set Print Area.

3 Clear the print area by pointing to Print Area on the File menu and clicking Clear Print Area.

Setting Other Print Options

THE BOTTOM LINE

Worksheets that print on two or more pages may benefit from having certain row and column labels (and even row numbers and column letters) repeated on every page. These can be helpful in clearly identifying data and eliminating the need to flip through pages to determine what the data represents. You also can save on ink or toner by selecting options to control the quality of printouts.

To further customize your worksheet printout, you can print row and column labels, gridlines, row numbers, and column letters on each page. You also can choose whether to print in color or black and white, and you can select the quality of the printing. These options appear on the Sheet tab of the Page Setup dialog box, shown in Figure 4-11.

FIGURE 4-11

Sheet tab in the Page Setup dialog box

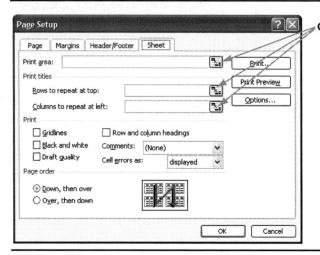

Collapse Dialog Button

Options include:

- **Rows To Repeat At Top or Columns To Repeat At Left** Print row or column text labels on each page by specifying the row or rows to repeat at the top of each page and the column or columns to repeat at the left of each page. Printing titles on each page of a multiple-page worksheet makes it easy to identify the data on subsequent pages.
- **Gridlines** Print the gridlines that appear in the worksheet window.
- **Black And White** Print color worksheets more quickly and save ink or toner by printing them in black and white.
- **Draft Quality** Print the worksheet at a reduced **resolution** in order to print faster and to save ink or toner.
- **Row And Column Headings** Print the row numbers and column letters that appear in the worksheet window.

Apply additional print settings

In this exercise, you apply print settings from the Sheet tab in the Page Setup dialog box.

1 **On the File menu, click Page Setup.**

The Page Setup dialog box appears with the Page tab displayed.

2 **In the Scaling section in the middle of the tab, click the Adjust To option, type 100 in the text box, and then click OK.**

The worksheet scale returns to 100%.

3 **On the View menu, click Page Break Preview. If the Welcome to Page Break Preview message box appears, click OK.**

The worksheet appears in Page Break Preview.

4 **Click and drag the dashed blue page break line to the left until it's between columns H and I.**

The worksheet should have a vertical page break between the columns for June and July.

5 **On the View menu, click Normal.**

The worksheet is displayed in Normal view.

6 **On the File menu, click Page Setup, and then click the Sheet tab.**

The Page Setup dialog box appears with the Sheet tab displayed.

 **7** **Click the Collapse Dialog button on the Print Area box.**

The Page Setup dialog box collapses, and you are returned to the worksheet.

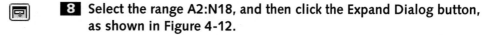 **8** **Select the range A2:N18, and then click the Expand Dialog button, as shown in Figure 4-12.**

FIGURE 4-12

Selecting the print area

Expand Dialog button

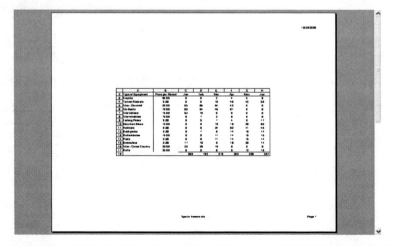

D	E										M	N
					Rentals per Month							
Feb	Mar	Apr	May	Jun	Jul	Aug	Sep	Oct	Nov	Dec		
0	2	4	5	8	18	12	6	2	0	0		
0	16	40	42	28	30	32	15	11	0	0		
65	54	42	0	0	0	0	0	0	17	78		
54	45	31	0	0	0	0	0	0	15	47		
13	0	0	0	0	0	0	0	0	23	35		
7	2	0	0	0	0	0	0	0	7	10		
5	7	4	9	17	13	23	5	2	0	0		
0	13	18	23	30	46	48	53	33	2	0		
0	24	32	41	45	58	65	75	41	2	0		
7	6	14	18	14	13	12	11	15	9	8		
0	11	14	18	15	12	17	22	8	0	0		
0	11	14	15	14	12	16	20	8	0	0		
13	9	16	20	14	18	17	21	25	9	13		
28	13	0	0	0	0	0	0	0	8	19		
0	0	3	12	16	15	13	12	0	0	0		
192	213	232	203	201	235	255	240	145	92	210		

The Page Setup dialog box redisplays with the range you selected in the Print Area box.

9 **Click the Collapse Dialog button on the Columns To Repeat At Left box.**

The Page Setup dialog box collapses, and you are returned to the worksheet. The mouse pointer icon changes to a down arrow.

10 **Position the mouse pointer on the column A selector and click, and then click the Expand Dialog button.**

The Page Setup dialog box redisplays with column A displayed in the Columns To Repeat At Left box.

11 **Click the Row And Column Headings box, and then click the Print Preview button.**

The worksheet appears in the Preview window with page 1, which contains the data for the first six months and the row and column headings, as shown in Figure 4-13.

FIGURE 4-13

Previewing the sheet

12 Click the Next button to preview page 2.

The column labels should be repeated on page 2, and the row and column headings should appear.

13 Click the Close button in the Print Preview window.

The worksheet appears in Normal view.

14 On the File menu, click Page Setup, and click the Sheet tab, if necessary.

15 Delete the selections in the Print Area box and the Columns To Repeat At Left box. Click the Row And Column Headings box to deselect it, and then click OK.

The additional print options are removed.

16 Save the workbook with the current name.

◆ Close Sports Income. If you are continuing to other lessons, leave Excel open. If you are not continuing to other lessons, save and close all open workbooks. Click the Close button in the top right corner of the Excel window.

Key Points

✔ *Headers and footers are useful for documenting important information about a worksheet, such as the date it was created or last modified, who prepared it, the page number, and so on.*

✔ *Margins are an effective way to control and optimize the white space on a printed worksheet.*

✔ *Centering the content in a worksheet can help you achieve balance between data and white space, which adds considerably to the readability and appearance of a worksheet.*

✔ *Printed worksheets are easiest to read and analyze when all of the data appears on one piece of paper. Excel's orientation and scaling features give you more control over the number of pages that worksheet data prints on.*

✔ *When worksheet data prints on more than one page, you can control where the page breaks occur. This allows you to break data where it's most logical, resulting in a well-organized, easy-to-read document.*

✔ *Defining an area or a section in a worksheet to print gives you more control over exactly what shows up on the printed page.*

✔ *Worksheets that print on two or more pages may benefit from having certain row and column labels (and even row numbers and column letters) repeated on every page. These can be helpful in clearly identifying data and eliminating the need to flip through pages to determine what the data represents.*

✔ *You can save on ink or toner by selecting options to control the quality of printouts.*

Quick Quiz

True/False

T F **1.** A header prints at the top of the first page only of a printed worksheet.

T F **2.** You can insert graphics in the header or footer of a worksheet.

T F **3.** In landscape orientation, the sheet appears longer than it is wide.

T F **4.** You can change margins by adjusting settings in the Page Setup dialog box or by dragging margin indicators in the Print Preview window.

T F **5.** Once you insert a manual page break, you cannot remove it.

Multiple Choice

1. If you wanted to change the point size of text in a custom header, which button in the Header dialog box would you click?
   a. Format
   b. Font
   c. Font Size
   d. Size

2. What are the default margin settings for a worksheet?
   a. top and bottom at .5 inch; left and right at 1 inch
   b. top and bottom at 1 inch; left and right at .5 inch
   c. top and bottom at .75 inch; left and right at 1 inch
   d. top and bottom at 1 inch; left and right at .75 inch

3. Which option lets you enlarge or reduce the size of a worksheet?
   a. orientation
   b. scaling
   c. resolution
   d. centering

4. In which view can you manually adjust page breaks?
   a. Print Preview
   b. Page Break Preview
   c. Zoom view
   d. Expand Dialog view

5. In which orientation does the page print longer than it is wide?
   a. Portrait
   b. Picture
   c. Landscape
   d. Horizontal

Short Answer

1. How can you automatically add the date to the bottom of every page when you print a worksheet?

2. How can you change a worksheet's page orientation?

3. What are two ways to print an area of a worksheet you've selected?

4. What are the default page margins of a worksheet?

5 Why would you want to repeat row or column labels on subsequent pages of a worksheet printout?

IMPORTANT

In the On Your Own section below, you must complete Exercise 1 before continuing to Exercise 2.

On Your Own

◆ **Open Sports Income from the Excel Core Practice/Lesson04 folder.**

Exercise 1

Delete the existing header and footer. Add the header Sports Income by Month, Year, and Activity in the top right corner of the worksheet. Add a footer that always prints the current date and time at the bottom center of the worksheet. Change the font of the header and footer to one of your choice.

◆ **Save Sports Income and leave the file open for Exercise 2.**

Exercise 2

Set the Sports Income workbook to print in Portrait orientation with gridlines, and adjust the scaling to print at 100% of normal size. Preview the location of the page breaks, and scale the worksheet to print on a single page. Set the print area to A1:P20, and preview the worksheet.

◆ **Close Sports Income.**

One Step Further

Exercise 1

You want to create a footer that includes your name, the file name (including its location), and the current page number out of the total number of pages. You want this information to be left-aligned, centered, and right-aligned. Briefly describe how you would do this.

Exercise 2

You want to create a header for your worksheet that includes the current date and time in the left corner and your company logo in the right corner. Briefly describe how you would you do this.

Exercise 3

On the Sheet tab of the Page Setup dialog box are a few additional options that were not discussed in this lesson. Explore this tab of the dialog box, and use the Help system, if necessary, to determine how you can choose to print cell comments and where they can be placed. Additionally, determine the significance of the Page Order section of this sheet. When would one page order be preferred over the other?

5

Organizing Worksheets and Window Display

After completing this lesson, you will be able to:

✔ *Magnify and shrink a worksheet on-screen.*
✔ *Hide and unhide rows and columns.*
✔ *Freeze and unfreeze rows and columns.*
✔ *Move between worksheets in a workbook.*
✔ *Add and delete worksheets in a workbook.*
✔ *Copy and move worksheets in a workbook.*
✔ *Sort data.*
✔ *Apply filters to data.*

KEY TERMS

- ascending order
- descending order
- filter
- freeze
- hide
- zoom

As you work with Excel, you will probably create worksheets that contain more data than can be viewed all at once on screen. You also might find that you need to distribute related data among several worksheets and workbooks. Fortunately, Excel provides several methods that allow you to work with the content in large worksheets or with the content spread across multiple worksheets and workbooks. These methods include assorted viewing options, the ability to add or delete worksheets in a workbook, and ways to sort and limit the data that's displayed.

The viewing options are particularly useful when you have a lot of data in your worksheet. You can magnify a worksheet to enlarge cells and see the content more easily, or you can shrink a worksheet so that you can see more of the content in the worksheet at once. Hiding worksheet rows and columns lets you focus on specific information in your worksheet by concealing data that is not relevant. When you want to see those rows and columns again, you unhide them. You can *freeze* one or more rows or columns so that they always remain in view, no matter how far you scroll down or across the worksheet. This is helpful when you want to keep data labels in sight. You can easily unfreeze the rows or columns to restore the look of your worksheet.

When you want to include related, but somewhat different, data in an existing workbook, you can add one or more worksheets. This allows you to keep the data in one workbook without creating overly large or complex worksheets. You can easily delete worksheets that are no longer necessary. You can also rearrange the order of worksheets and copy worksheets.

An important aspect of working with large amounts of data is the ability to organize it in a certain order and focus on the most important data in a worksheet, whether that data represents the best ten days of sales in a month or slow-selling product lines that you may need to reevaluate. Excel provides a number of powerful, flexible tools with which you can sort and limit the data displayed in your worksheet. In this lesson, you'll learn how to sort and *filter* the data that appears in your worksheets.

IMPORTANT

Before you can use the practice files in this lesson, you must install them from the book's companion CD to their default location. For additional information on how to find and open files used in this book, see the "Using the CD-ROM" section at the beginning of this book.

Magnifying and Shrinking a Worksheet On-Screen

THE BOTTOM LINE

Excel's Zoom feature lets you zoom in on a portion of a worksheet so that it appears larger and the data is easier to read. Or you can zoom out to get a better overall view of the worksheet, which makes it easy to identify formatting inconsistencies or awkward spacing or alignment.

If you've ever operated a video camcorder, you probably know how useful the zoom feature can be. You can zoom in to get a close-up view of your subject and zoom out to get a broader view of the subject and its surroundings. Excel's Zoom feature works in the same way.

When you create a worksheet, the cells and any data they contain appear at a standard size of 100%, which means basically that the size they appear on the screen is the size they appear on the printed page. You can magnify a worksheet to make each cell appear bigger. For example, in a large worksheet with cell after cell of numeric data, you might want to zoom in on a section so that the numbers are larger and, therefore, less stressful on your eyes to read. Or you can shrink the worksheet to see more rows and columns at a time. Again, in a large worksheet where all of the data does not fit on the screen, reducing the view of it lets you easily assess the overall appearance of the data.

To magnify or shrink a worksheet, you "**zoom**" it. To zoom in (magnify), you select a size greater than 100%; to zoom out (shrink), you select a size less than 100%.

◆ To complete the procedures in this lesson, you must use the files Sports Income05, Food, and Filter in the Lesson05 folder in the Excel Core Practice folder located on your hard disk.

◆ Open Sports Income05 from the Excel Core Practice/Lesson05 folder.

Zoom in and out

In this exercise, you zoom in and out on a worksheet.

1 Click cell C7. On the View menu, click Zoom.

The Zoom dialog box appears.

FIGURE 5-1

Zoom dialog box

2 Click the 200% option, and click OK.

Each cell of the worksheet appears twice its original size.

ANOTHER METHOD

On the Standard toolbar, click the down arrow on the Zoom button, and select 200%.

TROUBLESHOOTING

If the Zoom button doesn't appear on the Standard toolbar, click the Toolbar Options button, click Add Or Remove Buttons, click Standard, and then click Zoom on the list of buttons that appears.

100% ▾

3 On the Standard toolbar, click in the Zoom box.

4 In the Zoom box, type 60, and press Enter.

The worksheet shrinks to 60 percent of its original size and looks similar to the following illustration.

FIGURE 5-2

Zooming out

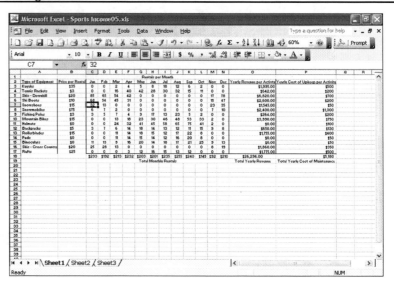

5 Click the down arrow on the Zoom box, and click 100%.

The worksheet returns to its original size.

◆ Keep this file open for the next exercise.

QUICK REFERENCE ▼

Zoom in and out on a worksheet

1 On the View menu, click Zoom.

2 In the Zoom dialog box, select the percentage by which you want to shrink or magnify the worksheet.

Hiding Rows and Columns

THE BOTTOM LINE

Not all of the data in a worksheet is relevant all of the time to all of the people who view it. You can hide specified rows and columns so that only the data you want to focus on is displayed.

Sometimes you have more rows or columns in a worksheet than you want to see at one time. In such situations, you can **hide** rows or columns so that they don't appear on your screen or in worksheet printouts. When you want to see them again, you unhide them.

For example, the activities coordinator at Adventure Works wants to focus on equipment rented during December, January, and February. On the worksheet, she hides the columns for the rest of the year. She already knows that no one rents kayaks during the winter, so she hides that row as well. When she's finished viewing the winter rentals, she reveals the hidden columns and the row so that she can view the rentals for the entire year.

Hide and unhide rows and columns

In this exercise, you hide and unhide worksheet rows and columns.

1 **Click the column selector for column D (Feb), hold the Shift key, and click the column selector for column L (Oct).**

Excel selects the columns.

ANOTHER METHOD

Click the column selector for column D, and drag the mouse pointer to the column selector for column L.

2 **On the Format menu, point to Column, and click Hide.**

The columns are hidden. Notice that the column labeling has not changed and that a dark line indicates where the hidden columns D through L are.

FIGURE 5-3

Hiding columns

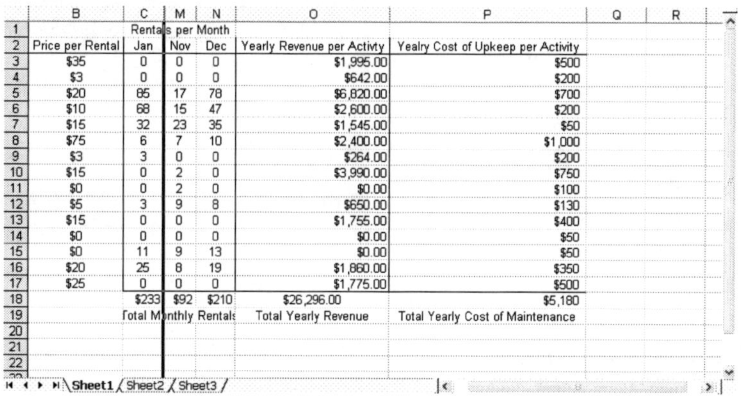

	B	C	M	N	O	P	Q	R
1			Rentals per Month					
2	Price per Rental	Jan	Nov	Dec	Yearly Revenue per Activity	Yearly Cost of Upkeep per Activity		
3	$35	0	0	0	$1,995.00	$500		
4	$3	0	0	0	$642.00	$200		
5	$20	85	17	78	$6,820.00	$700		
6	$10	68	15	47	$2,600.00	$200		
7	$15	32	23	35	$1,545.00	$50		
8	$75	6	7	10	$2,400.00	$1,000		
9	$3	3	0	0	$264.00	$200		
10	$15	0	2	0	$3,990.00	$750		
11	$0	0	2	0	$0.00	$100		
12	$5	3	9	8	$650.00	$130		
13	$15	0	0	0	$1,755.00	$400		
14	$0	0	0	0	$0.00	$50		
15	$0	11	9	13	$0.00	$50		
16	$20	25	8	19	$1,860.00	$350		
17	$25	0	0	0	$1,775.00	$500		
18		$233	$92	$210	$26,296.00	$5,180		
19		Total Monthly Rentals			Total Yearly Revenue	Total Yearly Cost of Maintenance		
20								
21								
22								

H ◀ ▶ H \ Sheet1 / Sheet2 / Sheet3 /

3 **Click the row selector for row 3 (Kayaks).**

The row is selected.

4 **On the Format menu, point to Row, and then click Hide.**

The row is hidden. Notice that the row numbering has not changed and that a dark line indicates where the hidden row 3 is.

5 **Click the column selector for column C, and drag to the column selector for column M.**

Excel selects columns C and M.

ANOTHER METHOD

Click the column selector for column C, hold the Shift key, and click the column selector for column M.

6 On the Format menu, point to Column, and click Unhide.

Columns D through L are redisplayed.

7 Click a blank area of the worksheet outside of the selected area.

The columns are deselected.

8 Click the row selector for row 2, and drag to the row selector for row 4.

Rows 2 and 4 are selected.

ANOTHER METHOD

Click the row selector for row 2, hold the Shift key, and click the row selector for row 4.

9 On the Format menu, point to Row, and then click Unhide.

Row 3 is redisplayed.

◆ Close the workbook without saving your changes.

QUICK REFERENCE ▼

Hide a row or column

1 Click the row or column selector for the row or column you want to hide.

2 On the Format menu, point to Row or Column, and click Hide.

Unhide a row or column

1 Select the rows or columns on both sides of the hidden row or column.

2 On the Format menu, point to Row or Column, and click Unhide.

Freezing Rows and Columns

THE BOTTOM LINE

When you scroll in a large worksheet to bring rows and columns of data into view, you can implement the freezing feature to keep specified data, such as row or column labels, from moving off the screen. With the label always visible, you can easily identify what the data represents.

When your worksheet is larger than you can display on-screen at once, you need to scroll right and down to see all of your columns and rows. If your leftmost column and top row contain labels, scrolling can make the labels disappear off the edge of your screen—leaving you to wonder what exactly is in the cells you're seeing.

To remedy this problem, you can **freeze** rows and columns so that they remain on the screen even when you scroll down and across the worksheet. For example, the chef at Adventure Works uses a workbook to track the amount of food that is prepared by the popular restaurant at the resort. Doing this helps him determine what supplies to order from month to month. He freezes the rows and columns that have labels so that he can keep them in view as he scrolls down and across a worksheet.

◆ **Open Food from the Excel Core Practice/Lesson05 folder.**

Freeze and unfreeze rows and columns

In this exercise, you freeze and unfreeze rows and columns.

1 Scroll the worksheet to the right and then back to column A.

When you scroll the worksheet to the right, the leftmost columns disappear.

2 Click cell B3.

This cell is just below the row you want to freeze and just to the right of the column you want to freeze.

3 On the Window menu, click Freeze Panes.

The month row and Type of Food column are now frozen.

4 Scroll the worksheet to the right.

The leftmost column, with the category labels, remains visible on the screen.

5 Scroll down the worksheet.

The month row remains visible on the screen.

FIGURE 5-4

Freezing the month row and category labels column

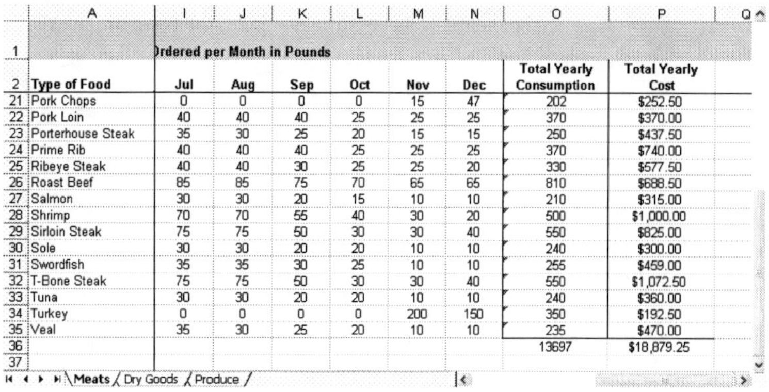

	A	I	J	K	L	M	N	O	P	Q
1		rdered per Month in Pounds								
2	Type of Food	Jul	Aug	Sep	Oct	Nov	Dec	Total Yearly Consumption	Total Yearly Cost	
21	Pork Chops	0	0	0	0	15	47	202	$252.50	
22	Pork Loin	40	40	40	25	25	25	370	$370.00	
23	Porterhouse Steak	35	30	25	20	15	15	250	$437.50	
24	Prime Rib	40	40	40	25	25	25	370	$740.00	
25	Ribeye Steak	40	40	30	25	25	20	330	$577.50	
26	Roast Beef	85	85	75	70	65	65	810	$688.50	
27	Salmon	30	30	20	15	10	10	210	$315.00	
28	Shrimp	70	70	55	40	30	20	500	$1,000.00	
29	Sirloin Steak	75	75	50	30	30	40	550	$825.00	
30	Sole	30	30	20	20	10	10	240	$300.00	
31	Swordfish	35	35	30	25	10	10	255	$459.00	
32	T-Bone Steak	75	75	50	30	30	40	550	$1,072.50	
33	Tuna	30	30	20	20	10	10	240	$360.00	
34	Turkey	0	0	0	0	200	150	350	$192.50	
35	Veal	35	30	25	20	10	10	235	$470.00	
36								13697	$18,879.25	
37										

H ◀ ▶ H \ Meats ⟨ Dry Goods ⟨ Produce /

6 Press Ctrl+Home.

Excel scrolls to the top left unfrozen cell.

7 On the Window menu, click Unfreeze Panes.

The panes are unfrozen.

◆ **Keep this file open for the next exercise.**

Freeze rows and columns

1 Click a cell below the bottom row you want to freeze and to the right of the rightmost column you want to freeze.

2 On the Windows menu, click Freeze Panes.

Unfreeze rows and columns

On the Windows menu, click Unfreeze Panes.

Managing Worksheets in a Workbook

Organizing Data

THE BOTTOM LINE

Each Excel workbook is made up of individual worksheets that you can add to, delete from, move, and copy as desired. This gives you the flexibility to group worksheets with similar subject matter together in one file and enables you to be more effective in organizing and managing data.

Storing related worksheet data in one workbook file has many organizational benefits. By using this method of organization, you can open all associated worksheets in a workbook at once, which saves time and ensures that all necessary data is available for a specific task. This also lets you quickly view related information and copy necessary data from one worksheet to the next without having to open and close various workbooks.

Moving between Worksheets

As you learned in Lesson 1, you can navigate from worksheet to worksheet by using the sheet tabs at the bottom of the worksheet window.

FIGURE 5-5

Using the sheet tabs to display different worksheets

Sheet tabs

18	Monkfish	$0.75	10	10
19	New York Strip Steak	$1.75	15	10
20	Pheasant	$3.00	10	10

I◄ ◄ ► ►I \Meats \ Dry Goods \ Produce /

The chef at Adventure Works uses several worksheets in one workbook. He orders different types of foods from different suppliers: one supplier provides meat, such as beef and poultry; another provides dry goods, such as flour and sugar; and a third provides produce. The chef tracks all of the food that he orders from each supplier on a separate worksheet in the same workbook. He can view each worksheet in the Food workbook by clicking the appropriate sheet tab.

Navigate among worksheets

You have learned how to customize the display of data in a single worksheet. In this exercise, you will display and view the various worksheets in a workbook.

1 **Click the Dry Goods tab.**

The Dry Goods worksheet is displayed.

2 **Click the Produce tab.**

The Produce worksheet is displayed.

3 **Click the Meats tab.**

The Meats worksheet is displayed.

◆ **Keep this file open for the next exercise.**

QUICK REFERENCE ▼

Navigate between worksheets in a workbook

Click the sheet tab of the worksheet you want to display.

Adding and Deleting Worksheets in a Workbook

By default, each new workbook contains three blank worksheets. If you don't need all three worksheets, you can easily delete the unnecessary ones. If you want more worksheets, you can insert as many new ones as you need. For example, the chef at Adventure Works decides to add a new worksheet to the Food workbook. Because he wants this new worksheet to contain summaries of figures from the other three worksheets, he names this worksheet *Summary*.

Add and delete a worksheet

In this exercise, you add and delete a worksheet.

1 **Click the Produce tab.**

The Produce worksheet is displayed.

2 **On the Insert menu, click Worksheet.**

A new worksheet named Sheet1 is inserted to the left of Produce.

ANOTHER METHOD

Right-click the sheet tab, select Insert, click Worksheet on the General tab of the Insert dialog box, and click OK.

3 Select any cell, type Test, and press Enter.

4 On the Edit menu, click Delete Sheet.

An alert message box opens.

FIGURE 5-6

Warning message

ANOTHER METHOD

Right-click the sheet tab, and select Delete on the shortcut menu.

5 Click Delete.

The new worksheet is deleted, and the Produce worksheet is redisplayed.

6 Click the Meats tab.

The Meats worksheet is displayed.

7 On the Insert menu, click Worksheet.

A new worksheet named Sheet2 is inserted to the left of Meats.

FIGURE 5-7

Inserting a new sheet

8 Double-click the Sheet2 tab.

9 Type Summary, and press Enter.

The name of the worksheet is changed.

◆ Keep this file open for the next exercise.

QUICK REFERENCE ▼

Add a worksheet to a workbook

On the Insert menu, click Worksheet.

Delete a worksheet in a workbook

1 In your workbook, click the sheet tab for the worksheet you want to delete.

2 On the Edit menu, click Delete Sheet.

Moving and Copying Worksheets

Just as you can move and copy data in a worksheet, you can move and copy the worksheets within a workbook. For example, you might want to move a worksheet in order to change the order of sheets in the workbook. You might want to copy a worksheet so that you can overwrite existing data with new data in the copy. When you copy the worksheet, you retain the structure and formatting of the original so that you don't need to "rebuild" it from scratch.

The chef at Adventure Works wants the Summary worksheet that was just added to appear as the last sheet in the workbook instead of the first. He also wants the workbook to include a worksheet for beverages. He decides to copy one of the existing sheets so that he can simply overwrite the data with the new beverage data.

Move and copy a worksheet

In this exercise, you move a worksheet to another location in the workbook and make a copy of a worksheet.

1 Click the Summary sheet tab, press and hold the mouse button, and drag until the small, black sheet insertion arrow is at the right corner of the Produce tab, as shown in Figure 5-8.

FIGURE 5-8

Moving a worksheet

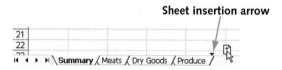

The Summary sheet is moved from its position as the first sheet to follow the Produce sheet.

ANOTHER METHOD

Right-click the sheet tab, select Move Or Copy on the shortcut menu, click (Move To End) in the Before Sheet list box, and click OK.

2 Click the Produce sheet tab, hold the Ctrl key, and drag until the sheet insertion arrow is between the Produce and the Summary sheet tabs, as shown in Figure 5-9.

FIGURE 5-9

Copying a worksheet

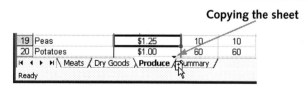

A copy of the Produce sheet, named *Produce (2)*, is inserted between the Produce and Summary worksheets.

Right-click the sheet tab, select Move Or Copy on the shortcut menu, click Summary in the Before Sheet list box, click the Create A Copy box, and then click OK.

3 **Double-click the Produce (2) sheet tab, type** Beverages, **and press Enter.**

The copied sheet is renamed.

4 **Click the Save button on the Standard toolbar.**

- Select Save on the File menu.
- Press Ctrl+S.

◆ **Close Food.**

QUICK REFERENCE ▼

Move a worksheet

1 Click the sheet tab.
2 Drag the sheet tab to the desired location.

Copy a worksheet

1 Click the sheet tab.
2 Hold the Ctrl key, and drag the copy to the desired location.

Sorting Data

THE BOTTOM LINE

The order in which you enter data is not necessarily the most logical order for interpreting or analyzing it. Sorting data (from highest to lowest or smallest to largest, for example) lets you quickly and easily identify trends and generate forecasts or predictions.

Sorting a Data List

The data you enter in a worksheet may be in an arbitrary order. For example, in a list of employees, an employee's name is added to the list as he or she joins the company. It might be more useful to the human resources manager, for example, to view the list of employees according to the department they're in or by their starting salary.

You can sort rows of data according to the contents of a particular column or columns. You can sort in **ascending order,** in which alphabetic data appears from A to Z, numeric data appears from lowest to highest or smallest to largest, and dates appear from the oldest to the most recent. If you sort in **descending order,** data appears just the opposite.

◆ **Open Sports Income05 from the Excel Core Practice/Lesson05 folder.**

Sort data

In this exercise, you sort equipment by the cost per rental and by the yearly revenue per type of equipment.

1 **Select the range A2:P17.**

This is the list you will sort.

2 **On the Data menu, click Sort to open the Sort dialog box.**

FIGURE 5-10

Sort dialog box

3 **Click the down arrow on the Sort By text box, and select Price per Rental.**

4 **Click OK.**

The data is sorted from lowest to highest price per rental.

FIGURE 5-11

Sorting by the Price per Rental column

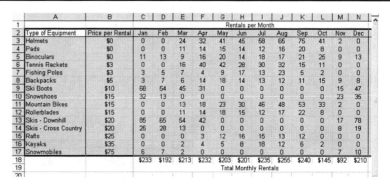

	A	B	C	D	E	F	G	H	I	J	K	L	M	N
1							Rentals per Month							
2	Type of Equipment	Price per Rental	Jan	Feb	Mar	Apr	May	Jun	Jul	Aug	Sep	Oct	Nov	Dec
3	Helmets	$0	0	0	24	32	41	45	58	65	75	41	2	0
4	Pads	$0	0	0	11	14	15	14	12	16	20	8	0	0
5	Binoculars	$0	11	13	9	16	20	14	18	17	21	25	9	13
6	Tennis Rackets	$3	0	0	16	40	42	28	30	32	15	11	0	0
7	Fishing Poles	$3	3	5	7	4	9	17	13	23	5	2	0	0
8	Backpacks	$5	3	7	6	14	18	14	13	12	11	15	9	8
9	Ski Boots	$10	68	54	45	31	0	0	0	0	0	0	15	47
10	Snowshoes	$15	32	13	0	0	0	0	0	0	0	0	23	35
11	Mountain Bikes	$15	0	0	13	18	23	30	46	48	53	33	2	0
12	Rollerblades	$15	0	0	11	14	18	15	12	17	22	8	0	0
13	Skis - Downhill	$20	85	65	54	42	0	0	0	0	0	0	17	78
14	Skis - Cross Country	$20	25	28	13	0	0	0	0	0	0	0	8	19
15	Rafts	$25	0	0	0	3	12	16	15	13	12	0	0	0
16	Kayaks	$35	0	0	2	4	5	8	18	12	6	2	0	0
17	Snowmobiles	$75	6	7	2	0	0	0	0	0	0	0	7	10
18			$233	$192	$213	$232	$203	$201	$235	$255	$240	$145	$92	$210
19							Total Monthly Rentals							
20														

5 On the Standard toolbar, click the Undo button.

The rows of data are returned to their original order.

6 Select the range A2:P17.

7 On the Data menu, click Sort.

The Sort dialog box opens.

8 Click the down arrow on the Sort By text box, and select Yearly Revenue per Activity.

9 Click the Descending button, and then click OK.

The data is sorted from the type of equipment with the highest yearly revenue to the lowest yearly revenue.

10 Click cell B3, and on the Window menu, click Freeze Panes.

You will freeze the column labels so that you can scroll to bring the Yearly Revenue per Activity column into view.

11 Click the right scroll arrow so that column O is next to column A.

You can now see which type of equipment rentals generated the most yearly revenue.

FIGURE 5-12

Sorting equipment by yearly revenues

	A	O	P	Q
1				
2	Type of Equipment	Yearly Revenue per Activity	Yearly Cost of Upkeep per Activity	
3	Skis - Downhill	$6,820.00	$700	
4	Mountain Bikes	$3,990.00	$750	
5	Ski Boots	$2,600.00	$200	
6	Snowmobiles	$2,400.00	$1,000	
7	Kayaks	$1,995.00	$500	
8	Skis - Cross Country	$1,860.00	$350	
9	Rafts	$1,775.00	$500	
10	Rollerblades	$1,755.00	$400	
11	Snowshoes	$1,545.00	$50	
12	Backpacks	$650.00	$130	
13	Tennis Rackets	$642.00	$200	
14	Fishing Poles	$264.00	$200	
15	Helmets	$0.00	$100	
16	Pads	$0.00	$50	
17	Binoculars	$0.00	$50	
18		$26,296.00	$5,180	
19		Total Yearly Revenue	Total Yearly Cost of Maintenance	
20				

12 On the Window menu, click Unfreeze Panes.

Columns B through N are redisplayed.

◆ Close the workbook without saving your changes.

QUICK REFERENCE ▼

Sort data

1 Select the range to be sorted.

2 Click Sort on the Data menu.

3 In the Sort dialog box, specify the column or columns by which the rows are to be sorted and the sort order.

4 Click OK.

Filtering Data

THE BOTTOM LINE

You can display a subset of rows that meet certain rules, or criteria, by applying a filter to data. The rest of the rows are temporarily "filtered out," enabling you to focus on the data that's pertinent to your review or analysis.

Excel spreadsheets can hold as much data as you need them to, but you may not want to work with all of the data in a worksheet at the same time. You can find data that meets certain rules by creating a filter. A **filter** is a rule or a set of criteria that when applied, temporarily filters out those entries that don't meet the criteria and displays only those that do. For example, you might want to see the entries for only those employees in the Marketing Department. You would set up a filter to temporarily hide the rows of those employees who are not in the Marketing Department.

To create a filter, you click the cell in the group you want to filter and use the Data menu to turn on AutoFilter. When you turn on AutoFilter, which is a built-in set of filtering capabilities, a down arrow button appears in the cell that Excel recognizes as the column's label, as shown in Figure 5-13.

FIGURE 5-13

Turning on AutoFilter

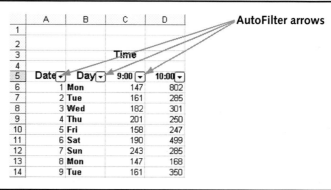

Limiting the Data That Appears on the Screen

TIP

When you turn on filtering, Excel treats the cells in the active cell's column as a range. To ensure that the filtering works properly, the column you want to filter should always have a label.

Clicking the down arrow displays a list of values and options, as shown in Figure 5-14. The Sort Ascending and Sort Descending options are new in Excel 2003. You can select them to sort the list according to the values in the selected column. The next few items on the menu are filtering options, such as whether you want to display the top ten values in the column, create a custom filter, or display all values in the column (that is, remove the filter). The rest of the items on the menu are the unique values in the column—clicking one of those values displays only the row or rows containing that value.

FIGURE 5-14

AutoFilter menu

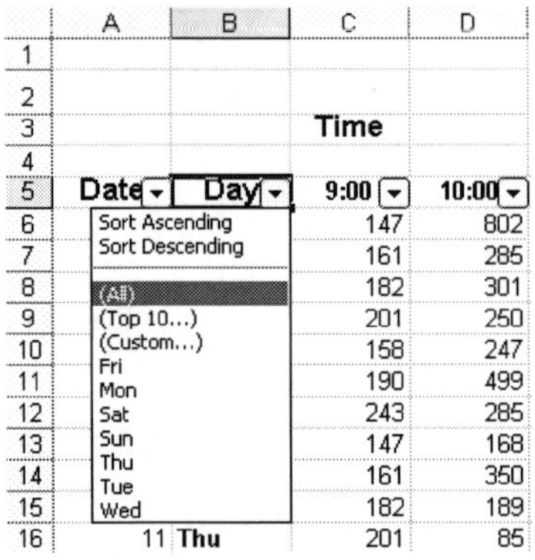

	A	B	C	D
1				
2				
3			**Time**	
4				
5	Date ▾	Day ▾	9:00 ▾	10:00 ▾
6	Sort Ascending		147	802
7	Sort Descending		161	285
8	(All)		182	301
9	(Top 10...)		201	250
10	(Custom...)		158	247
11	Fri / Mon		190	499
12	Sat		243	285
13	Sun		147	168
14	Thu		161	350
15	Tue / Wed		182	189
16	11	Thu	201	85

Choosing the Top 10 option from the list doesn't just limit the display to the top ten values. Instead, it opens the Top 10 AutoFilter dialog box. From within this dialog box, you can choose whether to show values from the top or bottom of the list, define the number of items you want to see, and choose whether the number in the middle box indicates the number of items or the percentage of items to be shown when the filter is applied. Using the Top 10 AutoFilter dialog box, you can find your top ten salespeople or identify the top 5 percent of your customers.

◆ **Open Filter from the Excel Core Practice/Lesson05 folder.**

Create a filter

In this exercise, you create a filter to show the top five sales days in January and show sales figures for Mondays during the same month.

1 If necessary, click the January sheet tab.

2 Click cell O5.

3 On the Data menu, point to Filter, and then click AutoFilter.

A down arrow appears in all the label cells.

4 In cell O5, click the AutoFilter arrow, and click (Top 10...) from the list that appears.

The Top 10 AutoFilter dialog box appears.

FIGURE 5-15

Top 10 AutoFilter dialog box

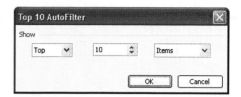

5 Click in the middle box, delete 10, type 5, and click OK.

Only the rows containing the five largest values in column O are shown.

FIGURE 5-16

Displaying the five largest values

	F	G	H	I	J	K	L	M	N	O
1										
2	es Summary for January									
3										
4										
5	12:00	13:00	14:00	15:00	16:00	17:00	18:00	19:00	20:00	Total
8	187	189	285	302	277	189	750	404	300	3766
11	150	206	189	602	401	206	601	388	135	3802
14	299	147	166	385	400	147	1028	385	243	4013
20	401	166	135	192	385	412	849	382	190	3794
21	187	187	206	166	277	602	1003	400	101	3710
37										
38	7276	8072	6948	8659	7553	7529	13930	8704	6111	97925
39										

6 In cell O5, click the AutoFilter arrow, and click Sort Descending.

The values are sorted from largest to smallest, with 4013 at the top.

7 On the Data menu, point to Filter, and then click AutoFilter.

The filtered rows reappear.

8 Click cell B5.

9 On the Data menu, point to Filter, and then click AutoFilter.

A down arrow appears in the label cells.

10 In cell B5, click the down arrow, and from the list of unique column values that appears, click Mon.

Only rows with *Mon* in column B are shown in the worksheet.

11 On the Data menu, point to Filter, and then click AutoFilter.

The filtered rows reappear.

◆ Close the workbook without saving your changes.

◆ If you are continuing to other lessons, leave Excel open. If you are not continuing to other lessons, save and close all open workbooks. Click the Close button in the top right corner of the Excel window.

QUICK CHECK

Q. How do you apply a filter that displays the 15 highest-paid employees in a list?

A: Click a cell in the column that shows the pay or salary for employees. On the Data menu, click Filter and then AutoFilter. Click the AutoFilter arrow on the column label cell, and click (Top 10...) from the list that appears. In the Top 10 AutoFilter dialog box, click in the middle box, delete 10, type 15, and click OK.

Key Points

✔ *Excel's Zoom feature works much like the zoom feature on a video camcorder. You can zoom in on a portion of a worksheet so that it appears larger and the data is easier to read. Or you can zoom out to get a better overall view of the worksheet.*

✔ *Not all of the data in a worksheet is relevant all of the time to all of the people who view it. You can hide specified rows and columns so that only the data you want to focus on is displayed.*

✔ *When you scroll in a large worksheet to bring rows and columns of data into view, you can implement the freezing feature to keep specified data, such as row or column labels, from moving off the screen. With the label always visible, you can easily identify what the data represents.*

✔ *Each Excel workbook is made up of individual worksheets that you can add to, delete from, move, and copy as desired. This gives you the flexibility to group worksheets with similar subject matter together in one file and enables you to be more effective in organizing and managing data.*

✔ *The order in which you enter data is not necessarily the most logical order for interpreting or analyzing it. Sorting data lets you quickly and easily identify trends and generate forecasts or predictions.*

✔ *You can display a subset of rows that meet certain rules, or criteria, by applying a filter to data. The rest of the rows are temporarily "filtered out," enabling you to focus on the data that's pertinent to your review or analysis.*

Quick Quiz

True/False

T F **1.** If you set your Zoom magnification at 50%, the cells in the worksheet would look about twice as large as normal.

T F **2.** The only way to reset the magnification of a worksheet to its default setting is to close the workbook and reopen it.

T F **3.** If you want to freeze columns A and B, you need to click a cell in column A before executing the Freeze Panes command.

T F **4.** In a descending sort, numbers appear from largest to smallest.

T F **5.** The AutoFilter menu contains options for sorting.

Multiple Choice

1. Which feature would you use if you wanted to enlarge the appearance of the worksheet?
   a. Zoom
   b. Freeze Panes
   c. AutoFilter
   d. Focus

2. Which feature would you use if you wanted to keep a column of row labels displayed as you scrolled other columns into view?
   a. Zoom
   b. Freeze Panes
   c. AutoFilter
   d. Hide

3. If you wanted to freeze the column headings in row 2 and the row headings in column A, which cell should you click on before executing the command to freeze?
   a. A1
   b. A2
   c. B2
   d. B3

4. How would you copy a worksheet using the keyboard and mouse?
   a. Click the sheet tab, hold the Ctrl key, and drag the sheet tab icon to the desired location.
   b. Click the sheet tab, hold the Shift key, and drag the sheet tab icon to the desired location.
   c. Click the sheet tab, hold the Alt key, and drag the sheet tab icon to the desired location.
   d. Click the sheet tab, and drag the sheet tab icon to the desired location.

5. Your workbook contains three sheets: Sheet1, Sheet2, and Sheet3. If you select the Sheet2 tab and insert a new worksheet, where would it be positioned?
   a. as the first sheet in the workbook
   b. as the last sheet in the workbook
   c. before Sheet2
   d. after Sheet2

Short Answer

1. How do you navigate between multiple worksheets in a workbook?

2. How can you display a worksheet on your screen at 60% of normal size?

3. Explain the difference between an ascending sort and a descending sort.

4. If your worksheet is so large that rows and columns with data labels disappear when you scroll down and to the right, what should you do?

5. If you want simultaneously to display certain columns or rows on your screen but columns or rows in the middle make it impossible, what should you do?

On Your Own

◆ **Open Sports Income05 from the Excel Core Practice/Lesson05 folder.**

Exercise 1

Zoom in on Sheet1 by 50%, and zoom out by 100%. Hide and then un-hide column B. Freeze column B and row 2, and then unfreeze them.

◆ **Close Sports Income05.**

◆ **Open Food from the Excel Core Practice/Lesson05 folder.**

Exercise 2 Open the Food workbook. On the Meats worksheet, sort the data in descending order by Total Yearly Consumption. Which type of meat generated the most orders? The fewest? Perform the same sort on the Dry Goods and Produce worksheets, and determine which items generated the most and the fewest orders.

Exercise 3

On the Meats worksheet in the Food workbook, apply an AutoFilter to the Total Yearly Consumption column that finds the top five items, and then sort them in ascending order. What are the top five meats? Apply the same AutoFilter on the Total Yearly Consumption columns in the Dry Goods and Produce worksheets. List the top five items on both of those sheets.

◆ **Close Food.**

One Step Further

Exercise 1

In this lesson, you learned how to insert and delete worksheets. You know that the default number of worksheets in a workbook is three, but is there a limit to the number of worksheets that can be added? If there is a limit, what determines this limit? Is there a limit to the number of rows or columns in a workbook? Use the Ask A Question box to determine the answer to these questions.

◆ **Open Filter from the Excel Core Practice/Lesson05 folder.**

Exercise 2

As you explored AutoFilter, you may have noticed the Custom option in the AutoFilter list. Use the Filter workbook to explore the Custom option. What can it be used for? If necessary, use Excel's Help files to determine the filtering possibilities made available through the Custom option. Briefly describe your findings.

◆ **Close Filter.**

6

Working with Charts

After completing this lesson, you will be able to:

- ✔ *Create charts using the Chart Wizard.*
- ✔ *Move, resize, and delete charts.*
- ✔ *Modify chart titles.*
- ✔ *Move and format chart elements.*
- ✔ *Change chart types and organize source data.*
- ✔ *Update data and format the axes.*
- ✔ *Add gridlines and arrows.*
- ✔ *Preview and print charts.*

KEY TERMS

- ▪ axis labels
- ▪ Category axis
- ▪ charts
- ▪ chart sheet
- ▪ embedded charts
- ▪ legend
- ▪ source data
- ▪ Value axis

Excel allows you to track and work with substantial amounts of data. At times, you may not be able to understand the larger picture from looking only at the details. With Excel **charts,** you can summarize, highlight, or reveal trends in your data that might not be obvious when looking at the raw numbers.

At the vacation resort Adventure Works, the sales manager records expense data and estimates future revenue in the Five Year Sales workbook. He intends to use charts to summarize the annual sales projections and quickly see which business area has the highest percentage of expenses. The activities coordinator tracks the pledges collected from members at resort events, and she uses charts to analyze the trend in pledge rates at various levels over the year.

In this lesson, you will learn what types of charts are available in Microsoft Excel and how to create them. Then you will learn how to modify, move, and format charts and chart elements. Finally, you will learn how to preview and print your charts.

IMPORTANT

Before you can use the practice files in this lesson, you must install them from the book's companion CD to their default location. For additional information on how to find and open files used in this book, see the "Using the CD-ROM" section at the beginning of this book.

Creating Charts Using the Chart Wizard

Creating a Chart

The Chart Wizard automates the tasks involved in creating a chart, saving you the time of manually adding elements such as titles, axis labels, and legends.

The Chart Wizard guides you through the process of creating a chart. As you complete each step, the wizard prompts you for your next selection. To start, you select the type of chart you want.

Excel offers 14 types of charts, with each type having two or more subtypes. Using the Chart Wizard, you can preview the chart types and choose the chart that best suits your data. For example, revenue and sales projections are easily summarized with a column, bar, or line chart, while expenses might be best represented as a pie chart.

The following table gives a brief description of each chart type.

Icon	Chart Name	Function
	Column	Compares individual values across time or other categories; represents values as vertical bars
	Bar	Compares individual values across time or other categories; represents values as horizontal bars
	Line	Shows the trend of values across time or other categories; represents values as points along a line
	Pie	Shows values as parts of a whole; represents values as sections of a circular pie
	XY (Scatter)	Compares the values of two sets of data across time or other categories; values are represented as data points, which might be connected by lines
	Area	Shows the trend of values across time or other categories; represents values as shaded areas
	Doughnut	Shows values as parts of a whole; represents values as sections of a circular band
	Radar	Shows the trend of values relative to a center point; represents values as points that radiate from the center; each category has its own axis; lines connect all of the values in the same series

	Surface	Shows the trend of values across two sets of data; values are represented as a 3-D surface that illustrates the relationship between the sets
	Bubble	Compares three sets of values
	Stock	Shows the trend of sets of values across time; often used to illustrate stock price changes with markers for High, Low, Close, and Open values; represents values as points, lines, or columns
	Cylinder	Compares individual values across time or other categories; represents values as vertical or horizontal cylinders
	Cone	Compares individual values across time or other categories; represents values as vertical or horizontal cones
	Pyramid	Compares individual values across time or other categories; represents values as pyramidal shapes

In preparation for a budget meeting, the sales manager for Adventure Works wants to create a chart to show the projected trend in each of four revenue categories over the next five years. A line chart clearly shows that the largest increase is expected in lodging sales.

In the Step 1 Of 4 – Chart Type dialog box, you can click the Press And Hold To View Sample button to see a preview of your chart.

◆ To complete the procedures in this lesson, you must use the files Five Year Sales and Member Pledges in the Lesson06 folder in the Excel Core Practice folder located on your hard disk.

◆ Open Five Year Sales from the Excel Core Practice/Lesson06 folder.

Create a chart using the Chart Wizard

In this exercise, you open a workbook and create a chart using the Chart Wizard.

1 Select cells A2:F6 in the Sales Projections worksheet.

 2 On the Standard toolbar, click the Chart Wizard button.

The Step 1 Of 4 – Chart Type dialog box appears.

FIGURE 6-1

Step 1 of 4 Chart Wizard

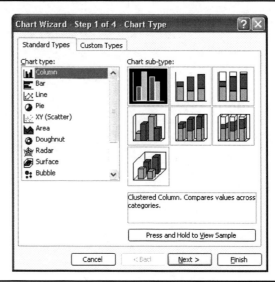

3 In the Chart Type list, click Column, if necessary.

4 In the Chart Sub-type box, click the Stacked Column sub-type in the center of the top row, and click Next.

The Step 2 Of 4 – Chart Source Data dialog box appears with a preview of your chart.

FIGURE 6-2

Step 2 of 4 Chart Wizard

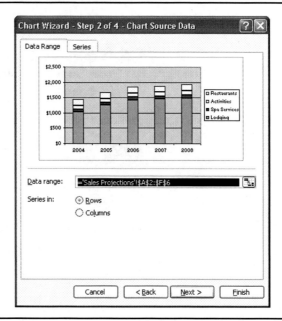

5 On the Data Range tab, verify that the Rows option is selected, and click Next.

The Step 3 Of 4 – Chart Options dialog box appears.

FIGURE 6-3

Step 3 of 4 Chart Wizard

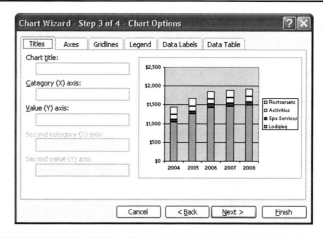

6 In the Chart Title box, type Yearly Sales, and click Next.

The Step 4 Of 4 – Chart Location dialog box appears.

FIGURE 6-4

Step 4 of 4 Chart Wizard

IMPORTANT

Charts are either embedded as objects in an existing worksheet or placed in a separate sheet. **Embedded charts** appear on a worksheet with other data. A **chart sheet** appears as a separate sheet in the workbook.

ANOTHER METHOD

To quickly create a chart with the default chart options, select a range of cells, and then press F11. The chart will be created in a new worksheet.

7 Click the As Object In option, if necessary, and click the Finish button.

The chart appears in the worksheet, and the Chart toolbar displays. The data that's charted is outlined in blue.

FIGURE 6-5

Creating a chart on the same sheet

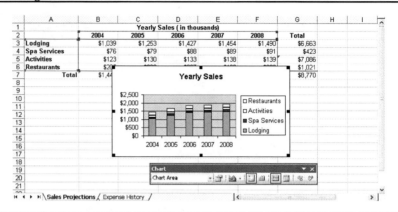

◆ **Keep this file open for the next exercise.**

QUICK REFERENCE ▼

Create a chart

1 Select the range of cells to be represented.

2 On the Standard toolbar, click the Chart Wizard button.

3 In the Step 1 Of 4 – Chart Type dialog box, click the chart type and
chart subtype, and click Next.

4 In the Step 2 Of 4 – Chart Source Data dialog box, click the Rows or
Columns option to specify whether the data is organized in rows
or columns, and click Next.

5 In the Step 3 Of 4 – Chart Options dialog box, type titles for the chart
and axes, and click Next.

6 In the Step 4 Of 4 – Chart Location dialog box, click As New Sheet to
create a chart sheet or As Object In to create an embedded chart.
Then click the Finish button.

Moving and Resizing Charts

THE BOTTOM LINE

You can reposition and change the size of a chart to present your
data more effectively and to enhance the overall appearance of a
worksheet.

Once a chart is created, you can position it in the worksheet, change its
size, or delete it altogether. It is often useful to place the chart just before
or immediately after the data it summarizes. For readability, detailed or
complex charts may need to be larger, while simple charts can be smaller.

To move, resize, or delete a chart, you must select the chart. You select a chart by clicking in the Chart Area, which is the background or blank area of a chart. Clicking in other areas of the chart might select an element or elements of the chart. You will work with chart elements later in this lesson.

When selecting or dragging a chart, be sure to click the Chart Area and not the legend, labels, or Plot Area itself. To find the Chart Area, point to different parts of the chart to display the ScreenTips.

Using Chart Templates
Did you know that many of the workbook templates available through Microsoft's Web site include chart sheets? For example, you can download a fitness workbook template and enter data for your measurements in one worksheet. The data you enter is automatically reflected in the Weight and Body Fat chart, the Weight and BMI chart, and the Measurements chart that are on chart sheets within the workbook template. There are also templates with charts for tracking costs, blood sugar counts, and a baby's growth. To download a template, click Templates on Office Online under the Templates section of the New Workbook task pane. Clicking this option takes you to Microsoft's Web site, which lists the templates available for download.

Modify a chart

In this exercise, you move, resize, delete, and restore a chart.

1 If necessary, click a blank area of the chart to select it.

2 Drag the chart to a position below the data and along the left edge of the worksheet.

FIGURE 6-6

Moving a chart

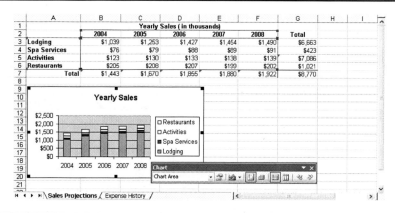

3 Drag the sizing handle on the right edge of the chart to the right side of column F to make the chart wider.

If the Chart toolbar is in the way, you can move it by dragging it by its title bar.

4 Drag the bottom sizing handle to the bottom of row 27 to make the chart longer.

FIGURE 6-7

Adjusting the size of the chart

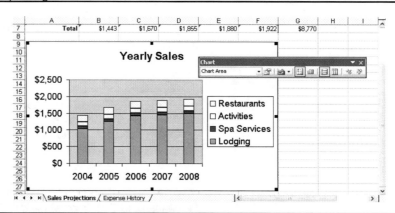

5 Click the Chart Area, and press the Delete key.

The chart disappears from the worksheet.

6 On the Standard toolbar, click the Undo button.

The chart reappears on the worksheet.

7 Save the workbook with the current name.

◆ Keep this file open for the next exercise.

QUICK REFERENCE ▼

Move a chart

1 Click the Chart Area to select the chart.
2 Drag the chart to the desired location.

Resize a chart

1 Click the Chart Area to select the chart.
2 Drag the appropriate sizing handle until the chart is the desired size.

Delete a chart

1 Click the Chart Area to select the chart.
2 Press the Delete key.

QUICK CHECK

Q. How do you resize a chart?

A: Click the chart to select it, and then drag a sizing handle in the desired direction.

Modifying Chart Titles and Adding Axis Labels

Customizing Chart Labels and Numbers

THE BOTTOM LINE

A meaningful title and descriptive labels can clarify the meaning of a chart and enhance its impact.

Charts are useful for displaying statistical data in an eye-catching manner. When you create a chart using the ChartWizard, category labels and a **legend** are added to the chart if the selected range of cells includes the necessary information. You also can add a title and **axis labels** during the wizard operation, or you can add them later by changing the chart options.

For example, the sales manager at Adventure Works can add a label to the value axis to clearly show that revenue figures are reported in thousands of dollars. He also can rephrase the chart title so that it is more descriptive of the data that's being charted.

Change the title of a chart and insert axis labels

In this exercise, you change the title of the chart and add labels for the X and Y axes.

1 **Right-click a blank area of the chart, and click Chart Options.**

The Chart Options dialog box appears with the Titles tab displayed.

TIP

If the Titles tab is not displayed, click it.

ANOTHER METHOD

Select the chart and on the Chart menu, select Chart Options.

2 **In the Chart Title box, select "Yearly Sales," and type** Five-Year Revenue Projection.

The new title appears in the chart preview.

3 **In the Category (X) Axis box, type** Fiscal Year.

The axis title appears in the chart preview.

FIGURE 6-8

Previewing the chart

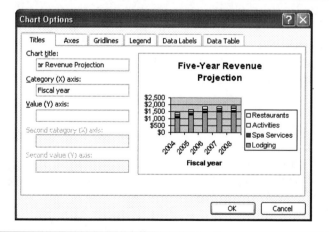

4 In the Value (Y) Axis box, type Revenue (in thousands), and click OK.

The chart appears with the new title and axis labels.

FIGURE 6-9

Changing the title and adding labels

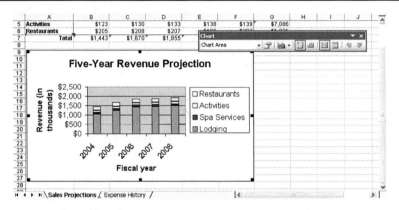

5 Right-click the chart title, and click Format Chart Title.

The Format Chart Title dialog box appears.

ANOTHER METHOD

- Click the chart title, and on the Chart toolbar, click the Format Chart Title button.
- On the Chart toolbar, click the Chart Objects down arrow, click Chart Title, and click the Format Chart Title button.

6 Click the Font tab, if necessary, and on the Size list, click 12. Click OK.

The chart title appears smaller.

ANOTHER METHOD

You can edit the chart title and axis labels like other text. Simply click the title or label to place your insertion point and begin typing. You also can format the chart title or axis labels by selecting the text and using the Formatting toolbar.

7 Save the workbook with the current name.

◆ Keep this file open for the next exercise.

QUICK REFERENCE ▼

Edit a chart title or an axis label

1 Right-click the Chart Area, and click Chart Options.

2 On the Titles tab, type the desired chart title or axis label, and click OK.

QUICK CHECK

Q. What are the two methods for editing the title of a chart?

A: You can edit a chart title by opening the Chart Options dialog box, selecting the Titles tab, and typing the new chart title in the Chart Title text box. Or you can click the chart title and click it again to place the insertion point within it and then start typing.

Moving and Formatting Chart Elements

THE BOTTOM LINE

Just as you format data to enhance the appearance of the worksheet and to highlight important entries, you can modify parts of a chart to make it easier to read and more effective in graphically depicting raw data and trends.

You can customize the appearance of your charts in many ways. To make the best use of the Chart Area, you can reposition the title or legend. To emphasize certain values, you can add labels to each data point on a line chart. To draw attention to a crucial piece of a pie chart, you can move that piece away from the rest of the chart. Other types of charts offer different formatting options.

The sales manager at Adventure Works has created a chart to represent data he needs for the budget meeting. Using a pie chart, he is able to show the percentage of costs spent in each business area for the past five years. To set the legend apart from the rest of the chart, he adds a border to it. He repositions other chart elements to highlight the least costly business area.

Format the legend and the pieces of a pie chart

In this exercise, you reposition and format the legend and draw out pieces of the pie chart.

1 Click the Expense History sheet tab.

The sheet contains a pie chart.

FIGURE 6-10

Sheet with a pie chart

	A	B	C	D	E
2		1999	2000	2001	2002
3	Lodging	$723	$857	$1,059	$1,061
4	Spa Services	$59	$62	$72	$74
5	Activities	$101	$106	$109	$111
6	Restaurants	$142	$147	$148	$144
7	Total	$1,025	$1,172	$1,388	$1,390

Expenses

- Lodging
- Spa Services
- Activities
- Restaurants

11%
8%
5%
76%

Sales Projections \ Expense History

2 Drag the chart legend to the lower left corner of the Chart Area.

3 Right-click the chart legend, and click Format Legend.

The Format Legend dialog box appears.

4 Click the Patterns tab, select the Shadow check box, and click OK.

The legend appears with a shadowed border.

FIGURE 6-11

Formatting the legend

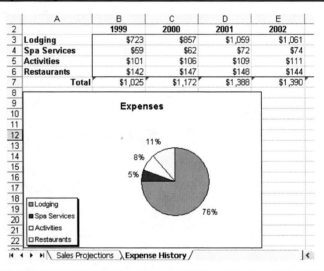

	A	B	C	D	E
2		1999	2000	2001	2002
3	Lodging	$723	$857	$1,059	$1,061
4	Spa Services	$59	$62	$72	$74
5	Activities	$101	$106	$109	$111
6	Restaurants	$142	$147	$148	$144
7	Total	$1,025	$1,172	$1,388	$1,390

Expenses

11%
8%
5%
76%

■ Lodging
■ Spa Services
□ Activities
□ Restaurants

Sales Projections \ **Expense History** /

5 Click the pie area, and click the smallest piece of the pie.

Sizing handles appear around the piece.

6 Drag the piece a short distance away from the pie.

The piece appears separated from the rest of the pie.

FIGURE 6-12

Manipulating a piece of the pie

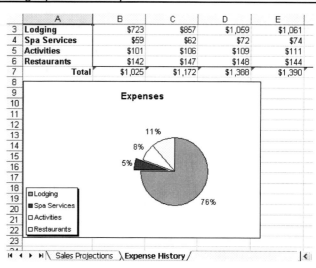

	A	B	C	D	E
3	Lodging	$723	$857	$1,059	$1,061
4	Spa Services	$59	$62	$72	$74
5	Activities	$101	$106	$109	$111
6	Restaurants	$142	$147	$148	$144
7	Total	$1,025	$1,172	$1,388	$1,390

QUICK CHECK

Q. How do you open the Format Legend dialog box using the Chart toolbar?

A: Click the legend, and then click the Format Legend button on the Chart toolbar. Or on the Chart toolbar, click the Chart Objects down arrow, click Legend, and click the Format Legend button.

◆ Save and close the Five Year Sales workbook.

Changing the Chart Type and Organizing the Source Data

THE BOTTOM LINE

You can manipulate data and chart it in different ways, which enables you to develop the most comprehensive assessment and analysis of it.

As you have learned, Excel offers a wide variety of chart types. Because each type emphasizes a particular aspect of the source data, several types might be useful for representing the same set of data. For budget discussions, a pie chart shows the proportion of expenses allocated to each category. For income projections, a column chart shows the trend of income over the past five years. You select a chart type when using the ChartWizard. After the chart is created, you can change it to a different chart type.

When you create a chart, the Chart Wizard interprets the **source data** as being organized in rows or columns. The organization of data in a chart depends on the range selected when creating the chart. When you select a range of cells with the same number of rows and columns, or more columns than rows, the data is plotted by rows. When you select a range that contains more rows than columns, the data is plotted by columns. For different chart types, it may be necessary to change the way the organization of the data is interpreted. In other words, you may need to indicate whether the data is organized in rows or columns. Also, when changing the chart type, you may want to exclude certain data (such as a column of totals) or include additional data.

By changing a column chart to a stacked area chart, the activities coordinator at Adventure Works can show the trend of member pledges collected at her events over the past year. Also, she has just recorded the final contributions for December, so she can include those figures in her chart.

◆ **Open Member Pledges from the Excel Core Practice/Lesson06 folder.**

Change the chart type, and organize the data

In this exercise, you change the chart type and organize the source data.

1 **Click the Chart sheet tab.**

The sheet contains a column chart showing pledges collected in each category.

FIGURE 6-13

Column chart showing pledges

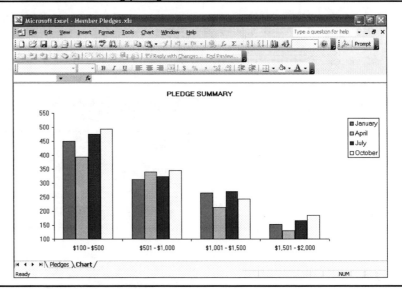

TIP

Close the Chart toolbar if it obscures your view of parts of the chart.

2 **Right-click the Chart Area, and click Chart Type.**

The Chart Type dialog box appears.

ANOTHER METHOD

Click the Chart Area, and on the Chart menu, click Chart Type.

3 **On the Chart Type list, click Area.**

4 **Click the Stacked Area chart sub-type in the center of the first row.**

FIGURE 6-14

Selecting the Stacked Area chart

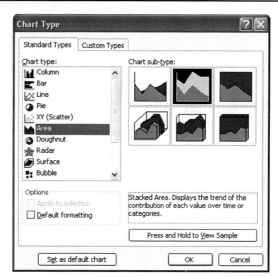

5 **Click OK in the Chart Type dialog box.**

A stacked area chart appears.

6 **Right-click the Chart Area, and click Source Data.**

The Source Data dialog box appears, and the worksheet from where the data was taken opens with a flashing marquee around the range of the source data.

FIGURE 6-15

Viewing the source data

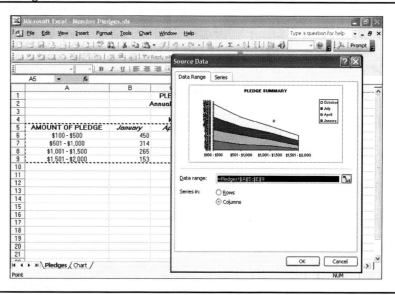

ANOTHER METHOD

Click the Chart Area, and on the Chart menu, click Source Data.

7 On the Data Range tab, click the Rows option, and click OK.

The updated chart appears.

FIGURE 6-16

Editing the source data

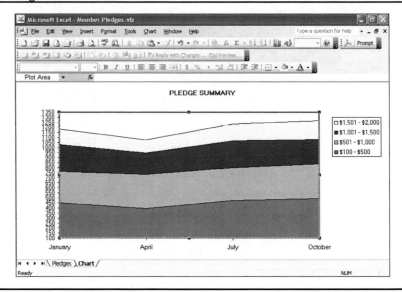

TIP

You might need to move the Source Data – Data Range dialog box in order to see the entire range of cells to be selected.

8 Right-click the Chart Area, and click Source Data.

The Source Data dialog box appears, and the source data worksheet opens.

9 On the Data Range tab in the Data Range box, click the Collapse Dialog button.

10 Select A5:F9, and click the Expand Dialog button in the Source Data – Data Range dialog box.

11 In the Source Data dialog box, click OK.

The chart appears with the data added for the month of December.

◆ Save and close the Member Pledges workbook.

QUICK REFERENCE ▼

Change a chart type

1 Right-click the Chart Area, and click Chart Type.

2 Select the chart type and chart sub-type, and click OK.

Reorganize the source data

1 Right-click the Chart Area, and click Source Data.

2 On the Data Range tab, click the Columns or Rows option, and click OK.

Updating Data and Formatting the Axes

THE BOTTOM LINE

The relationship between data and the chart that plots it is dynamic, so when you make changes to data entries, any charts that are based on that data are automatically updated. This saves you time and ensures that charts are accurate and up to date.

Typically, the data stored in Excel worksheets requires periodic updating. When you change any data that is source data, the corresponding chart updates automatically.

At Adventure Works, the sales manager learns that the new marketing campaigns are expected to increase restaurant revenues by 50 percent and spa revenues by 60 percent. When he enters the new figures on the Sales Projections sheet, the Five-Year Revenue Projection chart changes to reflect the new data.

As data values change, you may need to change various aspects of the axes in a chart. Using Scale options, you can format the **Value axis** (Y axis) to display a meaningful range of values for your data. Scale options for the **Category axis** allow you to control the display of category labels.

For example, the sales manager can set the minimum and maximum dollar values displayed on the Expected Annual Sales chart to be sure that the new values are properly represented.

Open Five Year Sales from the Excel Core Practice/Lesson06 folder.

Update source data, and format axes

In this exercise, you update the source data for a chart and format the axes.

1 Switch to the Sales Projections sheet, and type the following values.

Cell	B4	C4	D4	E4	F4
Value	122	126	141	142	146

Cell	B6	C6	D6	E6	F6
Value	308	312	311	299	303

The chart updates to reflect the new values.

FIGURE 6-17

Updating values in the chart

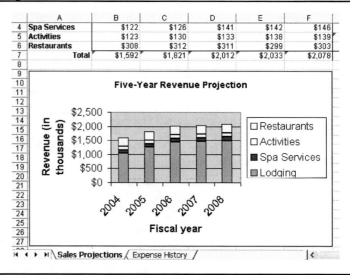

The Y axis is the Value axis, and the X axis is the Category axis.

2 **Right-click the Value axis, click Format Axis, and click the Scale tab in the Format Axis dialog box.**

The Format Axis dialog box appears with the Scale tab displayed.

FIGURE 6-18

Format Axis dialog box

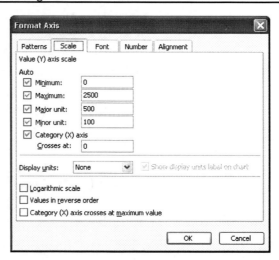

- Click the Value axis, and on the Chart toolbar, click the Format Axis button.
- On the Chart toolbar, click the Chart Objects down arrow, click Value Axis, and click the Format Axis button.

TIP

The Auto check boxes clear when you change the various default values (Minimum, Maximum, Major Unit, and so on). To use the default value, simply select the Auto check box to restore that value.

3 In the Minimum box, type 500.

4 In the Maximum box, type 2100, and click OK.

The chart appears with the updated axis.

FIGURE 6-19

Updating the chart's axis information

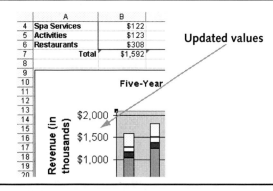

Keep this file open for the next exercise.

QUICK CHECK

Q. What does the Category axis typically display?

A: The Category axis typically displays labels that identify the categories of data you are plotting.

QUICK REFERENCE ▼

Change the scale of an axis

1 Right-click the axis, and click Format Axis.

2 On the Scale tab, type the desired values for minimum, maximum, major unit, and minor unit.

3 Click OK.

Adding Gridlines and Arrows

Adding a Graphic to a Worksheet

THE BOTTOM LINE

Horizontal and vertical gridlines help identify the value of each data marker in a chart. Arrows are useful for highlighting a particular data marker or for calling attention to certain information in a chart.

You can add gridlines to correspond with values on one or both axes in a chart. Gridlines are an effective tool for helping you identify more exact values for the categories of data being plotted on the chart. For example, you might have a line chart that plots income by week for the year. The Value axis is organized by units of $200, with $0 being the minimum and

$2000 being the maximum. Without the gridlines, you would more or less need to eyeball where the weekly values fall on the Value axis. You add major gridlines (appearing at bigger intervals) or minor gridlines (appearing at smaller intervals) using the Chart Options dialog box.

Using the Drawing toolbar, you can add picture objects, such as lines or arrows, to your chart. A well-placed arrow clearly indicates the most important piece of data in your chart.

You also can add a picture to the worksheet by clicking Picture on the Insert menu. Doing so displays a submenu that lists several sources from which you can choose to add a picture, including an existing file or clip art.

Once you've added a graphic element (picture, clip art, arrow, line, and so on) to your worksheet, you can change the graphic's location on the worksheet by dragging it to the desired location. You can change the graphic's size by right-clicking the picture and choosing Format Picture from the shortcut menu that appears. You also can resize a graphic by clicking the picture and then dragging one of the handles that appears on the graphic. However, using the Format Picture dialog box ensures that the aspect ratio (the relationship between the picture's height and width) doesn't change.

The sales manager would like to draw attention to the effects of the new marketing campaigns. Adding gridlines will more clearly define the impact of the new revenue levels. An arrow will emphasize the largest change in revenue.

Add gridlines and graphic objects to a chart

In this exercise, you add gridlines to the chart and add and move an arrow. You also add a text box to label the arrow.

1 Right-click the Chart Area, and click Chart Options.

The Chart Options dialog box appears.

2 Click the Gridlines tab, select the Minor Gridlines check box in the Value (Y) Axis section, and click OK.

The chart appears with major and minor horizontal gridlines.

FIGURE 6-20

Adding gridlines

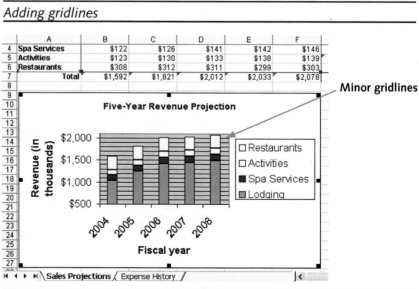

3 Click the Drawing button on the Standard toolbar.

The Drawing toolbar appears.

4 Click the Arrow button. Click a blank area in the upper right corner of the chart, drag the mouse pointer to the top of the tallest column on the chart, and click away from the chart.

An arrow appears on the chart.

FIGURE 6-21

Adding an arrow

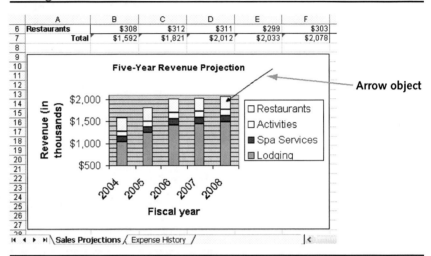

Arrow object

IMPORTANT

When you select a chart or any element of a chart that contains picture objects, the chart moves to the front, causing the picture objects to seemingly disappear. To bring the picture objects back to the front, simply click outside of (deselect) the chart and any of its elements.

5 Click the arrow to select it, and drag the arrow so that it points to the top of the center column on the chart.

6 On the Drawing toolbar, click the Text Box button.

TIP

If the text box isn't big enough, you can drag the resize handles to increase its size.

7 Click a blank area of the chart at the tail of the arrow, and drag to draw a rectangular text box.

8 In the text box, type Largest Projected Increase!

The text appears in the text box.

FIGURE 6-22

Adding text

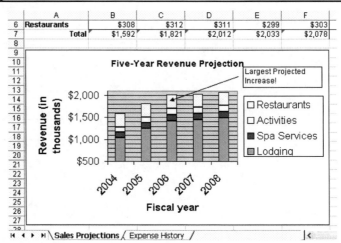

	A	B	C	D	E	F
6	Restaurants	$308	$312	$311	$299	$303
7	Total	$1,592	$1,821	$2,012	$2,033	$2,078

Five-Year Revenue Projection

Largest Projected Increase!

Revenue (in thousands)

$2,000
$1,500
$1,000
$500

□ Restaurants
□ Activities
■ Spa Services
▨ Lodging

2004   2005   2006   2007   2008

Fiscal year

H ◄ ► H \ Sales Projections / Expense History /

9 If all of the text is not displayed in the text box, click the text box, and drag its handles until you can see all of the text.

10 On the Standard toolbar, click the Drawing button.

The Drawing toolbar closes.

11 Save the workbook.

◆ Keep this file open for the next exercise.

QUICK REFERENCE ▼

Display gridlines

1 Right-click the Chart Area, and click Chart Options.

2 On the Gridlines tab, select the desired options, and click OK.

Add an object to a chart

1 On the Standard toolbar, click the Drawing button.

2 On the Drawing toolbar, click the desired object button.

3 Drag to create the object in the chart.

QUICK CHECK

Q. Which type of gridline appears at smaller intervals?

A: Minor gridlines appear at smaller intervals.

Previewing and Printing Charts

Printing a Chart

You should preview a chart before printing it, especially if the printout is part of a presentation to be reviewed by others. Previewing the chart, and any data that will print with it, helps you identify formatting problems and awkward page breaks.

You can preview and print Excel charts in the same way that you preview and print worksheets. Whether the chart is embedded or on a chart sheet, the Print Preview command displays the chart just as it will be printed, allowing you to verify the appearance and layout of your chart before printing.

As you have learned, you can choose to print the entire workbook, a single sheet in a workbook, a selected range of data, or a selected chart. If your chart appears as an object in a worksheet and you want to print a selected range of data, select the cells that include your chart. If your chart appears as an object in a worksheet and you want to print only the chart, select the chart before choosing the Print command. If your chart is on a chart sheet, simply go to the chart sheet and choose the Print command.

IMPORTANT

You must have a printer to complete the following exercise.

Preview and print a chart

In this exercise, you preview and print charts.

1 **Click a blank area of the Sales Projections worksheet, and click the Print Preview button on the Standard toolbar.**

The worksheet and embedded chart appear in the Preview window, as shown in Figure 6-23.

FIGURE 6-23

Previewing an embedded chart

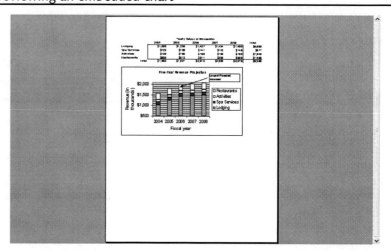

2 Click the Print button on the Preview toolbar.

The Print dialog box appears, and the Preview window closes.

3 Review your print settings, and click OK to print the chart.

4 Click a blank area of the chart, and then click the Print Preview button.

Only the chart appears in the Preview window, as shown in Figure 6-24.

FIGURE 6-24

Previewing a chart

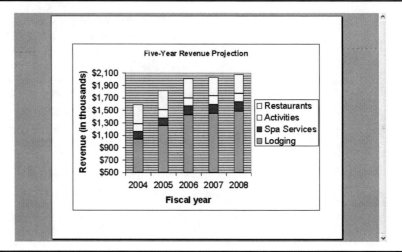

5 Click the Close button.

6 With the chart still selected, on the File menu, click Print.

ANOTHER METHOD

Press Ctrl+P.

7 Review your print settings, and click OK to print the chart.

◆ Save and close Five Year Sales.If you are continuing to other lessons, leave Excel Open. If you are not continuing to other lessons, save and close all open workbooks. Click the Close button in the top right corner of the Excel window.

QUICK REFERENCE ▼

Preview and print a chart

1 For an embedded chart, click the Chart Area to select the chart. For a chart on its own sheet, click the chart sheet tab.

2 On the Standard toolbar, click the Print Preview button.

3 On the Preview toolbar, click the Print button.

QUICK CHECK

Q. When you select a chart that's embedded on a worksheet, what do you see in the Print Preview window?

A: You see only the selected chart.

Key Points

✓ *The Chart Wizard automates the tasks involved in creating a chart, saving you the time of manually adding elements such as titles, axis labels, and legends.*

✓ *You can reposition and change the size of a chart so that it's easier to read and complements other data or elements on the sheet.*

✓ *You can apply formats to parts of a chart to highlight certain data and to enhance the overall appearance of the sheet.*

✓ *Excel has many different chart types. You can apply a different type of chart to your data and manipulate how the data is plotted. This enables you to interpret the data in different ways.*

✓ *When you make changes to data entries, any charts that are based on that data are automatically updated. This saves you time and ensures that charts are accurate and up to date.*

✓ *Horizontal and vertical gridlines help identify the value of each data marker in a chart.*

✓ *You can use graphics, such as lines, arrows, and text boxes, to highlight a particular data marker or to call attention to certain information in a chart.*

✓ *You should preview a chart before printing it. This helps you identify formatting problems and awkward page breaks.*

Quick Quiz

True/False

T F   **1.** A column chart represents values as vertical bars.

T F   **2.** A bar chart represents values as horizontal bars.

T F   **3.** An embedded chart is one that appears on its own sheet in the workbook.

T F   **4.** Every chart must have a legend.

T F   **5.** The Y axis also is referred to as the Value axis because it typically displays a range of values for your data.

Multiple Choice

1. Which chart type shows values as parts of a whole?
   a. column
   b. bar
   c. area
   d. pie

2. A(an) _____ chart appears on a worksheet with other data.
   a. filtered
   b. embedded
   c. source
   d. destination

3. A chart's X axis also is referred to as what?
   a. Value axis
   b. Category axis
   c. Data axis
   d. Legend

4. Which toolbar contains buttons for graphic objects, such as arrows and lines, that you can add to a chart?
   a. Chart
   b. Formatting
   c. Drawing
   d. Picture

5. What part of a chart do you click when you want to select the entire chart?
   a. Chart Area
   b. Plot Area
   c. Chart Title
   d. Legend

Short Answer

1. What are five types of charts you can create with the Chart Wizard?
2. How do you move a chart in a worksheet?
3. How do you move individual elements within a chart?
4. How can you format an axis of a chart?
5. How can you change the title of a chart?
6. How can you change the type of a chart?

IMPORTANT

In the On Your Own exercises that follow, you must complete Exercise 1 before continuing to Exercise 2.

On Your Own

◆ **Open Five Year Sales from the Excel Core Practice/Lesson06 folder.**

Exercise 1

On the Expense History worksheet, change the pie chart to a doughnut chart comparing the percentage of expenses allocated to each category in 1999–2003. View the ScreenTips to see what year the outer ring represents.

Exercise 2

In the Five Years Sales workbook, move the legend to the left side of the chart. Change the chart title to read *Cost Allocation, 1999–2003*. Add a text box to the chart explaining which ring represents which year. Preview and print the chart.

◆ **Close Five Year Sales.**

One Step Further

Exercise 1

In this lesson, Value (Y) axis major and minor gridlines were included in a chart for the Five Year Sales worksheet. Would major or minor Category (X) axis gridlines have been useful in this chart? Why or why not? In what types of charts are X axis gridlines likely to be most useful?

Exercise 2

In the Five Year Sales workbook, a section of the Expenses History pie chart was pulled apart from the rest of the pie. This is often referred to as an "exploded view." Is there a way to "explode" the entire pie without having to click and drag each component after the pie chart is made? Explore Excel's chart types or use Excel's Help files to find the answer.

Exercise 3

Most companies have a company logo—something that identifies them to their customers. To be effective, these logos need to be visible in as many locations as possible. This includes any worksheets that the company provides to customers, shareholders, and business partners. How would you include an existing logo in a worksheet?

7

Performing Basic Calculations

After completing this lesson, you will be able to:

✔ *Build formulas.*
✔ *Copy formulas.*
✔ *Use absolute and relative cell references.*
✔ *Edit formulas.*
✔ *Use the SUM function and AutoSum.*
✔ *Insert Date functions.*
✔ *Understand basic statistical functions.*
✔ *Work with three-dimensional formulas.*

KEY TERMS

- absolute reference
- AutoSum
- formula
- Formula bar
- function
- relative references
- three-dimensional formula

With Microsoft Excel, you can easily perform common and complex calculations. In addition to adding, subtracting, multiplying, and dividing, you can calculate the total and compute the average of a set of values. With basic calculations, you can figure profit values from revenue and expenses and you can compute an employee's wages from hours worked and pay rates. These are just a few examples of the calculations Excel can perform.

At the Adventure Works resort, the reservations manager is preparing a report on annual vacancy rates. To start, he finds the total number of nights that each type of room was occupied. Then he calculates the average number of rooms occupied per night. Finally, he figures the occupancy rate for each type of room. The results of these calculations help him plan the upcoming season and schedule cabin renovations for the time of year when demand is lowest.

Also at Adventure Works, the accountant is calculating income generated from equipment rentals for various activities. With those numbers, he can compute the average income earned from each activity each month. The activities coordinator uses these figures to plan her strategy for activities in the upcoming year.

In this lesson, you will learn how to perform basic Excel calculations with formulas and functions. You also will learn how to create and edit formulas, use mathematical operators, and use Excel's built-in functions.

Building Formulas

Creating Formulas to Calculate Values

THE BOTTOM LINE

The real strength of a spreadsheet program like Excel is its feature for calculating and crunching numbers. Simple to complex formulas entered in a worksheet are calculated instantaneously, giving you results and solutions that help you assess and analyze your data.

A **formula** is the written expression of a calculation to be performed by Excel. When you enter a formula in a cell, the formula is stored internally while the calculated result is what you see in the cell.

A formula consists of two elements: operands and mathematical operators. The operands identify the values to be used in the calculation. An operand can be a constant value, another formula, or a reference to a cell or range of cells. Mathematical operators specify what calculations are to be performed with the values.

You can use any of the following mathematical operators in a formula:

Operator	Meaning
^	Exponentiation
*	Multiplication
/	Division
+	Addition
-	Subtraction

When a formula contains two or more operators, operations are not necessarily performed in the order in which you read the formula—that is, left to right. The order in which operations are performed is determined by operator priority, as defined by the rules of mathematics. For example, exponentiation is performed before any other operation. Multiplication and division are next on the priority list, performed sequentially from left to right. Finally, addition and subtraction are performed, again from left to right. Consider the following equation:

$$2 + 4 * 6 / 3 - 1 = 9$$

First, four is multiplied by six, and the result is divided by three. Two is then added to the result, and one is subtracted. See Figure 7-1.

FIGURE 7-1

Structure of a formula

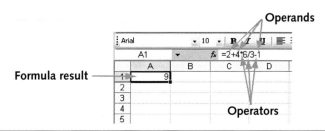

Formula result

Operands

Operators

You can override the standard operator priorities by using parentheses. Operations contained within parentheses are completed before those outside parentheses. Thus, the following equation is calculated differently than the previous one.

$$(2 + 4) * 6 / (3 - 1) = 18$$

In this formula, two and four are added first, and the result is multiplied by six. Finally, that result is divided by the result of three minus one. See Figure 7-2.

FIGURE 7-2

Using parentheses to control the order of operations

	A	B	C	D
1	18			
2				
3				
4				
5				

Creating a formula is similar to entering text and numbers in cells. To begin, you select the cell in which you want the formula to appear. To allow Excel to distinguish formulas from data, all formulas begin with an equal sign (=) or a plus sign (+).

Then you use one of two methods to create the formula:

- Type an equal sign to mark the entry as a formula. Then type the formula, including cell addresses, constant values, and mathematical operators, directly into the cell.
- Type an equal sign. When entering the formula, type any operators, constant values, or parentheses directly in the cell, but you can click a cell or range of cells included in the formula instead of typing the cell or range address. This method is typically quicker and eliminates the possibility of typing an incorrect cell or range address.

As you build a formula, it appears in the **Formula bar** and the cell itself. When you have completed the formula, the cell displays the result of the formula and the Formula bar displays the formula itself, as you saw in Figures 7-1 and 7-2.

The reservations manager at Adventure Works has tracked the number of nights each type of room was occupied each month for the last year. To calculate occupancy rates, he must find the total number of nights occupied for each month, divide that total by the number of rooms, and divide that result by the number of nights in the month.

◆ **To complete the procedures in this lesson, you must use the files Lodging Usage, Activity Rentals, and Food07 in the Lesson07 folder in the Excel Core Practice folder located on your hard disk.**

◆ **Open Lodging Usage from the Excel Core Practice/Lesson07 folder.**

Enter formulas in a worksheet

In this exercise, you open a worksheet and create basic formulas using different methods to enter the formulas.

1 Click cell C9, and type =C5+C6+C7.

As you type each cell address (or reference), the cell being referred to is selected and the selection border appears in a specific color. This color matches the color of the text used for the cell reference, as shown in Figure 7-3.

FIGURE 7-3

Color-coordinating cell references

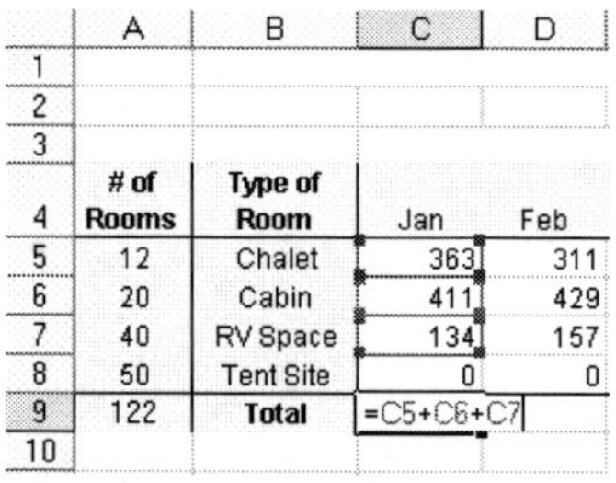

	A	B	C	D
1				
2				
3				
4	# of Rooms	Type of Room	Jan	Feb
5	12	Chalet	363	311
6	20	Cabin	411	429
7	40	RV Space	134	157
8	50	Tent Site	0	0
9	122	Total	=C5+C6+C7	
10				

TIP

When you type a cell address in a formula, you can use uppercase or lowercase letters. For example, references *B8* and *b8* refer to the same cell.

2 Press Enter.

The total of the cells (908) appears in cell C9.

3 Click cell C13, type =, and click cell C5.

C5 is added to the formula. The cell you click is color-coded and shows a flashing marquee border, as shown in Figure 7-4.

FIGURE 7-4

Referencing a cell in a formula

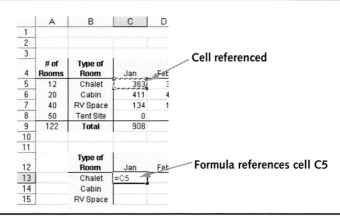

Cell referenced

Formula references cell C5

✓ **4** Type /, click cell A5, and click the Enter button on the Formula bar.

Excel completes the formula and displays the ratio of cells C5 and A5 (30.25).

5 Scroll down, if necessary, and click cell C21. Click in the Formula bar, type =C13/31, and click the Enter button on the Formula bar.

Excel calculates the occupancy rate of chalet rooms for the month of January (0.97581), and the results appear in cell C21.

6 On the Format menu, click Cells.

ANOTHER METHOD

- Right-click the selected cell, and select Format Cells on the shortcut menu.
- Press Ctrl+1.

---

7 Switch to the Number tab, if necessary, and click Percentage in the Category list.

8 Click OK to accept the default number of decimal places (2).

The value in C21 appears as a percentage.

FIGURE 7-5

Formatting formula results

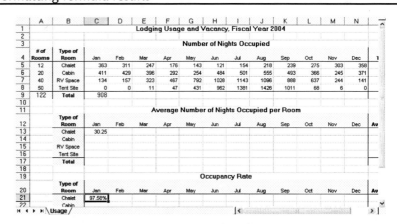

◆ **Keep this file open for the next exercise.**

> **TIP**
>
> By default, Excel calculates formulas automatically. To change when a formula is calculated, open the Tools menu and click Options; on the Calculation tab, select the desired option.

QUICK REFERENCE ▼

Enter a formula in a cell

1 Click the cell and type =.

2 Type the formula, including cell references, constant values, mathematical operators, functions, and parentheses.

3 Press Enter.

Copying Formulas

> **THE BOTTOM LINE**
>
> You can avoid entering formulas repeatedly and save a considerable amount of time by copying a cell with a completed formula and pasting it in the destination cells.

You may find that a similar formula is needed in several adjacent cells. For example, if you have a list of items and each item contributes to the total income for one year, you might want to add the items to total the income for that year. To total the income for consecutive years, you can create formulas to sum the income for each year.

Instead of entering the formula repeatedly for each year, you can simply copy it and paste it in the destination cells. You also can use the Fill feature to copy formulas to adjacent cells.

When selecting a cell, you may have noticed the small black square in the bottom right corner, as shown in Figure 7-6. This is the Fill handle. When you click a cell containing a formula and drag the Fill handle, the formula is copied to the cells. When the formula contains cell references, Excel changes them to match those of the column or row to which the formula has been copied.

FIGURE 7-6

Fill handle on a selected cell

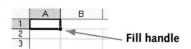

Fill handle

The reservations manager does not want to type the same formula over and over to calculate the occupancy rate for each type of room for each month. Instead, he copies his formulas to several locations.

Copy formulas

In this exercise, you copy formulas in your worksheet.

1 **Click cell C13, and on the Edit menu, click Copy.**

A flashing marquee border appears around the cell.

ANOTHER METHOD

- Select the cell you want to copy, and then click the Copy button.
- Select the cell you want to copy, and press Ctrl+C.

2 **Click cell C14, and on the Edit menu, click Paste.**

The formula is pasted in cell C14, and the Paste Options button appears next to the cell.

ANOTHER METHOD

- Select the cell to which you want to paste, and then click the Paste button.
- Select the cell to which you want to paste, and press Ctrl+V.

TIP

For more information on the Paste Options button, see Lesson 2, "Editing and Formatting Worksheets."

3 **Repeat step 2 for cells C15 and C16.**

ANOTHER METHOD

To copy data, including a formula, that is in the cell directly above the selected cell, press Ctrl+D. To copy data that is in the cell to the immediate left of the selected cell, press Ctrl+R.

4 **Click cell C9, and point to the Fill handle.**

The mouse pointer turns into a crosshair pointer when properly positioned.

TIP

When you copy a formula to a different cell, Excel also copies the formatting.

5 **Drag the Fill handle to cell D9.**

The formula in cell C9 is copied to cell D9, and the Auto Fill Options button appears next to the cell.

FIGURE 7-7

Copying a formula using the Fill handle

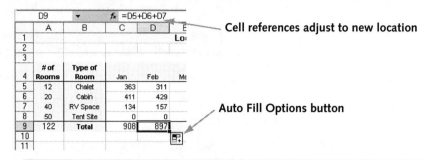

Cell references adjust to new location

Auto Fill Options button

6 **Click cell D9, and observe its formula in the Formula bar.**

The formula is copied from C9, and the column letter is adjusted to match the column of the new cell.

7 **Point to the Fill handle in cell D9, and drag the handle to cell N9.**

The formula is copied to cells E9:N9. The total number of nights occupied for each month is displayed in cells E9:N9.

FIGURE 7-8

Formula copied to a range of cells

	B	C	D	E	F	G	H	I	J	K	L	M	N	O
1		Lodging Usage and Vacancy, Fiscal Year 2004												
2														
3				Number of Nights Occupied										
4	Type of Room	Jan	Feb	Mar	Apr	May	Jun	Jul	Aug	Sep	Oct	Nov	Dec	Total
5	Chalet	363	311	247	176	143	121	154	218	239	275	303	358	
6	Cabin	411	429	396	292	254	484	501	555	493	366	245	371	
7	RV Space	134	157	323	467	792	1028	1143	1096	888	637	244	141	
8	Tent Site	0	0	11	47	431	962	1381	1426	1011	68	6	0	
9	Total	908	897	966	935	1189	1633	1798	1869	1620	1278	792	870	
10														
11				Average Number of Nights Occupied per Room										

◆ **Save the file, and leave it open for the next exercise.**

Q. If you wanted to copy a formula from cell A5 to cell C5, would you use the Fill handle method or would you use the Copy and Paste commands?

A: You would use the Copy and Paste commands because you can use the Fill handle only to copy to adjacent cells.

TROUBLESHOOTING

If you inadvertently delete or change a formula, press Ctrl+Z or click the Undo button on the Standard toolbar to reverse the action.

QUICK REFERENCE ▼

Copy a formula using the Fill handle

1 Select the cell that contains the formula you want to copy.

2 Drag the Fill handle to the last cell in the desired range.

CHECK THIS OUT ▼

Using Auto Fill
Excel's Auto Fill feature takes the Fill capabilities one step further. When you enter data that forms a recognizable series or pattern, such as the days in the week or a sequential list of numbers, you can use Auto Fill to automatically complete the series for you. Simply type the first two or three entries, select the range of cells containing the entries, click the Auto Fill Options button on the Fill handle, and select Fill Series. Other Auto Fill options include copying the formatting only of the selected cell or range to the target cells and filling the target cells with unformatted values.

Working with Cell References

THE BOTTOM LINE

Cell references are frequently used in formulas. Being able to copy formulas without having to manually change cell references is a time-saver as well as an effective way to ensure accuracy in your calculations.

As you have learned, you can copy (and move) cells that contain formulas with cell references, and the references automatically adjust to reflect their new location. These are referred to as **relative references**. For example, if you enter =(C4+C5) in cell C6, the resulting value in C6 will be the sum of the values in C4 and C5. If you copy this formula to cell D6, the formula in D6 will appear as =(D4+D5) and the resulting value in cell D6 will be the sum of the values in D4 and D5. Excel automatically adjusts the cell references relative to their new location, which is why they are called "relative" cell references.

In some cases, however, you need cell references that don't change when you copy them from one location to another. For example, a formula might refer to a rate of interest that is always stored in a particular cell. This is referred to as an **absolute reference**. A cell reference also may have an absolute reference to a row but not to a column, and vice versa. To make a cell reference absolute, type a dollar sign ($) before either or both of the column or row references.

For example, C1 is an absolute reference to cell C1. $C1 is an absolute reference to column C, but the reference to row 1 is relative. C$1 is a relative reference to column C, but the reference to row 1 is absolute.

At Adventure Works, the reservations manager is having trouble copying the formulas in his worksheet that calculate simple averages. Using a combination of absolute and relative references, however, he is able to replicate easily the formulas to compute the necessary averages.

Use cell references in formulas

In this exercise, you use absolute references and relative references to build and copy a formula.

1 **Double-click cell C13.**

2 **Type a dollar sign ($) before the A in the reference to cell A5, and press Enter.**

The formula reads =C5/$A5.

3 **Copy the formula in cell C13 to cell D13, and click cell D13, if necessary, to select it.**

The formula in cell D13 reads =D5/$A5. Because the column reference to cell A5 is absolute, that reference does not change when the formula is copied. The reference to the first cell in the formula is entirely relative.

4 Copy the formula in cell C13 to cell C14, and click cell C14.

The formula in cell C14 reads =C6/$A6. Because the reference to column A is absolute, that reference does not change when the formula is copied. However, the row reference is still relative, so that value is updated when the formula is copied. The reference to the first cell is entirely relative.

5 Using the Fill handle, copy the formula in cell C14 to cells C15 and C16. Click cell D13 and use its Fill handle to copy the formula to E13:N13. Use the Fill handles on C14, C15, and C16 to copy their formulas to D14:N14, D15:N15, and D16:N16, respectively. That section of the worksheet should look like the worksheet shown in Figure 7-9.

FIGURE 7-9

Copying formulas with cell references

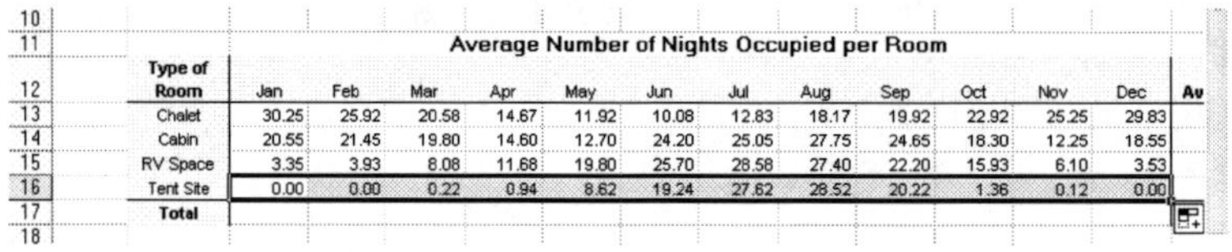

	Type of Room	Jan	Feb	Mar	Apr	May	Jun	Jul	Aug	Sep	Oct	Nov	Dec	Av
11					*Average Number of Nights Occupied per Room*									
13	Chalet	30.25	25.92	20.58	14.67	11.92	10.08	12.83	18.17	19.92	22.92	25.25	29.83	
14	Cabin	20.55	21.45	19.80	14.60	12.70	24.20	25.05	27.75	24.65	18.30	12.25	18.55	
15	RV Space	3.35	3.93	8.08	11.68	19.80	25.70	28.58	27.40	22.20	15.93	6.10	3.53	
16	Tent Site	0.00	0.00	0.22	0.94	8.62	19.24	27.62	28.52	20.22	1.36	0.12	0.00	
17	Total													

◆ Save and close Lodging Usage.

QUICK REFERENCE ▼

Create an absolute reference

- Type a dollar sign ($) before the column reference to make the column reference absolute.
  Or

- Type a dollar sign ($) before the row reference to make the row reference absolute.
  Or

- Type a dollar sign ($) before the column and row references to make the entire cell reference absolute.

QUICK CHECK

Q. Which type of cell reference changes to reflect a location to which it is copied or moved?

A: A relative cell reference changes "relative" to its new location.

Editing Formulas

You may want to change a formula to produce a different result on specified data or because an error was made in entering a formula.

You can edit a formula just like you edit any data you've already entered in a cell. For example, instead of summing the values in a range of cells, you may want to find the average for the range. You can edit a formula using one of the following methods:

- Double-click the cell, type your changes directly in the cell, and press Enter.

  Or

- Click the cell, click in the Formula bar, type your changes, and click the Enter button on the Formula bar or press Enter.

To delete a formula, click the cell and press the Delete key or the Backspace key.

◆ **Open Food07 from the Excel Core Practice/Lesson07 folder.**

Edit formulas

In this exercise, you revise formulas.

1 **Click cell P3, and click to the right of the formula in the Formula bar.**

The insertion point flashes at the end of the formula.

2 **Press the Backspace key three times, click cell O3, and then press Enter.**

The Total Yearly Consumption figure, which also is shown in cell O3, is deleted from the formula, and the cell reference for that data replaces it. Using a cell reference in the formula instead of a constant allows you to copy the formula.

Double-click the cell, edit the formula by typing the new values or by referencing other cells, and press Enter.

3 **Copy the formula to cells P4:P35 by using the Fill handle in cell P3.**

Excel calculates and displays the yearly costs per item.

Before you drag the Fill handle, make sure the mouse pointer icon is the shape of a crosshair. If it's the shape of a four-headed arrow, you will move the cell when you drag.

FIGURE 7-10

Edited worksheet

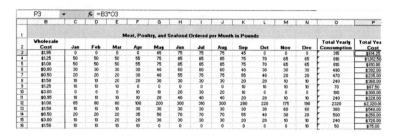

P3						=B3*O3								

Wholesale Cost	Jan	Feb	Mar	Apr	May	Jun	Jul	Aug	Sep	Oct	Nov	Dec	Total Yearly Consumption	Total Yearly Cost
$1.95	0	0	0	0	45	75	75	75	45	0	0	0	315	$614.25
$1.25	50	50	50	55	75	85	85	85	75	70	65	65	810	$1,012.50
$1.00	50	50	50	55	75	85	85	85	75	70	65	65	810	$810.00
$0.80	30	30	30	30	40	60	80	60	40	30	30	30	490	$392.00
$0.50	20	20	20	30	40	55	75	75	55	40	20	20	470	$235.00
$1.50	10	10	20	20	30	30	30	30	20	20	10	10	240	$360.00
$1.25	10	10	10	0	0	0	0	0	10	10	10	10	70	$87.50
$3.00	0	0	0	10	10	20	30	20	10	0	0	0	100	$300.00
$0.95	10	10	10	10	20	40	40	40	20	20	10	10	240	$228.00
$1.00	85	80	80	100	200	300	310	300	280	220	175	190	2320	$2,320.00
$1.50	10	10	10	30	30	30	30	30	30	30	60	60	360	$540.00
$0.50	20	20	20	35	50	70	70	70	55	40	30	20	500	$250.00
$3.00	10	10	20	20	30	30	30	30	20	20	10	10	240	$720.00
$1.50	10	10	10	10	0	0	0	0	0	0	0	10	50	$75.00

Meat, Poultry, and Seafood Ordered per Month in Pounds

◆ Save and close Food07.

QUICK REFERENCE ▼

Revise a formula

1 Click the cell that contains the formula.

2 Click in the Formula bar.

3 Edit the necessary formula, functions, or arguments, and click the Enter button on the Formula bar or press Enter.

Exploring Functions

THE BOTTOM LINE

Functions are designed to perform all sorts of calculations—from simple to complex. When you apply one of Excel's built-in functions to specified data, you eliminate the time involved in manually constructing a formula and ensure the accuracy of the formula's result.

One of the most common calculations performed in a worksheet is adding a range of cells. You can add a range of cells by creating a formula that includes each cell label separated by the addition (+) operator. An easier way to achieve the same result is to use the SUM function.

A **function** is a predefined formula that performs a calculation. For example, the SUM function adds values or a range of cells. A typical SUM function totaling cells C13 through C16 looks like this: *=SUM(C13:C16)*.

A function consists of two components: the *function name* and, in most cases, an *argument list*. See Figure 7-11. The argument list, which is enclosed in parentheses, contains the data (or operands) that the function requires to produce the result. Depending on the function, an argument can be a constant value, a single-cell reference, a range of cells, a range name, or even another function. When a function contains multiple arguments, the arguments are separated by commas. In this lesson, you explore some of the more commonly used functions, including the SUM, AVERAGE, and various date functions.

FIGURE 7-11

Structure of a function

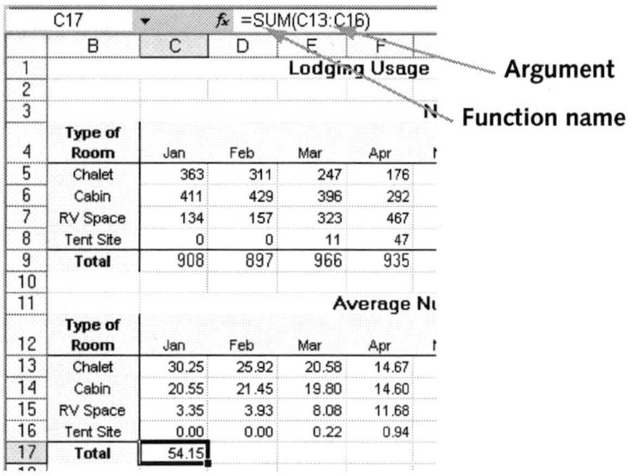

	B	C	D	E	F	
1				Lodging Usage		
2						
3						
4	Type of Room	Jan	Feb	Mar	Apr	
5	Chalet	363	311	247	176	
6	Cabin	411	429	396	292	
7	RV Space	134	157	323	467	
8	Tent Site	0	0	11	47	
9	Total	908	897	966	935	
10						
11				Average Nu		
12	Type of Room	Jan	Feb	Mar	Apr	
13	Chalet	30.25	25.92	20.58	14.67	
14	Cabin	20.55	21.45	19.80	14.60	
15	RV Space	3.35	3.93	8.08	11.68	
16	Tent Site	0.00	0.00	0.22	0.94	
17	Total	54.15				

C17 f_x =SUM(C13:C16)

Argument — Function name

Inserting a Function

You can enter a function in a cell just as you enter any formula: by typing it directly in the cell or in the Formula bar. With this method, you must know the exact name and syntax (or structure) of the function. You might find that an easier way to enter a function is to use the Insert Function feature, which guides you through the process of "building" the formula that the specified function will execute.

Once you've selected a function in the Insert Function dialog box, the Function Arguments dialog box opens. This is where you build your function. The Function Arguments dialog box lists the selected function's arguments, provides a description of each argument, and shows the calculated result of the function.

At Adventure Works, the accountant uses the Insert Function feature to calculate the annual income generated through the rental of various types of sporting equipment.

◆ **Open Activity Rentals from the Excel Core Practice/Lesson07 folder.**

Insert functions

In this exercise, you use the Insert Function feature to enter functions in a worksheet.

1 **Click cell O3, and click the Insert Function button on the Standard toolbar.**

The Insert Function dialog box opens.

FIGURE 7-12

Insert Function dialog box

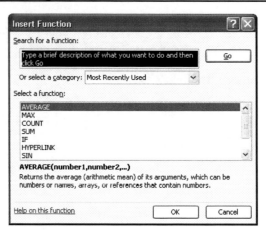

- On the Insert menu, click Function.
- Click the cell, and click the Insert Function button on the Formula bar.

If the Office Assistant appears asking if you want help with this feature, click No, Don't Provide Help Now.

2 In the Or Select A Category box, click the down arrow, and select Most Recently Used, if necessary.

3 In the Select A Function list, click SUM, and then click OK.

The Function Arguments dialog box appears, showing the SUM function totaling cells C3:N3.

FIGURE 7-13

Function Arguments dialog box

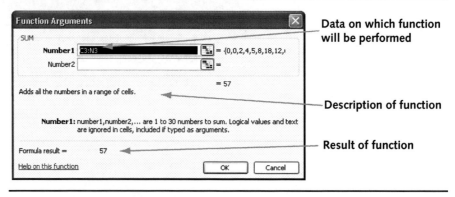

Data on which function will be performed

Description of function

Result of function

If you do not see the SUM function in the Select A Function list, click the arrow on the *Or Select A Category* box, and click All. All of Excel's functions are listed alphabetically in the Select A Function list.

4 **Click OK in the Function Arguments dialog box.**

The Function Arguments dialog box closes, and the result of the calculation (57) appears in cell O3.

5 **Click cell A20, and then click the Insert Function button on the Standard toolbar.**

The Insert Function dialog box appears.

6 **In the Or Select A Category box, click the down arrow, and select Statistical.**

7 **In the Select A Function list, click COUNT, and then click OK.**

The Function Arguments dialog box appears.

8 **In the Value1 text box, type A3:A17, and click OK.**

Excel counts 15 numeric entries in cells 3 through 17 of column A.

◆ **Save Activity Rentals, and then close the workbook.**

QUICK REFERENCE ▼

Enter a function using the Function Arguments dialog box

1 Click the cell that will contain the function.

2 On the Standard toolbar, click the Insert Function button.

3 Select the function, and enter arguments into the Function Arguments dialog box.

4 Click OK.

Using AutoSum

Excel's **AutoSum** feature offers a shortcut for entering SUM functions to total ranges of cells. When you click the AutoSum button on the Standard toolbar, Excel totals cells directly above or to the left of the cell containing the function.

If there are any nonnumeric cells within the range of cells you want to total, AutoSum will, by default, calculate the total only from the active cell to the first nonnumeric cell. To get around this problem, either alter the arguments to include the full range of cells or select only the range of cells you want to total.

The reservations manager learns that AutoSum makes it even easier for him to complete his occupancy calculations. He can use AutoSum to calculate the many totals he needs.

◆ Open Lodging Usage from the Excel Core Practice/Lesson07 folder.

Use AutoSum

In this exercise, you use AutoSum to total a range of cells.

Σ ▾

1 **Click cell C17, and click the AutoSum button on the Standard toolbar.**

A SUM formula appears in cell C17 and the Formula bar, and the range C13:C16 is surrounded by a flashing marquee border.

2 **Press Enter.**

The formula is entered in cell C17, and the result (54.15) is displayed.

3 **Click cell O5, and then click the AutoSum button.**

A SUM formula is displayed in cell O5 and in the Formula bar, and the range C5:N5 is surrounded by a flashing marquee border.

4 **Press Enter.**

The formula is entered in cell O5, and the result (2908) is displayed.

FIGURE 7-14

Applying the AutoSum feature

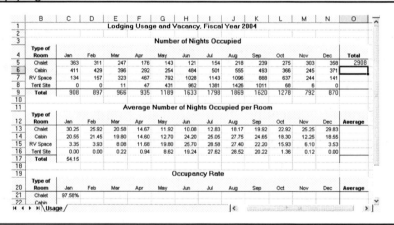

◆ Leave the file open for the next exercise.

QUICK CHECK

Q. Which Excel function does AutoSum use?

A: **AutoSum incorporates the SUM function.**

QUICK REFERENCE ▼

Automatically total a row or column of cells

1 Select the cell that will contain the total.

2 On the Standard toolbar, click the AutoSum button.

3 Modify the arguments, if desired, and press Enter.

Using Date Functions

Excel's Date and Time functions allow you to use dates and times in formulas. To perform calculations on these values, Excel converts each date and time to a serial number. The Date function performs that conversion for any year, month, and day combination you enter. The Time function converts any hour, minute, and second combination you enter.

NOW and TODAY are two of the most frequently used date functions. NOW returns the date and time that the function was entered in a worksheet. TODAY returns only the date. Each time you open a workbook that uses one of these functions, the date or time is updated automatically.

In March, the reservations manager needs to figure the occupancy rate for the winter season, which runs from November 1 through the end of February. He wants to confirm the number of days in that season.

Enter Date functions

In this exercise, you use Date functions to calculate the amount of time between two dates.

1 Click cell A20, and click the Insert Function button.

2 Select Date & Time from the Or Select A Category list.

3 Select DATE from the Select A Function list, and click OK.

The Function Arguments dialog box opens.

4 In the Year box, type 2004.

5 In the Month box, type 2.

6 In the Day box, type 29.

The serial number for the date 02/29/2004 appears as the formula result at the bottom of the Function Arguments dialog box.

7 With the Function Arguments dialog box still open, click to the right of the function in the Formula bar, press the spacebar, and type a minus sign (-).

TROUBLESHOOTING

Be sure you include a space between the closing parenthesis of the DATE argument and the minus sign.

8 On the Functions list to the left of the Formula bar, click Date, as shown in Figure 7-15.

The Function Arguments dialog box opens.

FIGURE 7-15

Entering a second DATE function

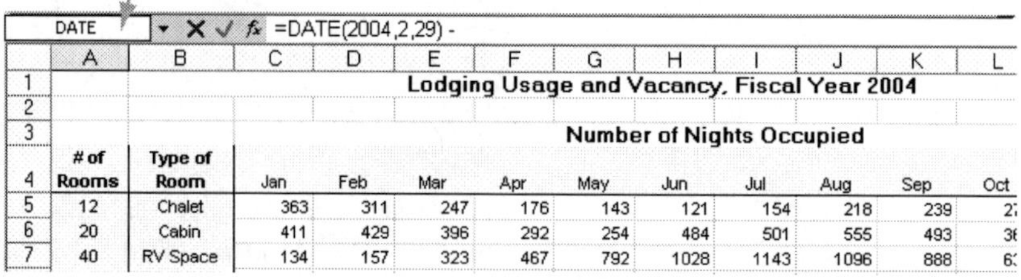

Functions list

	A	B	C	D	E	F	G	H	I	J	K	L
1					Lodging Usage and Vacancy, Fiscal Year 2004							
2												
3						Number of Nights Occupied						
4	# of Rooms	Type of Room	Jan	Feb	Mar	Apr	May	Jun	Jul	Aug	Sep	Oct
5	12	Chalet	363	311	247	176	143	121	154	218	239	2:
6	20	Cabin	411	429	396	292	254	484	501	555	493	3(
7	40	RV Space	134	157	323	467	792	1028	1143	1096	888	6:

(Formula bar: DATE ▼ ✕ ✓ ƒx =DATE(2004,2,29) -)

TIP

Date functions are most useful when the date arguments are formulas rather than constants.

9 In the Year, Month, and Day boxes, type 2003, 11, and 1, respectively, and click OK.

The total number of days (120) between 11/1/2003 and 2/29/2004 appears in the cell. The formula reads =DATE(2004,2,29) - DATE(2003,11,1).

10 In the Formula bar, click the first Date function.

A ScreenTip appears with a description of each item in that portion of the formula.

11 Click the word year in the ScreenTip to select 2004, and type 2005.

12 In the Formula bar, click to the right of the formula.

13 Press the Backspace key to remove the second date function of DATE(2003,11,1).

14 Type TODAY(), and press Enter.

The total number of days between 2/29/2005 and the current date appears in the cell.

◆ Close the workbook without saving your changes.

TIP

To calculate quickly the number of days between two dates that already appear in cells in your worksheet, simply subtract one cell from the other. For example, if cell A1 contains the date 11/1/2004 and cell A2 contains the date 2/29/2005, the number of days between them will be calculated with the following formula: =A2-A1.

Make sure you choose the number format for the cell containing this formula. Otherwise, Excel displays the result in the same format as the cells used in the calculation (in this case, as a date).

QUICK REFERENCE ▼

Use the NOW or TODAY function

1 Click the cell in which you want the date or date and time to appear.

2 Type **=NOW()** or **=TODAY()** in the cell, and press the Enter key.

Using Basic Statistical Functions

Statistical functions are typically used to compile and classify data so as to present significant information. For example, a teacher wants to determine the highest score (MAX) and the lowest score (MIN) on an exam, a sales manager wants to set pay increases based on sales reps' average sales over a 12-month period (AVERAGE), and a market researcher wants to figure out the middle income for a group of survey participants (MEDIAN). Some of the more commonly used statistical functions are shown in the following table.

QUICK **CHECK**

Q. What is the difference between the NOW and the TODAY functions?

A: The NOW function displays the current date and time; the TODAY function displays the current date.

Function	Meaning	Example
SUM	Totals the numeric arguments	=SUM(B5:B10)
AVERAGE	Computes the average (arithmetic mean) of the numeric arguments	=AVERAGE(B5:B10)
COUNT	Within the argument list, counts only the cells that contain numbers	=COUNT(B5:B10)
MIN	Returns the smallest number within the arguments	=MIN(B5:B10)
MAX	Returns the largest number within the arguments	=MAX(B5:B10)

The activities manager at Adventure Works is learning which Excel functions can help her devise a strategy for activities in the upcoming year.

◆ **Open Activity Rentals from the Excel Core Practice/Lesson07 folder.**

Insert statistical functions

In this exercise, you create formulas using the AVERAGE, MIN, and MAX functions.

fx

1 Click cell A21, and click the Insert Function button.

The Insert Function dialog box appears.

2 Select Statistical in the Or Select A Category list, click AVERAGE in the Select A Function list, and click OK.

The Function Arguments dialog box appears.

3 In the Number 1 box, click the Collapse Dialog button.

The Function Arguments dialog box collapses, allowing you to select the range of cells to be averaged.

4 Select cells C15:N15, and click the Expand Dialog button in the Function Arguments dialog box.

The Function Arguments dialog box appears with the completed AVERAGE function.

FIGURE 7-16

Entering the AVERAGE function

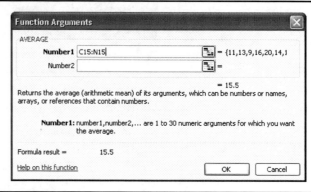

5 **In the Function Arguments dialog box, click OK.**

The average number of pairs of binoculars rented per month (15.5) appears in cell A21.

6 **Click in the Formula bar, and select the word AVERAGE.**

7 **Click the Functions down arrow to the left of the Formula bar (currently displaying the text AVERAGE), and click MAX.**

The Function Arguments dialog box opens with the range previously used already entered.

TROUBLESHOOTING

If MAX does not appear in your list of functions, click More Functions. This opens the Insert Functions dialog box, from which you can select MAX in the Statistical category.

FIGURE 7-17

Entering the MAX function

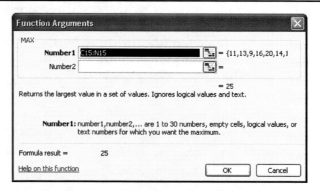

TIP

If you forget the syntax for a function you want to use, type = and the name of the function in a cell and press Ctrl+A. The Function Arguments dialog box appears so you can enter the arguments for your function.

8 **In the Function Arguments dialog box, click OK.**

The highest number of pairs of binoculars rented in a month (25) appears in cell A21.

9 **Click cell A22, type =MIN(C15:N15), and press Enter.**

The lowest number of pairs of binoculars rented in a month (9) appears in cell A22.

10 **Delete the entries in cells A20:A22.**

◆ **Save and close Activity Rentals.**

QUICK CHECK

Q. If you wanted a tally of the cells in a specified range that contained numbers, which function would you use?

A: **You would use the COUNT function.**

Creating a Three-Dimensional Formula

THE BOTTOM LINE

Formulas can reference cells in any worksheet within a workbook as well as in other workbooks. Using three-dimensional formulas, you can compile data and prepare summaries that are vital to forecasts and analyses.

So far you've learned how to enter formulas and functions that calculate data on a single worksheet. You also can enter formulas to calculate data from multiple worksheets within a workbook. A formula that contains a reference (referred to as a 3-D reference) to data or cells on one or more other worksheets is called a **three-dimensional formula**. When data is adjusted on a worksheet, any formula that references that data also is adjusted.

Three-dimensional formulas are widely used to create a summary sheet that totals figures from different sheets in a workbook file. For example, the chef at Adventure Works wants to see how much the restaurant has paid for food in a year. To calculate the total amount spent, he uses a three-dimensional formula on the Summary worksheet. The formula refers to the cells in each worksheet that contain the amount spent in a particular food category and adds these amounts together.

As with any formula, you can specify a reference by typing the cell coordinates. The references in the formula, however, must begin with the name of the worksheet to which the formula is linking, followed by an exclamation point and then the cell coordinates. Commas separate the references.

IMPORTANT

When a worksheet has a name consisting of two or more words, the name must be put in single quotation marks in the formula.

◆ **Open Food07 from the Excel Core Practice/Lesson07 folder.**

Create a three-dimensional formula

In this exercise, you create a formula in one worksheet that adds together data in other worksheets.

1   **Click the Summary sheet tab, click cell A3, type** Total Cost of Food, **and press Enter.**

Excel adds the text to cell A3 and moves the insertion point to cell A4.

2   **In cell A4, type** =SUM(.

3   **Click the Meats sheet tab, click cell P36, and type a plus sign (+).**

In the Formula bar on the Meats worksheet, the first argument and addition operator are added to the formula, as shown in Figure 7-18.

FIGURE 7-18

Building a three-dimensional formula

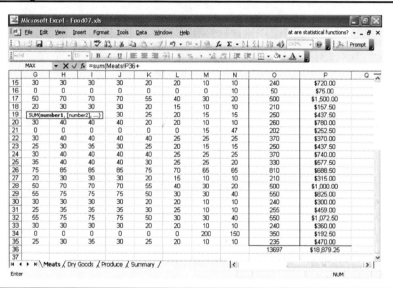

4   **Click the Dry Goods sheet tab, click cell P26, and type a plus sign (+).**

The second argument is added to the formula.

5   **Click the Produce sheet tab, click cell P28, and press Enter.**

The last argument is added to the formula, and the result of the formula appears in cell A4 on the Summary worksheet.

FIGURE 7-19

Result of a three-dimensional formula

A4	▾	*fx* =SUM(Meats!P36+Dry Goods!P26+Produce!P28)				
	A	B	C	D	E	F	G
1							
2							
3	Total Cost of Food						
4	$33,296.30						
5							
6							

◆ Save and close Food07. If you are continuing to other lessons, leave Excel open. If you are not continuing to other lessons, save and close all open workbooks. Click the Close button in the top right corner of the Excel window.

QUICK REFERENCE ▼

Create a three-dimensional formula

1 Click the cell where you want to insert the formula.
2 Enter the formula using the appropriate worksheet and cell references.
3 Press Enter.

Key Points

✔ *In a spreadsheet program like Excel, formulas that range from simple to complex are calculated instantaneously, giving you results and solutions that are timely and accurate. You can enter and edit formulas just as you enter and edit other data.*

✔ *You can avoid entering formulas repeatedly and save a considerable amount of time by copying a cell with a completed formula and pasting it in the destination cells. You also can copy a cell's contents by using the Fill feature.*

✔ *Cell references are frequently used in formulas. Being able to copy formulas without having to manually change cell references is a time-saver as well as an effective way to ensure accuracy in calculations.*

✔ *Excel comes with hundreds of functions that are designed to perform all sorts of calculations. When you apply one of Excel's built-in functions, you eliminate the time involved in manually constructing a formula and ensure the accuracy of the formula's result.*

✔ *You can use three-dimensional formulas to compile data from multiple worksheets and to prepare summaries.*

Quick Quiz

True/False

T F 1. A lowercase *x* is the multiplication operator.

T F 2. In a formula with addition and multiplication operators, the multiplication operation is performed first.

T F 3. You can use the Fill handle to copy a cell's contents only to adjacent cells.

T F 4. In a function, the argument includes the name of the function.

T F 5. You would use the DATE function if you wanted to display the current date in a worksheet.

T F 6. The COUNT function is an example of a statistical function.

Multiple Choice

1. Which of the following is *not* a mathematical operator?
   a. ^
   b. @
   c. +
   d. *

2. If you entered the formula, =(2 + 4) * 6 / (3 − 1) in a cell, what would the result be?
   a. 7.6
   b. 9
   c. 11
   d. 18

3. Which function automatically totals cells directly above or to the left of the cell containing it?
   a. AutoSum
   b. Auto Fill
   c. AutoComplete
   d. COUNT

4. Which character designates a cell reference as absolute?
   a. ^
   b. @
   c. #
   d. $

Short Answer

1. How can you enter a formula in a cell?

2. What is the quickest way to total a column of values?

3. How can you copy a formula to a range of adjacent cells?

4. What are two ways to edit a formula in a cell?

5. List and identify the five mathematical operators discussed in this lesson.

On Your Own

◆ **Open Lodging Usage from the Excel Core Practice/Lesson07 folder.**

Exercise 1

In cell O5, use AutoSum to total the data in C5:N5. Do the same for the data in C6:N9. Complete the row of totals in the next table, and then create a formula to compute the average number of nights occupied in each room type for the year. In the third table, compute the occupancy rates. To do this, divide the average number of nights occupied per room by the number of days in the month (use 29 days for February). Then figure the average occupancy rate of each room type for the year.

◆ **Close Lodging Usage.**

◆ **Open Activity Rentals from the Excel Core Practice/Lesson07 folder.**

Exercise 2

Calculate the total number of rentals each month, the total yearly rentals, the yearly income for each type of activity/equipment, and the total annual income. Use the NOW function to display the current date and time in cell A1. Insert a column to the right of Yearly Rentals, label it Average Monthly Rentals, and use the AVERAGE function to find the average monthly rentals for each type of equipment.

◆ **Close Activity Rentals.**

One Step Further

Exercise 1

In this lesson, you used the COUNT function, which is a statistical function. Review the other categories of functions available from the Insert Function dialog box. What category would you likely use the most?

Exercise 2

This lesson illustrated how to find the number of days between two days by entering the dates in a formula that subtracted one date from the other. Is there a function that can do this automatically? Is there a way to calculate just the number of workdays between two dates (not counting weekends)? Explore the Date & Time category of the Insert Function dialog box or use Excel's Help files to find the answers to these questions. Write a brief summary of your findings.

Exercise 3

This lesson briefly touched on the Auto Fill feature and the Auto Fill Options button that appears whenever you fill cells. Return to the Activity Rentals workbook, and explore the filling and copying options available through the Auto Fill Options button. Briefly describe how these options can be useful.

LESSON

8

Using Basic Financial and Logical Functions

After completing this lesson, you will be able to:

✔ *Use the PMT function to forecast loan payments.*
✔ *Calculate cumulative interest.*
✔ *Compute investment value.*
✔ *Use the IF function.*

KEY TERMS

- conditional formula
- cumulative interest
- future value

- logical_test
- present value
- principal

Microsoft Excel is an invaluable tool for performing financial calculations. Using basic functions, you can easily calculate the monthly payments for a loan, figure the accrued value of an investment, and set the value of a cell by comparing the values of two other cells. With advanced financial functions, you can figure the rate of return on an investment, amortize a loan or mortgage over time, and track the depreciation of an asset.

In this lesson, you will use the PMT function to calculate loan payments, compute the cumulative interest paid on a loan using the CUMIPMT function, and figure the future value of a periodic investment with the FV function. Finally, you will compare investment options using the IF function.

At Adventure Works, the chief financial officer (CFO) is weighing the options for financing the upcoming chalet renovation. The mortgage broker offered two possible loan scenarios, but the financial adviser suggested some short-term investments. Using Excel's financial and logical functions, the CFO can calculate payment amounts, **cumulative interest** paid, and **future value** to determine the most cost-effective financing option.

IMPORTANT

Before you can use the practice files in this lesson, you must install them from the book's companion CD to their default location. For additional information on how to find and open files used in this book, see the "Using the CD-ROM" section at the beginning of this book.

Using the PMT Function to Forecast Loan Payments

THE BOTTOM LINE

The PMT function calculates the payment required to repay a loan for a specified number of periods at a set interest rate. This function is often used to help determine how much you can afford to borrow, primarily for big-ticket items such as cars and homes.

The PMT (payment) function calculates payments for a loan based on a series of constant payments and a constant interest rate. Thus, it returns the borrower's required payments for a loan. For example, you want to buy a $20,000 car. You've saved $2,000 to put toward the purchase price, and you need to borrow $18,000. Your lender has given you an interest rate of 9 percent, and you will repay the loan in 48 months. Using the PMT function, after you plug in these numbers, your monthly payment for the 48 months is instantaneously calculated.

The PMT function requires the following syntax:

   PMT(rate,nper,pv,fv,type)

The following table explains the meaning of each argument:

Argument	Explanation
Rate	*The interest rate per payment period; when you are calculating monthly payments, divide the annual interest rate by 12; when calculating semimonthly payments, divide the annual rate by 24*
Nper	The total number of loan payments; when the loan is issued for a number of years and requires monthly payments, you can enter the number of payments as 12*<number of years>
Pv	The **present value** (principal) of the loan
Fv	The value of the loan after all payments are made; in general, this value is zero, and if this variable is omitted, it is assumed to be zero
Type	The timing of the loan payments; when the loan payment is due at the end of the payment period, use the default value of 0; when payment is due at the beginning of the payment period, set this value to 1

The Adventure Works CFO has narrowed her choices to two possible loans. Using the payment function, she determines the monthly payment for each loan based on the term and quoted interest rate.

◆ To complete the procedures in this lesson, you must use the file **Financing** in the **Lesson08** folder in the Excel Core Practice folder located on your hard disk.

◆ Open **Financing** from the Excel Core Practice/Lesson08 folder.

Use the PMT function

In this exercise, you use the PMT function to calculate loan payments.

1 On the Loans sheet, click cell B10, and then click the Insert Function button on the Standard toolbar.

The Insert Function dialog box appears.

FIGURE 8-1

Insert Function dialog box

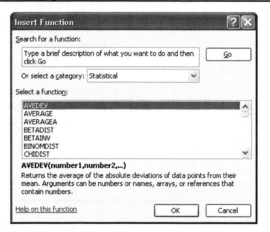

ANOTHER METHOD

- Open the Insert menu, and select Function.
- Click the Insert Function button on the Formula bar.

2 In the Or Select A Category list, click Financial.

The Select A Function list displays the available financial functions.

3 In the Select A Function list, scroll down, and click PMT. Then click OK.

The Function Arguments dialog box appears.

FIGURE 8-2

Function Arguments dialog box for the PMT function

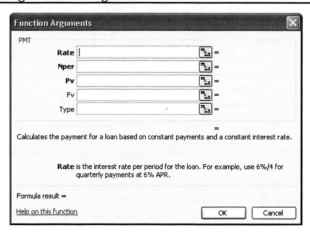

4 In the Rate box, click the Collapse Dialog button, and click cell B6.

5 Click the Expand Dialog button.

6 In the Rate box, to the right of B6, type /12.

You must divide the annual interest rate by 12 when calculating a monthly payment.

7 In the Nper box, click the Collapse Dialog button, click cell B8, and press Enter or click the Expand Dialog button.

8 In the Pv box, click the Collapse Dialog button, click cell B4, and press Enter or click the Expand Dialog button.

FIGURE 8-3

Completing the PMT arguments

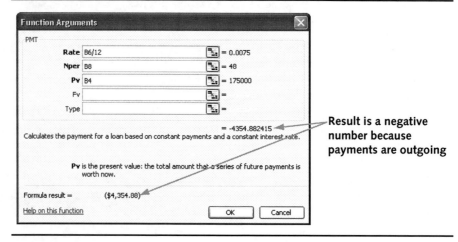

Result is a negative number because payments are outgoing

9 Click OK.

The monthly payment of (negative) $4,354.88 appears in cell B10.

10 Copy the formula in cell B10 to cell C10.

The monthly payment of (negative) $3,485.89 appears in cell C10.

FIGURE 8-4

Copying the function

	C10	▾	*fx* =PMT(C6/12,C8,C4)	
	A	B	C	
1	Real Estate Improvement Loan			
2				
3		Option A	Option B	
4	Principal:	$ 175,000.00	$ 175,000.00	
5				
6	Annual Percentage Rate	9.00%	7.25%	
7				
8	Number of Payments:	48	60	
9				
10	Monthly Payment:	($4,354.88)	($3,485.89)	
11				
12	Cumulative Interest Paid:			
13				

◆ **Save the workbook with the current name, and leave the file open for the next exercise.**

QUICK REFERENCE ▼

Use the Payment (PMT) function

1 Click the cell that will contain the formula.

2 Click the Insert Function button on the Standard toolbar.

3 Click Financial in the *Or Select A Category* list.

4 Click PMT in the Select A Function list, and click OK.

5 Enter the interest rate, number of payments, and principal.

6 Click OK.

QUICK CHECK

Q. What is the meaning of the Nper argument in the PMT function?

A: Nper is the total number of loan payments.

Calculating Cumulative Interest

THE BOTTOM LINE

Determining the amount of interest that will be paid over the term of a loan can be an effective tool for comparing and evaluating loan options.

For tax and accounting purposes, it's often necessary to calculate the total amount of interest paid over a series of loan payments. Excel's CUMIPMT function performs this task for you. The CUMIPMT function can also be used to compare loan options. For example, you can determine how much you would save in interest paid by making a bigger down payment on the loan. Going back to the new car example, you could use the CUMIPMT function to figure out the interest you'll pay over the 48-month period at 9 percent interest if you put $4,000 down instead of $2,000.

The CUMIPMT function requires the following syntax:

CUMIPMT(rate,nper,pv,start_period,end_period,type)

The following table explains the meaning of each argument.

Argument	Explanation
Rate	The interest rate per payment period; when you are calculating monthly payments, divide the annual interest rate by 12; when calculating semimonthly payments, divide the annual rate by 24
Nper	The total number of loan payments; when the loan is issued for a number of years and requires monthly payments, you can enter the number of payments as 12*<*number of years*>
Pv	The present value (principal) of the loan
Start_period	The first payment period in the calculation; the first period in a series of payments is numbered 1; the calculation can start with any period
End_period	The last payment period in the calculation; this value can be any value greater than the Start_period; the value of the final period in a series is equal to the total number of payments
Type	The timing of the loan payments; when the loan payment is due at the end of the payment period, use the default value of 0; when payment is due at the beginning of the payment period, set this value to 1

IMPORTANT

The CUMIPMT function is part of the Excel Analysis Toolpak. If the Analysis Toolpak is installed on your computer, it will appear on the list of Add-Ins accessible from the Tools menu. If the Analysis Toolpak is not installed, install it from the Microsoft Office 2003 or Microsoft Excel 2003 installation CD before continuing.

At Adventure Works, the CFO wants to compare the total amount of interest paid for each of the loans offered.

Use the CUMIPMT function

In this exercise, you activate the Analysis Toolpak and use the CUMIPMT function to calculate total interest paid for a loan.

1 **On the Tools menu, click Add-Ins.**

The Add-Ins dialog box appears.

FIGURE 8-5

Add-Ins dialog box

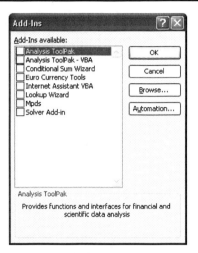

Your list of available add-ins may vary from what is shown in Figure 8-5.

2 **On the Add-Ins Available list, select the Analysis Toolpak check box, and click OK.**

Excel activates the Analysis Toolpak. Its functions are now available.

3 **Click cell B12, and click the Insert Function button.**

The Insert Function dialog box appears.

4 **In the Or Select A Category list, click Financial, if necessary.**

The Select A Function list displays the available financial functions.

5 **In the Select A Function list, click CUMIPMT, and click OK.**

The Function Arguments dialog box appears.

6 **Click in the Rate box, and type** B6/12.

7 **Click in the Nper box, and type** B8.

8 **Click in the Pv box, and type** B4.

9 **In the Start_period box, type** 1.

10 **In the End_period box, type** 48.

This formula will calculate the cumulative interest paid over the time between the given start and end periods. In this case, you are calculating cumulative interest for the entire life of the loan, so you begin with the first payment period (1) and end with the final payment period (48).

11 **Scroll down in the Function Arguments dialog box, and in the Type box, type** 0.

Excel will assume that each payment is due at the end of its payment period.

FIGURE 8-6

Arguments for the CUMIPMT function

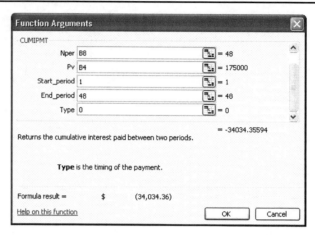

12 **Click OK.**

The amount of interest paid over the life of loan Option A ($34,034.36) appears in cell B12.

13 **Copy the formula in cell B12 to cell C12.**

The amount of interest paid over the life of loan Option B ($32,555.86) appears in cell C12.

FIGURE 8-7

Calculation of cumulative interest

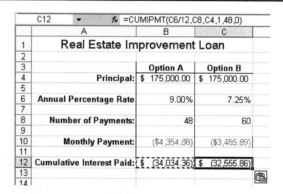

Q. What is the difference between the PMT function and the CUMIPMT function?

A: The PMT function calculates the amount you must pay per period on a loan, whereas the CUMIPMT function calculates the interest you will pay over the term of the loan.

◆ **Save the workbook, and leave it open for the next exercise.**

QUICK REFERENCE ▼

Use the CUMIPMT function

1 Click the cell that will contain the formula.

2 Click the Insert Function button.

3 Click Financial in the *Or Select A Category* list.

4 Click CUMIPMT in the Select A Function list, and click OK.

5 Enter the interest rate, number of payment periods, and principal.

6 Enter the start period, end period, and type, and click OK.

Computing Investment Value

The FV function determines the future value of an investment. This function is useful for formulating a savings plan because it helps you figure out the amount of money that can accumulate on an investment.

The FV (future value) function calculates the value of an investment based on a series of periodic, constant payments at a constant interest rate. The FV function shows the income that results from an interest-bearing investment or loan. For example, you would use the FV function to determine how much money you will save if you deposit $200 a month for two years in a savings account that pays 5 percent interest. The FV function requires the following syntax:

FV(rate,nper,pmt,pv,type)

The following table explains the meaning of each argument.

Argument	Explanation
Rate	The interest rate per period; when you are calculating monthly deposits, divide the annual interest rate by 12; when calculating semimonthly deposits, divide the annual rate by 24
Nper	The total number of deposits
Pmt	The amount deposited in each period
Pv	The present value or lump sum amount that a series of deposits is worth now; by default, this amount is 0, and the Pmt argument is used
Type	The timing of the deposits; when the deposit is made at the end of the period, use the default value of 0; when deposits are made at the beginning of the payment period, set this value to 1

As an alternative to conventional loans, a financial adviser suggests that Adventure Works fund the planned chalet renovations by investing in short-term annuities. The CFO is evaluating the future value of the investment.

Use the FV function

In this exercise, you calculate the future value of an investment.

1 In the Financing workbook, click the Investments sheet tab.

2 Click cell B10, if necessary, and click the Insert Function button.

The Insert Function dialog box appears.

3 **In the Or Select A Category list, click Financial, if necessary.**

The Select A Function list displays the available financial functions.

4 **In the Select A Function list, click FV, and click OK.**

The Function Arguments dialog box appears.

5 **Click in the Rate box, and type B4/12.**

6 **Click in the Nper box, and type B6.**

7 **Click in the Pmt box, and type B8.**

8 **Click OK in the Function Arguments dialog box.**

The future value of the investment ($125,133.70) appears in cell B10.

FIGURE 8-8

Computing the future value of an investment

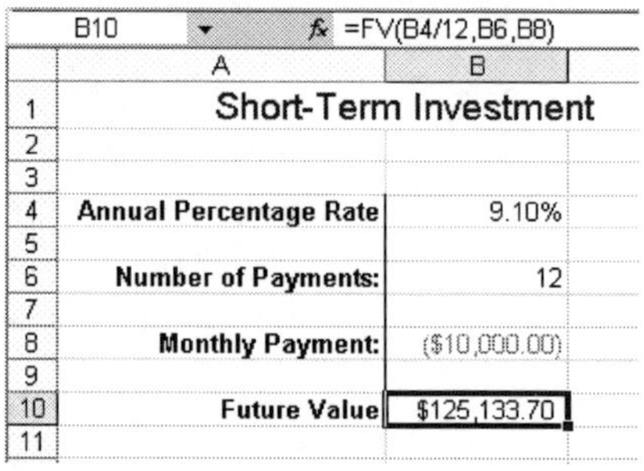

B10	▼	*fx* =FV(B4/12,B6,B8)	
	A	B	
1	Short-Term Investment		
2			
3			
4	Annual Percentage Rate	9.10%	
5			
6	Number of Payments:	12	
7			
8	Monthly Payment:	($10,000.00)	
9			
10	Future Value	$125,133.70	
11			

◆ **Save the workbook, and leave the file open for the next exercise.**

QUICK REFERENCE ▼

Use the FV function

1 Click the cell that will contain the formula.

2 Click the Insert Function button.

3 Click Financial in the *Or Select A Category* list.

4 Click FV in the Select A Function list, and click OK.

5 Enter the interest rate, number of payment periods, and payment amount.

6 Enter the present value and type, and click OK.

Using the IF Function

THE BOTTOM LINE

The IF function is an effective mechanism for determining results if certain conditions are met.

Suppose you are considering a loan that offers an interest rate of 9 percent *if* the **principal** is over $20,000 or an interest rate of 10 percent *if* the principal is less than $20,000. Using the IF function, you can create a formula that incorporates this rule when calculating payments of interest for various principal amounts.

Using the IF function creates a **conditional formula.** The result of a conditional formula is determined by the state of a specific condition or the answer to a logical question.

> **TIP**
>
> Excel includes three functions that calculate results based on conditions. The other two are COUNTIF and SUMIF.

The IF function requires the following syntax:

IF(logical_test,value_if_true,value_if_false)

The following table explains the meaning of each argument.

Argument	Explanation
Logical_test	The expression to be evaluated as true or false
Value_if_true	The value returned if the logical_test expression is true
Value_if_false	The value returned if the logical_test expression is false

The **logical_test** is an expression to be evaluated as true or false. One example of a logical_test is

D5>20000

With this test, Excel compares the value in cell D5 with the static value of 20000. If the value in D5 is greater than 20000, the test is true and the result of the formula is the Value_if_true. If the value in D5 is less than 20000, the logical test is false and the result of the formula is the Value_if_false. Using the IF function, the syntax of one such formula is

=IF(D5>20000,0.10,0.09)

The CFO at Adventure Works has learned that the investment she is considering offers many monthly payment options with slightly different interest rates. She creates a formula to calculate the future value of her investment at various payment levels.

Use the IF function

In this exercise, you use the IF function to evaluate the available investment options.

1 On the Investments sheet, click cell B4, and press DELETE.

2 Click the Insert Function button.

The Insert Function dialog box appears.

3 On the Or Select A Category list, click Logical.

The Select A Function list displays the available logical functions.

4 In the Select A Function list, click IF, and then click OK.

The Function Arguments dialog box appears.

5 In the Logical_test box, type B8<=-10000.

6 In the Value_if_true box, type 8.25%.

7 In the Value_if_false box, type 9.10%, and click OK.

The applicable interest rate (8.25%) appears in cell B4. Excel recalculates the future value of the investment.

FIGURE 8-9

Applying the IF function

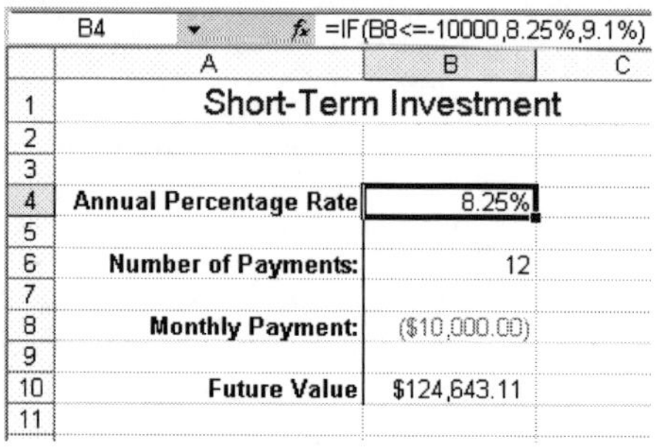

	B4	▼	*fx* =IF(B8<=-10000,8.25%,9.1%)	
		A	B	C
1		Short-Term Investment		
2				
3				
4		Annual Percentage Rate	8.25%	
5				
6		Number of Payments:	12	
7				
8		Monthly Payment:	($10,000.00)	
9				
10		Future Value	$124,643.11	
11				

8 Click cell B8, type -8500, and press Enter.

Excel recalculates the interest rate, and the updated future value of the investment ($106,363.65) appears in cell B10.

FIGURE 8-10

Finding the future value if the monthly payment is decreased

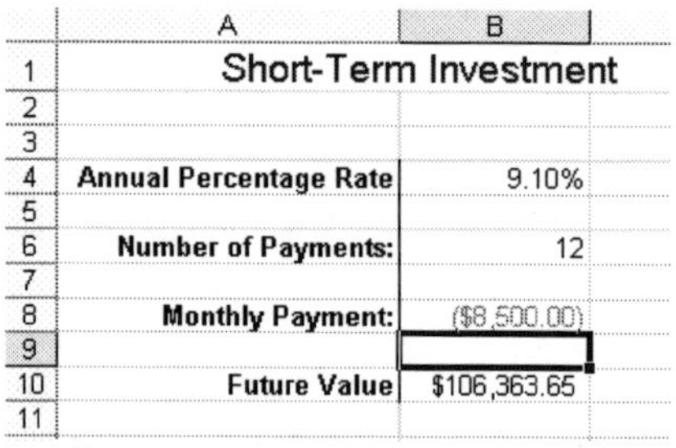

	A	B
1	Short-Term Investment	
2		
3		
4	Annual Percentage Rate	9.10%
5		
6	Number of Payments:	12
7		
8	Monthly Payment:	($8,500.00)
9		
10	Future Value	$106,363.65
11		

◆ Save and close Financing. If you are continuing to other lessons, leave Excel open. If you are not continuing to other lessons, save and close all open workbooks, and then click the Close button in the top right corner of the Excel window.

QUICK CHECK

Q. What is the meaning of the Logical_test argument in the IF function?

A: The Logical_test argument is the expression that will be evaluated as true or false.

QUICK REFERENCE ▼

Use the IF function

1 Click the cell that will contain the formula.

2 Click the Insert Function button.

3 Click Logical in the Or Select A Category list.

4 Click IF in the Select A Function list, and click OK.

5 Enter the Logical_test expression, the Value_if_true, and the Value_if_false.

6 Click OK.

Key Points

✔ *The PMT (payment) function calculates payments for a loan based on a series of constant payments and a constant interest rate.*

✔ *Determining the amount of interest that will be paid over the term of a loan using the CUMIPMT function can be an effective tool for comparing and evaluating loan options.*

✔ *The FV (future value) function calculates the value of an investment based on a series of periodic, constant payments at a constant interest rate. The FV function shows the income that results from an interest-bearing investment or loan.*

✔ *Using the IF function, you can determine results of investment options if, for example, certain conditions are met.*

Quick Quiz

True/False

T F **1.** The PMT function calculates payments for a loan based on a series of constant payments at a constant interest rate.

T F **2.** You would use the FV function to determine monthly payments on a new car loan over 36 months at an interest rate of 9.5 percent.

T F **3.** The CUMIPMT function calculates the total amount of interest paid over a series of loan payments.

T F **4.** The Nper argument, which is used in several financial functions, represents the interest rate.

T F **5.** If you wanted to figure out how much money you could save if you deposited $500 a month in a savings account that earned 6 percent interest, you would use the PMT function.

T F **6.** The Start_period argument in a financial formula must always be 1.

Multiple Choice

1. What is the initial (or present) value of a loan referred to?
   a. start_value
   b. cumulative value
   c. principal
   d. down payment

2. If you are calculating monthly payments in a function, what must you divide an annual interest rate by?
   a. 6
   b. 12
   c. 24
   d. 0; you don't need to divide by anything.

3. Which financial function uses the syntax *(rate,nper,pv,start_period,end_period,type)?*
   a. PMT
   b. FV
   c. CUMIPMT
   d. CUMULAT

4. In which type of function is a conditional formula created?
   a. FV
   b. PV
   c. CONDIT
   d. IF

Short Answer

1. What does the CUMIPMT function compute?

2. What function can be used to compare the value of two cells?

3. What are two ways to add cell addresses to a function?

4. What are the required arguments of the PMT function?

5. What does it mean if you use the PMT function and get a negative number?

On Your Own

Exercise 1

Calculate the monthly payments and cumulative interest for a 20-year $100,000 loan at an annual interest rate of 8 percent. Use an IF function to indicate that the interest rate for a 30-year loan is 7.5 percent.

Exercise 2

Calculate the future value of 24 monthly payments of $500 each at an annual interest rate of 6.5 percent.

Exercise 3

Calculate the monthly payments for a 30-year $150,000 home loan at an annual rate of 6 percent. Compare this to the monthly payments on the same house with a 15-year loan at 5 percent. What is the difference in monthly payment? What is the difference in cumulative interest?

One Step Further

Exercise 1

Many of the tasks in this lesson involved the development of function formulas useful in calculating loan values. Since the calculation of loans is such a common need for many users of Excel, a ready-made template is available for your use. Create a new worksheet based on this template, and explore the functions that are used within this worksheet. Which of the functions that you used in this lesson are used in that worksheet?

Exercise 2

Calculate the future value of an investment if you contribute $100 per month for the next five years in an account that earns 3 percent interest. Calculate the future value on an investment in which you contribute only $50 per month for five years and earn 6 percent interest. Which investment would be worth more at the end of the five-year period?

LESSON

Using Excel with the Internet

After completing this lesson, you will be able to:

✔ *Create and edit hyperlinks in worksheets.*
✔ *Save worksheets and workbooks as Web pages.*
✔ *Send workbooks via e-mail.*
✔ *Add comments to workbook cells.*
✔ *View and edit comments..*

KEY TERMS

- hyperlink
- Hypertext Markup Language (HTML)

With Microsoft Excel, you can easily share your data with others using the Internet. You can send Excel workbooks via e-mail. You also can save Excel files as Web pages to be viewed in a Web browser, even by people who don't have Excel. And you can enhance your worksheet using hyperlinks to refer to related files or Web pages. Finally, you and your colleagues can enhance workbook data by adding comments that offer insight into why sales were so good on a particular day or whether a product might be discontinued.

In this lesson, you will learn how to use Excel with the Internet. You will insert and modify hyperlinks in a worksheet, save a workbook as a Web page, and send a workbook via e-mail. You'll also learn how to manage comments to workbook cells.

At Adventure Works, the human resources department is gathering information to post on the company intranet. The administrative assistant is compiling a list of useful online resources and creating a table in Excel of the company's holiday schedule.

IMPORTANT

Before you can use the practice files in this lesson, you must install them from the book's companion CD to their default location. For additional information on how to find and open files used in this book, see the "Using the CD-ROM" section at the beginning of this book.

Inserting and Editing Hyperlinks

THE BOTTOM LINE

Hyperlinks enable you to augment worksheet data with additional information and resources, thus bringing another dimension and interactivity to a workbook file.

A **hyperlink** is an image or a sequence of characters that opens another file or Web page when you click it. The target file or Web page can be on the World Wide Web, on an intranet, or on your own computer. In a workbook containing personal financial data, for example, you might insert a hyperlink to jump you to the Web site of your stockbroker so you can regularly check the performance of your investments. All you need to do is click the hyperlink to automatically launch your Web browser and connect to the specified Web site.

Inserting a Hyperlink

Excel makes it easy for you to embed hyperlinks in worksheet cells. Each hyperlink appears as blue underlined text in the cell. When you point to a hyperlink, a ScreenTip describing the link or giving the location of the file appears.

Many of the staff members at Adventure Works use Microsoft Office in their everyday work, so the administrative assistant wants to add a link to the Microsoft Office Web site to her list of online resources.

◆ To complete the procedures in this lesson, you must use the file Intranet in the Lesson09 folder in the Excel Core Practice folder located on your hard disk.

◆ Open Intranet from the Excel Core Practice/Lesson09 folder.

IMPORTANT

You must have access to the Internet to complete this exercise. If you need to establish this connection manually, you should do so before beginning the exercise.

Insert a hyperlink

In this exercise, you create a hyperlink in a worksheet.

1 Click cell A4.

2 On the Standard toolbar, click the Insert Hyperlink button.

The Insert Hyperlink dialog box appears.

FIGURE 9-1

Insert Hyperlink dialog box

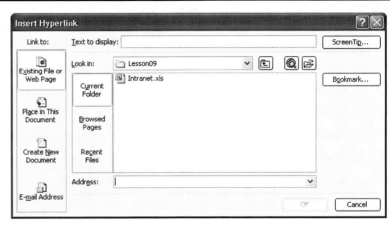

ANOTHER METHOD

- Open the Insert menu, and select Hyperlink.
- Right-click the selection, and click Hyperlink on the shortcut menu.
- Press Ctrl+K.

3 **In the Text To Display box, type** Microsoft.

TIP

Since you are typing an Internet address, *http://* is automatically added to the address for you.

4 **In the Address box, type** www.microsoft.com, **and click OK.**

The hyperlink appears in cell A4.

5 **Point to the cell with the hyperlink.**

The default ScreenTip appears, which lists the full address of the hyperlink and provides instructions for following the hyperlink or selecting the cell.

6 **Click the hyperlink.**

Your Web browser opens and connects to the Microsoft Web site.

7 **On the taskbar, click the Excel button to return to your workbook.**

◆ **Save the workbook, and leave it open for the next exercise.**

QUICK REFERENCE ▼

Insert a hyperlink

1 Click the cell in which you want to place the hyperlink.

2 Click the Insert Hyperlink button on the Standard toolbar.

QUICK CHECK

Q. What does hyperlink text in a cell look like?

A: **The hyperlink text is blue and underlined.**

3 In the Text To Display box, type the text that you want to appear as the text of the hyperlink.

4 In the Address box, type the path or URL; or click the Browse button to navigate to the file or Web page you want.

5 Click OK.

Editing and Removing a Hyperlink

You can easily change the target file or Web site address of a hyperlink as well as its ScreenTip text. For example, you might want to change the hyperlink in your personal finances workbook from your stockbroker's Web site to the Web site for one of the stock exchanges. You might want to edit the ScreenTip to display just the name of the stock exchange instead of its URL.

To edit a cell containing a hyperlink, you can't just click it to select it and then start typing like you do other cell data. If you left-click it, you will be "jumped" to the target file or Web site. You can select a hyperlink to edit by right-clicking the cell and selecting Edit Hyperlink on the shortcut menu. You can delete a hyperlink by right-clicking the cell and selecting Remove Hyperlink on the shortcut menu.

Edit and remove a hyperlink

In this exercise, you edit the hyperlink's target address and ScreenTip text and remove the hyperlink.

1 **Right-click cell A4, and click Edit Hyperlink.**

TROUBLESHOOTING

If you left-click a cell containing a hyperlink to a Web site, your Web browser will open and connect you to the site.

ANOTHER METHOD

Select the cell containing the hyperlink using one of the following methods: (1) click an adjacent cell, and use the arrow keys to select the cell; (2) click on the cell, and hold the mouse button down until the cell is selected; or (3) hold down the Ctrl key while you click the cell. Then click in the Formula bar to edit the hyperlink text.

2 **In the Text To Display box, click to the right of the word Microsoft, press the spacebar, and type** Office.

3 **In the Address box, click to the right of www.microsoft.com, and type** /office.

TIP

If there is already a backslash after www.microsoft.com, you do not need to type a second one.

4 **Click the ScreenTip button.**

The Set Hyperlink ScreenTip dialog box appears. This dialog box allows you to type the text you want to appear when the mouse pointer is hovered over the hyperlink.

FIGURE 9-2

Set Hyperlink ScreenTip dialog box

5 **Click in the ScreenTip Text box, type** Microsoft Office Home Page, **and click OK.**

The Set Hyperlink ScreenTip dialog box closes.

6 **In the Edit Hyperlink dialog box, click OK.**

The updated hyperlink appears in cell A4.

7 **Point to the hyperlink.**

The edited ScreenTip with the words *Microsoft Office Home Page* appears, as shown in Figure 9-3.

FIGURE 9-3

Edited ScreenTip text

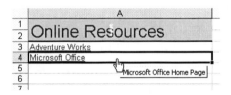

8 **Click the hyperlink.**

Your Web browser opens and connects to the Microsoft Office site.

9 **Close both instances of your browser, and return to the worksheet.**

10 **Right-click the hyperlink, and click Remove Hyperlink.**

The text remains in cell A4, but the hyperlink is removed.

◆ **Save the workbook, and leave the file open for the next exercise.**

QUICK REFERENCE ▼

Edit a hyperlink

1 Right-click the cell containing the hyperlink.

2 On the shortcut menu, point to Hyperlink, and click Edit Hyperlink.

3 To change the text of the link, edit the text in the Text To Display box.

4 To change the target of the link, edit the text in the Address box.

5 Click OK.

Remove a hyperlink

1 Right-click the cell containing the hyperlink.

2 On the shortcut menu, point to Hyperlink, and click Remove Hyperlink.

Saving Worksheets and Workbooks as Web Pages

THE BOTTOM LINE

You can save workbooks and individual worksheets in a format that enables anyone with Internet access to open and view them using a Web browser. This feature provides a great way to share workbook data with others who do not use Excel.

By saving a worksheet or workbook as a Web page, you can quickly create a file that others can view in a Web browser without using Excel. When you save a file as a Web page, Excel uses **Hypertext Markup Language (HTML)** to format the data for display in a Web browser.

Before you save a worksheet or workbook as a Web page, you can use Web Page Preview to view the page as it will appear when it is viewed in a browser. To preview a worksheet as a Web page, on the File menu, click Web Page Preview. The worksheet opens as a Web page in your default browser.

IMPORTANT

Before you save a worksheet as a Web page, make sure you save the file to a disk.

At Adventure Works, the administrative assistant is ready to create Web pages from the links and holidays worksheets she created.

Save a workbook and worksheets as Web pages

In this exercise, you save a worksheet and a workbook as a Web page.

1 **On the File menu, click Save As.**

The Save As dialog box appears.

Saving a Workbook for the Web

2 **Click the Save As Type down arrow, and click Web Page.**

The Save As dialog box changes to offer options specific to saving in Web page format.

FIGURE 9-4

Specifying the Web Page file format

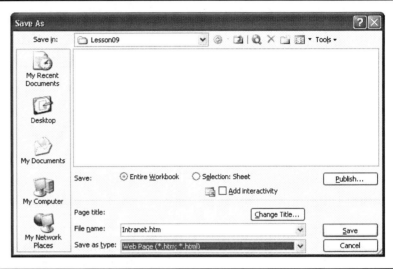

3 **Click the Selection: Sheet option.**

4 **In the File Name box, select the current text, type Links.htm, and click Save.**

Excel saves the worksheet as a file in HTML format.

5 **On the File menu, click Save As.**

The Save As dialog box appears.

6 **Click the Save As Type down arrow, and click Web Page.**

7 **Click the Entire Workbook option, if necessary, and click Save.**

Excel saves the entire workbook (with the name *Intranet*) as a file in HTML format. A folder also is created with the same name as the file. This folder contains any associated files that are needed to produce the Web page.

8 **Close the workbook.**

TIP

If you open the Links.htm file in Excel, it will not start your Web browser. It will simply appear in an Excel worksheet.

9 **Open Windows Explorer, navigate to the Lesson09 folder in the Excel Core Practice folder, and double-click the file Links.htm to open it.**

The Links worksheet appears in your Web browser.

FIGURE 9-5

Opening a worksheet in your Web browser

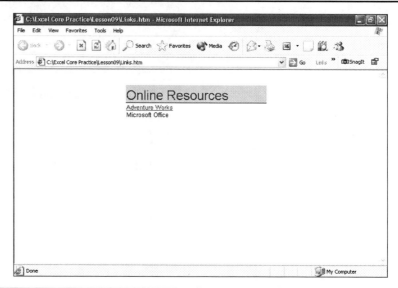

10 **From Windows Explorer, open the file Intranet.htm.**

The Intranet workbook appears in your Web browser, with the Links worksheet in front.

11 **At the bottom of the page, click the Holidays link.**

The Holidays worksheet appears.

FIGURE 9-6

Displaying a worksheet in your Web browser

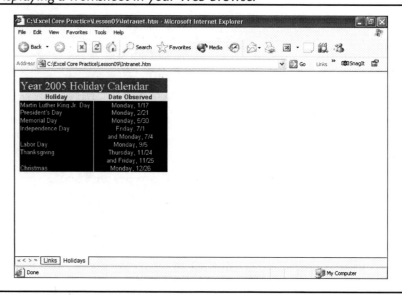

12 **Close both Web browser windows.**

By default, others will be able to view, but not edit, the worksheets you save as Web pages. To allow others to edit these worksheets, use the Add Interactivity option in the Save As dialog box.

QUICK REFERENCE ▼

Save a workbook as a Web page

1 On the File menu, click Save As.

2 Click the Save As Type down arrow, and click Web Page.

3 Click the Entire Workbook option.

4 If necessary, change the path and the file name.

5 Click Save.

Save a worksheet as a Web page

1 On the File menu, click Save As.

2 Click the Save As Type down arrow, and click Web Page.

3 Click the Selection: Sheet option.

4 If necessary, change the path and the file name.

5 Click Save.

Q. If you want to save an individual worksheet within a workbook as a Web page, what option in the Save As dialog box must you select?

A: You must select the Selection: Sheet option.

Sending Workbooks via E-mail

E-mail is a quick and easy way to transfer workbook files and share data with others.

With Excel, you have two options for sending a workbook via e-mail. You can send a worksheet or workbook in the body of an e-mail message without leaving Excel, or you can send an Excel file as an attachment to an e-mail message. Either way, e-mail represents an efficient way to transfer files and give others quick access to workbook data.

At Adventure Works, the administrative assistant wants to send the contents of the Intranet workbook to the human resources manager for approval before posting them to the intranet.

You must have access to the Internet to complete this exercise. If you need to establish this connection manually, you should do so before beginning the exercise.

When your e-mail program is set up to store messages to send later, Excel displays a message box to remind you.

Send and receive a worksheet

In this exercise, you e-mail a workbook to yourself and then open the file from your e-mail program.

1 **Open the Intranet workbook.**

2 **On the File menu, point to Send To, and click Mail Recipient.**

An E-Mail message box appears.

3 **Click the Send The Current Sheet As The Message Body option.**

An e-mail header form appears, as shown in Figure 9-7.

FIGURE 9-7

E-mail header form

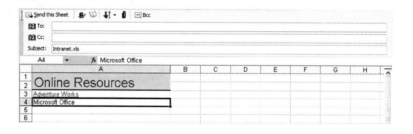

Click the E-Mail button on the Standard toolbar, which will give you the option of sending the workbook as an attachment or sending the workbook as the message body.

4 **In the To box, type your e-mail address, and click the Send This Sheet button.**

Excel sends the message and closes the e-mail header.

5 **Start your e-mail program, and check for new messages.**

6 **Open the message you sent.**

The Excel worksheet appears in the body of your message.

FIGURE 9-8

Viewing the worksheet e-mail

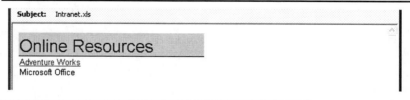

7 Close the message, and return to the worksheet.

8 On the File menu, point to Send To, and click Mail Recipient
(As Attachment).

An e-mail message form appears.

FIGURE 9-9

E-mail message form when sending an attachment

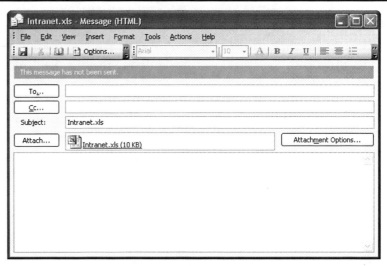

9 In the To box, type your e-mail address, and click Send.

10 Close the workbook.

11 Switch to your e-mail program, and check for new messages.

12 Open the message you sent, and double-click the attachment.

The workbook opens in Excel.

13 Close the e-mail message, but leave the workbook open for the next
exercise.

QUICK REFERENCE ▼

Send a workbook via e-mail

1 Open the workbook you want to send.

2 On the File menu, point to Send, and click Mail Recipient; or click Mail
Recipient (As Attachment) if you want to send the workbook as an
attachment.

3 In the To box, type the e-mail address to which you want to send the
workbook.

4 If desired, fill in the Subject and message body boxes.

5 Click the Send button.

QUICK CHECK

Q. How would you send a
workbook as an attach-
ment using File menu
commands?

A: On the File menu, point
to Send To, and then
click Mail Recipient (As
Attachment).

Managing Comments

Managing Comments

THE BOTTOM LINE

Comments are a handy tool for calling out or noting important or significant data and for providing insights from users of the workbook that go beyond the cell data.

Comments are like electronic sticky notes—they enable anyone who uses a workbook to point out specific items of interest and to share information in addition to the raw data contained in the file. For example, if rental equipment sales were exceptionally high for a particular day, the manager on duty could add a comment to the cell in which she records the sales for that day, noting that two exceptionally large groups visiting the resort accounted for the disparity.

When you add a comment to a cell, a flag appears in the upper right corner of the cell. When the mouse pointer hovers over a cell with a comment, the comment appears in a box next to the cell, along with the name of the user logged on to the computer at the time the comment was inserted.

TIP

The name attributed to a comment may not be the same as the person who actually created it. Enforcing access controls, such as requiring users to enter account names and passwords when they access a computer, can help track who made a comment or change.

The tools to insert, edit, delete, or move between existing comments as well as to show or hide them are available on the Reviewing toolbar. To open the Reviewing toolbar, point to Toolbars on the View menu and click Reviewing or right-click in the toolbar area and click on Reviewing in the pop-up list.

TIP

When someone other than the original user edits a comment, that person's input is marked with the new user's name and is added to the original comment.

Insert and review comments

In this exercise, you add a comment to a cell. You then review and delete the comment.

1 In the Intranet workbook, switch to the Holidays worksheet, and click cell B6.

2 Display the Reviewing toolbar, if necessary, by clicking the View menu, pointing to Toolbars, and clicking Reviewing.

The Reviewing toolbar is displayed.

3 Click the New Comment button on the Reviewing toolbar.

A comment field appears, as shown in Figure 9-10.

FIGURE 9-10

Comment field for cell B6

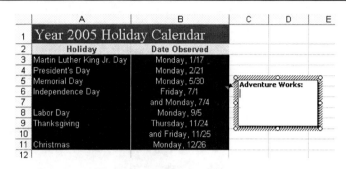

ANOTHER METHOD

- Open the Insert menu, and click Comment.
- Right-click the selection, and click Insert Comment on the shortcut menu.

4 In the comment field, type This date was added to provide a long weekend. Then click cell B7.

A red comment flag appears in the upper right corner of cell B6.

5 Move the mouse pointer over cell B6.

The comment in cell B6 appears.

TIP

If you want comments always to be displayed while the workbook is open, click the Show/Hide Comments button on the Reviewing toolbar. Click the button again to hide the comments.

6 Click cell B6, and then click the Edit Comment button on the Reviewing toolbar.

The cursor is placed at the end of the existing comment.

ANOTHER METHOD

Right-click the selection, and click Edit Comment on the shortcut menu.

7 Double-click the word was in the comment to select it, and then type and the following Monday were.

The existing comment is edited to include the new phrase.

8 Click cell B6, and then click the Delete Comment button on the Reviewing toolbar.

The comment is deleted from cell B6.

ANOTHER METHOD

Right-click the selection, and click Delete Comment on the shortcut menu.

◆ **Save and close Intranet. If you are continuing to other lessons, Leave Excel open. If you are not continuing to other lessons, save and close all open workbooks. Click the Close button in the top right corner of the Excel window.**

QUICK REFERENCE ▼

Add a comment to a worksheet

1 Click the cell in which you want to make a comment.

2 Click the New Comment button on the Reviewing toolbar.

3 Type in the comment field.

4 Click in another cell.

Edit a comment in a worksheet

1 Click the cell that contains the comment you want to edit.

2 Click the Edit Comment button on the Reviewing toolbar.

3 Insert, edit, or delete the contents of the comment.

4 Click in another cell.

Delete a comment in a worksheet

1 Click the cell that contains the comment you want to delete.

2 Click the Delete Comment button on the Reviewing toolbar.

QUICK CHECK

Q. How do you know when a cell contains a comment?

A: The cell has a small red triangle in its upper right corner.

Key Points

✔ *A hyperlink is an image or a sequence of characters that opens another file or Web page when you click it. Hyperlinks enable you to augment worksheet data with additional information and resources, thus bringing another dimension and interactivity to a workbook file.*

✔ *You can save workbooks and individual worksheets in a format that enables anyone with Internet access to open and view them using a Web browser, even if that person does not have the Excel application.*

✔ *E-mail is a quick and easy way to transfer workbook files and give others quick access to workbook data.*

✔ *Comments enable anyone who uses a workbook to note data of significance and to share information in addition to the raw data contained in the file.*

Quick Quiz

True/False

T   F   **1.** A hyperlink is always a picture or an image.

T   F   **2.** You can identify a hyperlink in a worksheet because it appears as blue underlined text.

T   F   **3.** The ScreenTip for a hyperlink to a Web site must always display the site's complete Web address.

T   F   **4.** Web Page Preview lets you view a worksheet as it will appear when it is opened in a Web browser.

T   F   **5.** Excel uses HTML to format worksheet data for display in a Web browser.

T   F   **6.** To send a workbook as an e-mail attachment, you must close the workbook and attach it to an e-mail that you compose in your e-mail program.

Multiple Choice

1. How is a hyperlink in a worksheet cell formatted?
   a. The text is red and bold.
   b. The text is red and underlined.
   c. The text is blue and bold.
   d. The text is blue and underlined.

2. Which of the following is *not* a method for selecting a cell containing a hyperlink?
   a. Click an adjacent cell, and use the arrow keys to select the cell.
   b. Click the cell, and hold the mouse button down until the cell is selected.
   c. Hold down the Ctrl key while you click the cell.
   d. Simply click the cell.

3. What does HTML stand for?
   a. Hyperlink Markup Language
   b. Hyperlink Management Language
   c. Hypertext Markup Language
   d. Hypertext Management Language

4. What appears in a cell to signify that it contains a comment?
   a. small red triangle
   b. small blue triangle
   c. red border on all four sides
   d. blue border on all four sides

Short Answer

1. What are two ways to insert a hyperlink in a selected worksheet cell?

2. How can you send a workbook via e-mail?

3. How can you save a workbook or worksheet as a Web page?

4. How can you edit the text of a hyperlink without using the shortcut menu?

5. How can you edit a comment in a worksheet cell?

On Your Own

◆ **Open Intranet from the Excel Core Practice/Lesson09 folder.**

Exercise 1

On the Links worksheet, create a hyperlink to a file on your hard disk. Edit the text of the hyperlink, and add a descriptive ScreenTip. Preview the workbook as a Web page, and save the Links worksheet as a Web page. Close the workbook, and open the Links Web page in your Web browser.

> **IMPORTANT**
>
> To complete On Your Own Exercise 2, you must have access to the Internet. If you need to establish this connection manually, you should do so before beginning the exercise.

◆ **Open Intranet from the Excel Core Practice/Lesson09 folder.**

Exercise 2

In the Intranet workbook, remove the hyperlink you added to the Links worksheet. Send the workbook to one of your classmates in the body of an e-mail message.

◆ **Save Intranet, and leave it open for the next exercise.**

Exercise 3

Open the Reviewing toolbar. Use the Insert Comment button to insert a comment in cell B11. Type Should we add another day here to provide a long weekend? Click cell B6, and insert a comment. Type I'd rather not have this day off, but get another day at Christmas instead. Use the Reviewing toolbar, and move to the next comment.

◆ **Close Intranet.**

One Step Further

Exercise 1

In this lesson, you created a hyperlink to a Web site. Is it possible to create a hyperlink to another spot within the worksheet or to another worksheet on your hard drive? Explore the Insert Hyperlink dialog box or use Excel's Help files to find the answer to this question.

Exercise 2

Is there a quick way to establish a hyperlink to a Web page without having to type in all of the text to get to the specific page? Explore the Insert Hyperlink dialog box or use Excel's Help files to find the answer to this question.

Glossary

A

absolute reference In a formula, a reference to a specific cell. Absolute references point to the same cell even when the formula that contains the reference is copied or moved to a different cell.

active cell The cell in which you can enter data in a worksheet. The active cell is surrounded by a thick black border.

ascending order Sort order in which alphabetic data appears A to Z, numeric data appears from lowest to highest or smallest to largest, and dates appear from the oldest to the most recent.

attribute A formatting characteristic of text or a cell.

Auto Fill An Excel feature that automatically fills cells with a series.

AutoFormat A feature you can use to apply predefined formats to ranges of cells.

AutoSum An Excel feature that automatically creates a SUM formula in a cell.

axis labels Descriptive text associated and aligned with an axis.

C

Category axis The chart axis along which the categories of data appear. It is typically the X, or horizontal, axis.

cell The intersection of a row and a column in a worksheet.

chart sheet A worksheet containing only a chart.

charts Graphical representations of numeric data in a worksheet.

clear To remove a cell's formatting, contents, or both.

collect and paste The ability to use the Office Clipboard to copy multiple selections (up to 24 at one time) and paste the selections separately.

column width The number of characters that can fit within the cells of a column. You can change column width by using the Column Width dialog box or by dragging the right edge of a column selector.

conditional formula A formula where the result is determined by the state of a particular condition.

copy To place a duplicate of a selection on the Windows Clipboard (and the Office Clipboard if the Clipboard task pane is displayed).

cumulative interest The total amount of interest paid over a given loan period.

cut To move a selection to the Windows Clipboard (and the Office Clipboard if the Clipboard task pane is displayed).

D

descending order Sort order in which alphabetic data appears from Z to A, numeric data appears from highest to lowest or largest to smallest, and dates appear from the most recent to the oldest.

E

embedded charts Charts that appear with data on an existing worksheet.

F

filter A rule that Excel uses to determine which worksheet rows to display.

font A set of text characters designed to appear a certain way. Times New Roman and Arial are two examples of fonts.

footer A line of text that appears at the bottom of each page of a printed worksheet. Footers can include numbers, dates, and the results of formulas.

Format Painter A feature that allows you to copy formatting from a cell or range of cells to another cell or range of cells.

Formula bar The area in the Excel window where you can enter or edit cell entries.

formula A sequence of operands and operators that performs a calculation and returns the result.

freeze To make certain rows or columns remain visible on your screen even when you scroll your worksheet.

function A predefined formula used to perform specific calculations.

future value The value of an investment or a loan at the end of the final payment period.

H

header A line of text that appears at the top of each page of a printed worksheet. Headers can include numbers, dates, and the results of formulas.

hide To make a row or column invisible so that you can display other rows and columns simultaneously on your screen.

hyperlink An image or a sequence of characters that opens another file or Web page when you click it.

Hypertext Markup Language (HTML) The primary language used to format text and graphics for display in a Web browser.

L

legend A guide to the data in a chart.

logical_test An expression to be evaluated as true or false.

M

merge cells The ability to combine multiple cells into a single cell, which can then be formatted as a single cell.

O

Office Clipboard An area in memory available in some Microsoft Office applications for storing multiple copied or cut items so they can be selectively pasted at other locations.

orientation A setting that specifies in what direction a worksheet appears on a printed page: either vertically (portrait orientation) or horizontally (landscape orientation).

P

Paste Special A command and corresponding dialog box that can be used to insert different elements of copied cells into a different location.

paste To insert a cut or copied selection stored on the Windows Clipboard or on the Office Clipboard.

points A measurement of the height of characters in a cell or the height of a row. One point is equal to 1/72 inch.

present value The value of an investment or a loan at the beginning of the first payment period.

principal The initial value of a loan.

Print Preview The window in Excel that allows you to view a full-page preview of what your worksheet will look like when it is printed.

R

range A group of adjacent cells that you select to perform operations on all of the selected cells.

relative references In formulas, cell references that change "relative" to the location to which they are copied or moved.

resolution The degree of detail, or number of dots per inch, in a character or an image printed on a page.

row height The top-to-bottom height of a row, given in points or in pixels. You can change the height of a row by using the Row Height dialog box or by dragging the bottom of the row selector.

D

scaling Expanding or shrinking how a worksheet appears on a printed page.

selecting Identifying the cell or range of cells in which you want to enter data.

source data The range of data cells represented in a chart.

string Any sequential entry of letters or numbers that you type.

style A set of formatting attributes you can apply as a group to a cell or range of cells.

T

task pane A pane that allows you to access quickly commands related to a specific task without having to use menus and toolbars.

templates Files that are already set up to track certain kinds of data, such as invoices and purchase orders.

three-dimensional formula A formula that contains a reference (called a 3-D reference) to a cell or range of cells in another worksheet in the workbook.

V

Value axis The chart axis along which the values of data appear. It is typically the Y, or vertical, axis.

W

workbook An Excel file that can contain multiple worksheets.

worksheets Individual sheets within a workbook.

zoom To make a worksheet appear bigger (zoom in) or smaller (zoom out) on your screen.

Index

A

B

C

System Requirements

Your computer system must meet the following minimum requirements for you to install the practice files from the CD-ROM included with this book and to run Microsoft Excel 2003.

- A personal computer running Microsoft Excel 2003 on a Pentium 233-megahertz (MHz) or higher processor.
- Microsoft Windows® 2000 with Service Pack 3 (SP3), Windows XP, or later.
- 128 MB of RAM or greater.
- At least 2 MB of available disk space (after installing Excel 2003 or Microsoft Office).
- A CD-ROM or DVD drive.
- A monitor with Super VGA (800 X 600) or higher resolution with 256 colors.
- A Microsoft mouse, a Microsoft IntelliMouse, or other compatible pointing device.

Get a **Free**
e-mail newsletter, updates,
special offers, links to related books,
and more when you
register online!

Register your Microsoft Press® title on our Web site and you'll get a FREE subscription to our e-mail newsletter, *Microsoft Press Book Connections.* You'll find out about newly released and upcoming books and learning tools, online events, software downloads, special offers and coupons for Microsoft Press customers, and information about major Microsoft® product releases. You can also read useful additional information about all the titles we publish, such as detailed book descriptions, tables of contents and indexes, sample chapters, links to related books and book series, author biographies, and reviews by other customers.

Registration is easy. Just visit this Web page and fill in your information:

http://www.microsoft.com/mspress/register

Microsoft·

Proof of Purchase

Use this page as proof of purchase if participating in a promotion or rebate offer on this title. Proof of purchase must be used in conjunction with other proof(s) of payment such as your dated sales receipt—see offer details.

**Microsoft® Official Academic Course:
Microsoft Office Excel 2003 Core Skills**
0-07-225569-2

CUSTOMER NAME

Microsoft Press, PO Box 97017, Redmond, WA 98073-9830